First World War
and Army of Occupation
War Diary
France, Belgium and Germany

50 DIVISION
Divisional Troops
250 Brigade Royal Field Artillery
17 April 1915 - 4 July 1919

WO95/2817/3

The Naval & Military Press Ltd
www.nmarchive.com
Published in association with The National Archives

Published by

The Naval & Military Press Ltd

Unit 10 Ridgewood Industrial Park,
Uckfield, East Sussex,
TN22 5QE England
Tel: +44 (0) 1825 749494

www.naval-military-press.com
www.nmarchive.com

This diary has been reprinted in facsimile from the original. Any imperfections are inevitably reproduced and the quality may fall short of modern type and cartographic standards.

Contents

Document type	Place/Title	Date From	Date To
Heading	WO95/2817-3		
Heading	50th Division R.A 1st Northumbrian Bde RFA Vol I 17.4-6.6.15		
War Diary		17/04/1915	19/04/1915
War Diary	Chestre	20/04/1915	06/06/1915
Map	Identification Trace For Use With Artillery Maps		
Map	Map		
Miscellaneous	Appendix I		
Map			
Heading	50th Division 1st Northbrn Bde RFA Vol II 7-30.6.15		
War Diary		07/06/1915	30/06/1915
Heading	50th Division 1st Northbn Bde RFA Vol III 1-31-7-15		
War Diary		01/07/1915	31/07/1915
Heading	50th Division 1st North'bn Bde RFA Vol IV From 1-31.8.15		
War Diary	Armentieres	01/08/1915	31/08/1915
Heading	50th Division 1st North'bn Bde RFA Vol V Sept 15		
War Diary	Armentieres	01/09/1915	30/09/1915
Heading	1st North'bn Bde RFA Vol VI Oct 15		
War Diary	Armentieres	01/10/1915	31/10/1915
Heading	1/1 Northumbrian Bde RFA Nov 1915 Vol VII		
War Diary	Hazebrouck La K Reule	01/11/1915	30/11/1915
Heading	1/1 Northumbrian Bde RFA Dec 1915 Vol. VIII		
War Diary	Millain	06/12/1915	22/12/1915
War Diary	Kruistraat	23/12/1915	31/01/1916
Heading	1st Northumbrian Bde RFA Jan 1916 Vol IX		
War Diary	Kruistraat	01/01/1916	29/02/1916
Heading	1/1 Northbrn Bde RFA Vol XI		
War Diary		01/03/1916	23/03/1916
War Diary	Ouderdom	02/04/1916	03/04/1916
War Diary	Eecke	04/04/1916	06/04/1916
War Diary	Millekruis	07/04/1916	30/05/1916
Operation(al) Order(s)	250th (Northumbrian) Brigade R.F.A. Operation Order No. 3 issued by Lt Col H.S. Bell D.S.O. Commanding	27/05/1916	27/05/1916
War Diary		01/06/1916	30/06/1916
Miscellaneous	250th (Northumbrian) Brigade R.F.A.	03/06/1916	03/06/1916
Miscellaneous	Time Table For 50th D.A.		
Miscellaneous	O.C., 250th (Northbn) Bde. R.F.A.	03/06/1916	03/06/1916
Operation(al) Order(s)	250th (Northumbrian) Brigade R.F.A. Operation Order No. 4	07/06/1916	07/06/1916
Operation(al) Order(s)	250th (Northumbrian) Brigade R.F.A. Operation Order No. 5	24/06/1916	24/06/1916
Miscellaneous	Day Hour. Battery Task		
Miscellaneous	250th (Northumbrian) Brigade R.F.A.		
Operation(al) Order(s)	149th Infantry Brigade Operation Order No. 89	05/06/1916	05/06/1916
War Diary		01/04/1916	31/05/1916
Heading	250th. Brigade R.F.A. 50th. Divisional Artillery September 1916		
War Diary		01/09/1916	31/03/1917
War Diary	Sheet 51B.S.W. Hqrs M.3.c.4 1/2. 1/2	01/04/1917	01/04/1917

War Diary	A/250 M.9.D.9 1/4.1/4 B/250 M.9.D.8 3/4. 1/2 C/250 M.10.C.1.1/2	02/04/1917	02/04/1917
War Diary	D/250 H.9.7 1/4.3/4	03/04/1917	11/04/1917
War Diary	Sheet 51B.S.W. A/250, B/250, C/250 N.13. C & D, D/250 N.19.A	12/04/1917	31/12/1917
Miscellaneous	Details Of Artillery Support	31/12/1917	31/12/1917
War Diary		01/01/1918	28/02/1918
Heading	50th Divisional Artillery 250th (Northumbrian) Brigade R.F.A. March 1918		
War Diary		01/03/1918	31/03/1918
Heading	50th Divisional Artillery. 250th (Northumbrian) Brigade R.F.A. April 1918		
War Diary		01/04/1918	30/04/1918
Heading	50th Division War Diary 250th Brigade R.F.A. May 1918		
War Diary		01/05/1918	31/05/1918
Miscellaneous	Statements Regarding Circumstances	27/05/1918	27/05/1918
Miscellaneous	Narrative Of Events On Position Occupied By 250th. Bde. R.F.A.	27/05/1918	27/05/1918
Miscellaneous	Narrative Of Events On Position Occupied By "B" Battery	26/05/1918	26/05/1918
Miscellaneous	Reference Your No. S/25/6.	04/06/1918	04/06/1918
Miscellaneous	50th. Division "G"	02/06/1918	02/06/1918
Miscellaneous	Demolition Of Brigade Over Aisne And Canal	02/06/1918	02/06/1918
Miscellaneous	(Copy Of Telegram.)		
Miscellaneous	(Copy Of Telegram.)	27/05/1918	27/05/1918
Miscellaneous	(Copy Of Telegram.)	26/05/1918	26/05/1918
War Diary		01/06/1918	30/06/1918
Miscellaneous	Accounts On The Operations	06/06/1918	06/06/1918
Miscellaneous	50th. Division. G.X. 80		
Miscellaneous	A Form Messages And Signals	11/06/1918	11/06/1918
Miscellaneous	Compte Rendu Des Evenements	07/06/1918	07/06/1918
Miscellaneous	149th. Infantry Brigade	14/06/1918	14/06/1918
Miscellaneous	Account Of The Operations	06/06/1918	06/06/1918
Miscellaneous	Relief Table		
War Diary		01/07/1918	31/11/1918
War Diary	Le Carnoy	01/01/1919	28/02/1919
Heading	War Diary Of 250th (Northumbrian) Bde R.F.A. For March Volume XLVIII		
War Diary	Le Carnoy	01/03/1919	04/07/1919

WO95/2817(3) WO 95/2817(3)

50th Division

R.A.

121/5617

50th Division

1st Northumbrian Bde. RFA.

Vol I 17.4 — 6.6.15

(1) 1st Northumbrian Bde. R.F.A.

WAR DIARY
or
INTELLIGENCE SUMMARY
(Erase heading not required.)

50 Div

Apl & May 1915.

Army Form C. 2118.

Instructions regarding War Diaries and Intelligence Summaries are contained in F. S. Regs., Part II. and the Staff Manual respectively. Title pages will be prepared in manuscript.

Hour, Date, Place	Summary of Events and Information	Remarks and references to Appendices
April 17 1915	The Brigade embarked at SOUTHAMPTON between 12 noon and 5 pm.	[illegible]
April 18th	Disembarked at HAVRE 7 a.m. [illegible] 11 a.m. entrained at night.	[illegible]
April 19th	Bde H.Q. and 1st Battery left HAVRE at 1.30 a.m. 2nd and 3rd Batteries and Ammunition Column travelled independently. All units arrived at HAZEBROUCK during the night of 19-20 and went into billets — H.Q. and Column at CAESTRE, the three Batteries in farms near that village	[illegible]
April 20th CAESTRE	Nothing of importance occurred.	
April 21st	do	[illegible]
April 22nd	do.	
April 23rd	The Brigade received orders to be ready to move at short notice. The C.R.A. [illegible] the Adjutant forward to reconnoitre positions [illegible] to the East of POPERINGHE astride the POPERINGHE – YPRES road along the line of the [illegible] The Brigade left CAESTRE at [illegible] and [illegible] as far as BOESCHEPE [illegible]	[illegible]

1247 W 3299 200,000 (E) 8/14 J.B.C. & A. Forms/C. 2118/11.

Instructions regarding War Diaries and Intelligence Summaries are contained in F. S. Regs., Part II. and the Staff Manual respectively. Title pages will be prepared in manuscript.

WAR DIARY
or
~~INTELLIGENCE~~ SUMMARY
(Erase heading not required.)

Army Form C. 2118.

Hour, Date, Place	Summary of Events and Information	Remarks and references to Appendices
April 23 (cont)	returned and ordered the Brigade to [illegible]; the Batteries [illegible] on the BOESCHEPE – BERTHEN road and the Ammunition Column in BERTHEN.	[illegible]
April 24.	At 6 a.m. orders were received for the Batteries to advance to the PO-BAARSBEEK [illegible] to Brig.-General RIDDELL. The Ammunition Column was to remain & await orders. The Batteries [illegible] ready to move [illegible] but the road was blocked with cavalry moving through BOESCHEPE. At 9 a.m. the Brigade passed through POPERINGHE which was being shelled. Six shells fell into the town during the passage of the Brigade; two men of the 3rd Northumberland Battery were wounded & one horse killed by a shell which burst under a team. The Brigade halted on the YPRES road to the WEST of POPERINGHE and the C.O. [illegible] went forward to report to Brig.-Gen. RIDDELL who ordered the Brigade to occupy positions to the North of the YPRES road in support of infantry trenches in the line [illegible] – DE DRIE GOEN.	[illegible] [illegible] map sheet 28.

(3)

Instructions regarding War Diaries and Intelligence Summaries are contained in F. S. Regs., Part II. and the Staff Manual respectively. Title pages will be prepared in manuscript.

WAR DIARY
or
~~INTELLIGENCE SUMMARY~~
(Erase heading not required.)

Army Form C. 2118.

Hour, Date, Place	Summary of Events and Information	Remarks and references to Appendices
April 24 (cont.)	Positions were selected and occupied as follows — 1st Battery on ROOBAARSBEEK, 2nd Battery to the south and 3rd on the right. Bde HQ in a farm near the railway. Telephone communication was established between H.Q. & the Batteries. At 10.30 p.m. a message was received from General RIDDELL saying that the Brigade was no longer under his command.	P.M.
April 25th	Very heavy firing on the left front between 3 & 4 a.m. The Brigade stood to arms at dawn. Headquarters was moved to a farm on the South where observation was easier. As no orders had been received a message was sent to the CRA asking for orders. The ammunition column reported itself in a position to the West of POPERINGHE. The Batteries completed the entrenchment & concealment of their guns.	P.M.
April 26	Nothing of importance occurred. 2 German aeroplanes appeared over the positions but retired after being fired at by anti-aircraft guns. POPERINGHE was again shelled, apparently by a gun quite close.	

1247 W 3299 200,000 (E) 8/14 J.B.C. & A. Forms/C. 2118/11.

(4)

Instructions regarding War Diaries and Intelligence Summaries are contained in F. S. Regs., Part II. and the Staff Manual respectively. Title pages will be prepared in manuscript.

WAR DIARY
or
~~INTELLIGENCE SUMMARY~~
(Erase heading not required.)

Army Form C. 2118.

Hour, Date, Place	Summary of Events and Information	Remarks and references to Appendices
April 27	Nothing of importance occurred.	[illegible]
April 28	German aeroplanes were observed early in the morning but they were again driven off. The D.A. Ammunition Column arrived & reported. The SAA section was sent along the YPRES road to get in touch with the Northumberland Infantry Brigade and the gun sections were placed in a field to the South of POPERINGHE. Owing to the bad state of the ground and the number of troops camped in the vicinity it was found impossible to place the column more than a mile in rear. Communication with the CRA which had been interrupted for some days owing to no information ~~[illegible]~~ as to his whereabouts having been received, was re-established.	[illegible]

1247 W 3299 200,000 (E) 8/14 J.B.C. & A. Forms/C. 2118/11.

Instructions regarding War Diaries and Intelligence Summaries are contained in F. S. Regs., Part II. and the Staff Manual respectively. Title pages will be prepared in manuscript.

WAR DIARY

or

~~INTELLIGENCE SUMMARY~~

(Erase heading not required.)

Army Form C. 2118.

Hour, Date, Place	Summary of Events and Information	Remarks and references to Appendices
April 29 – 30	Nothing of importance occurred.	[illegible]
May. 1 – 4th	Nothing of importance occurred.	[illegible]
May 4th	Orders were received at 11.20 am for the Brigade to march at 8 pm. to STEENVOORDE. a billeting officer being sent in advance. The Brigade moved punctually at 8 pm. & reached STEENVOORDE at 11.30 pm. Batteries then moved into billets on the North and West of STEENVOORDE.	[illegible]
May 5th 6th	Nothing of importance occurred.	[illegible]
May 6 – 10th	Nothing of importance occurred.	[illegible]
May 10th	The Brigade moved to WATOU starting at 9.30 am. was delayed on the road by Infantry transport & arrived at 11.30 am. and went into billets in the village	[illegible]

6.

Army Form C. 2118.

Instructions regarding War Diaries and Intelligence Summaries are contained in F. S. Regs., Part II. and the Staff Manual respectively. Title pages will be prepared in manuscript.

WAR DIARY

or

~~INTELLIGENCE SUMMARY~~

(Erase heading not required.)

Hour, Date, Place	Summary of Events and Information	Remarks and references to Appendices
May 11 — 12th	Nothing of importance occurred.	C.W.O.
May 13	Nothing of importance occurred.	C.W.O.
May 14.	The Brigade marched to St JAN TER BIEZEN at 10 am + went into billets in that village	C.W.O.
May 15 — 16	Nothing of importance occurred	C.W.O.
May 16 – 27	Nothing of importance occurred.	C.W.O.
May 27	The Brigade received orders to move to G a 10 on the POPERINGHE - YPRES road. Marched at 8pm and went into ~~billets~~ bivouac close to the main road.	C.W.O.

1247 W 3299 200,000 (E) 8/14 J.B.C. & A. Forms/C. 2118/11.

7. 1st Northumbrian Bde RFA

Army Form C. 2118.

WAR DIARY
or
INTELLIGENCE SUMMARY.

(*Erase heading not required.*)

Instructions regarding War Diaries and Intelligence Summaries are contained in F. S. Regs., Part II, and the Staff Manual respectively. Title pages will be prepared in manuscript.

Hour, Date, Place.	Summary of Events and Information.	Remarks and references to Appendi
May 20.	Orders were received that the Brigade was to relieve the 7th Bde RHA & the Warwickshire H.A.(T) on the north east of YPRES. The CO. & B.Cs. went forward to ascertain the positions of Batteries.	
	They were as ~~[illegible]~~ shown on attached artillery trace.	Map I.
	The zone allotted to the Brigade was from the VELORENHOEK road to the ROULERS railway. At 8.30 pm. one section from each Battery was moved up into position replacing a corresponding battery of the H.A.	
	The sections were not fired at. Wagon lines were established on the YPRES–POPERINGHE road. The Ammunition Column was moved to H 13 d 5 5.	

8

Instructions regarding War Diaries and Intelligence Summaries are contained in F. S. Regs., Part II, and the Staff Manual respectively. Title pages will be prepared in manuscript.

WAR DIARY
or
~~INTELLIGENCE SUMMARY.~~

(Erase heading not required.)

Army Form C. 2118.

Hour, Date, Place.	Summary of Events and Information.	Remarks and references to Appendices
May 29.	The sections in position carried out registration under orders of O.C. 7th Bde R.H.A. at 8.30 pm. the remaining sections were moved up without casualties. The enemy's artillery were firing on the road leading to the positions which delayed the operation for about half an hour after which it was carried out without difficulty. O.C. 7th Bde R.H.A. then formally handed over the command. at ~~4~~ 7 pm. a very violent bombardment opened on our left. This was in support of a French attack. All was quiet in the Brigade Zone during the night.	See map I for points registered. + App. I
May 30	Registration was continued with satisfactory results, until the enemy's sniping fire rendered the observation post untenable when it was thought advisable to suspend further operations.	

9

Instructions regarding War Diaries and Intelligence Summaries are contained in F. S. Regs., Part II, and the Staff Manual respectively. Title pages will be prepared in manuscript.

WAR DIARY

or

~~INTELLIGENCE~~ SUMMARY.

(Erase heading not required.)

Army Form C. 2118.

Hour, Date, Place.	Summary of Events and Information.	Remarks and references to Appendices
May 30. (Cont)	At 12 midnight a message was received that 300 Germans were moving about in front of the Royal Fusiliers Trenches with a request to open fire on them. No definite information was received as to the exact position of the trenches referred to & fire was not opened as it was thought inadvisable to do so without more definite information. The Infantry holding the trenches in front of the Brigade were 2nd Royal Fusiliers with 1st Northumberland Fusiliers in support. An officer of the Brigade was kept in constant communication with the Infantry at POTIJZE. There was again heavy bombardment on our left at 9 pm.	C.W.

Instructions regarding War Diaries and Intelligence Summaries are contained in F. S. Regs., Part II, and the Staff Manual respectively. Title pages will be prepared in manuscript.

WAR DIARY

or

INTELLIGENCE SUMMARY.

(Erase heading not required.)

Army Form C. 2118.

Hour, Date, Place.	Summary of Events and Information.	Remarks and references to Appendices
June 1st	Registration was continued. Some of the telephone lines were doubled. A house from which Germans were reported to be observing was shelled with apparently good effect. The 2nd Battery only shot today. The day passed quietly. Reconnaissance with a view to discovering a fresh observation post was carried out without success & it was decided to ask the Infantry to make a communication trench to the old one.	[illegible]
June 2nd	The 2nd Battery re-registered its targets. The old observation post was used. The infantry had not done anything towards making a communication trench. The H.Q. dug-outs were shelled in the afternoon with small H.E. shell. No damage was done. A line was laid at night to the 1st line trenches to facilitate communication	[illegible]

Army Form C. 2118.

WAR DIARY

or

~~INTELLIGENCE SUMMARY.~~

(Erase heading not required.)

Instructions regarding War Diaries and Intelligence Summaries are contained in F. S. Regs., Part II, and the Staff Manual respectively. Title pages will be prepared in manuscript.

Hour, Date, Place.	Summary of Events and Information.	Remarks and references to Appendices
June 3rd.	The 1st Battery registered targets on the South side of its zone. Fuzes were irregular. Several H.E. shell fell around the 2nd & 3rd Battery positions & a wagon was destroyed in the 2nd Battery. No casualties.	RWO
June 4th.	Nothing of importance occurred during the day. Fire was opened in the Evening on the roads leading to the German trenches ~~[illegible]~~ in Square I 6 (Sheet 28 N.W.). Salvoes were fired from 9 p.m. to 11.30 p.m. A telephone line was laid towards an observation post in I 10.d 7 8 but owing to the shortness of the night & difficulties with the telephone line it was not found possible to complete the work.	RWO
June 5	At 2 a.m. a warning was received of an expected attack &	

Army Form C. 2118.

WAR DIARY

or

~~INTELLIGENCE SUMMARY.~~

(Erase heading not required.)

Instructions regarding War Diaries and Intelligence Summaries are contained in F. S. Regs., Part II, and the Staff Manual respectively. Title pages will be prepared in manuscript.

Hour, Date, Place.	Summary of Events and Information.	Remarks and references to Appendices
June 5th	Batteries stood to arms. All remained quiet. At 12.45 p.m. a German working party was reported at – & fire was opened on it by the 1st B.G.	
June 6th	A quiet day. The Brigade received orders to move back to billets on the POPERINGHE – ABEELE road. No firing took place during the day except in the 1st Battery which again fired at the working party. The Brigade was withdrawn without accidents at 9 p.m. & marched to Square L 29 on map 27	

Identification Trace for use with Artillery Maps.

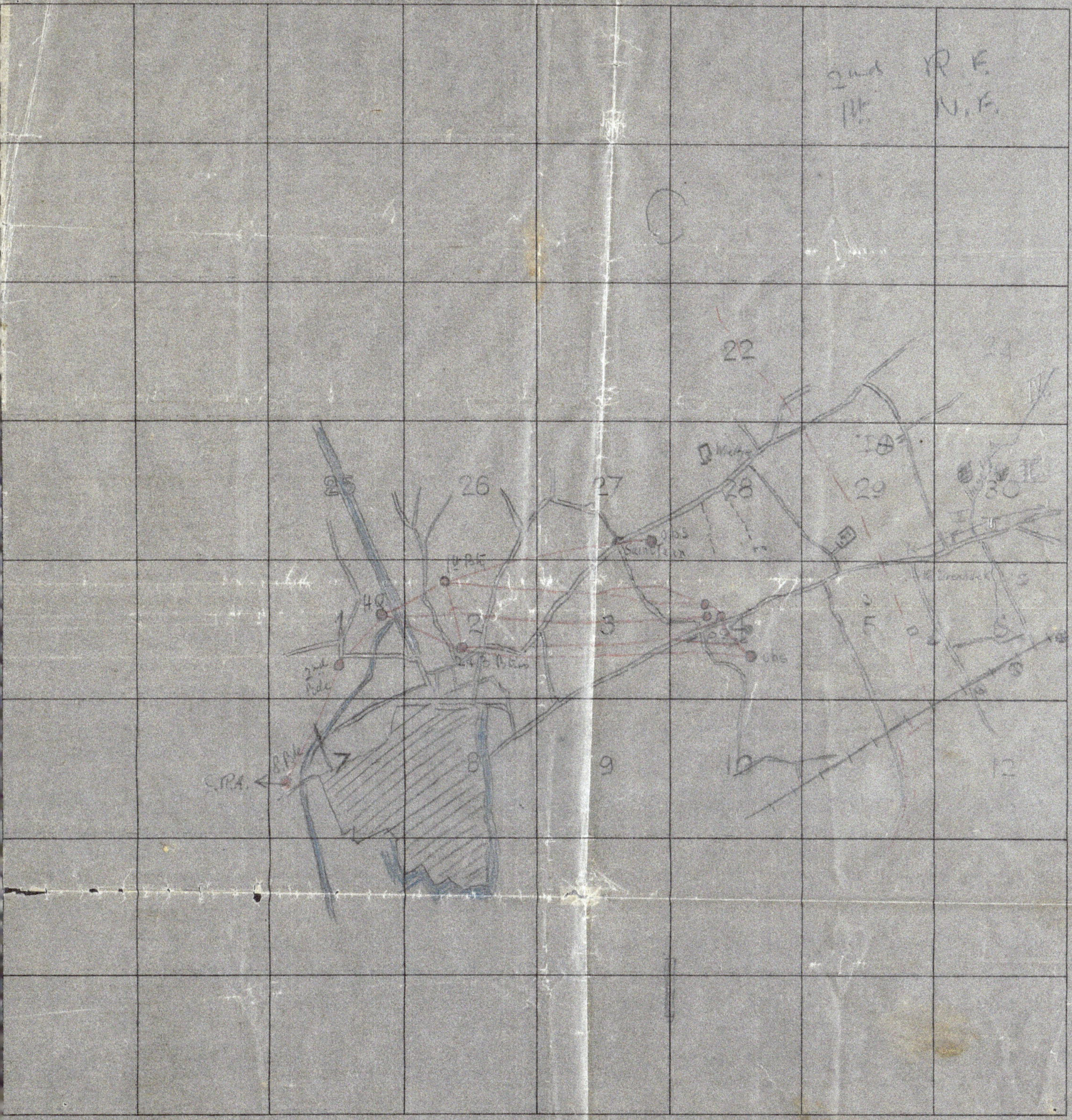

NOTE.—(1). These traces are intended to facilitate the communication of information as to the position of targets, which have been located on a squared map.

(2). The squares on this trace are 1,000 yards in length on the 1/20,000 scale, and 2,000 yards in length on the 1/40,000 scale.

(3). The squares on the trace are fitted to the squares of the map showing the targets, which are then drawn on the trace. Sufficient letters and numbers must also be added to enable the recipient to place the trace in the correct position on his own map. A little detail may also be traced, but this is not essential. The name and scale of the map to which the trace refers must be always given. The trace can be used for either the 1/20,000 or 1/40,000 scale.

G.S.G.S. 3022

approx British trenches — — —
points registered — ⊗
telephone stations ●
telephone lines ——

Tracing taken from Sheet 28 N.W.

of the 1/20,000 map of Ypres

Signature [illegible] Date 3.5.15

NOTE.—(1). These traces are intended to facilitate the communication of information as to the position of targets, which
map.

(2). The squares on this trace are 1,000 yards in length on the 1/20,000 scale, and 2,000 yards in length on the 1/

(3). The squares on the trace are fitted to the squares of the map showing the targets, which are then dr
letters and numbers must also be added to enable the recipient to place the trace in the correct position on h
may also be traced, but this is not essential. The name and scale of the map to which the trace refers mus
can be used for either the 1/20,000 or 1/40,000 scale.

G.S.G.S. 3023

Tracing of British Trenches
taken from Sheet 28 YPRES
Scale $\frac{1}{40,000}$

1–6–15

R Taylor RA

Appendix I

No	Target		
Ia	C 29 b 66	Night	Farm.
IIa	C 30 c 44	Night	Farm on Velorenhoek Rd.
IIIa	C 30 d 52		1st Battery
IVa	C 24 d 41		Velorenhoek Rd
Va	C 5 b 64		Hanebeek
Ib	I 6 b 4 8.	night	farm
IIb	I 5 d 10.10.		
IIIb	C 29 d 9.0.	night	2nd Battery
IVb	I 6 c 42		
Vb	I 6 d 26		
Ic	I 6 d 26	night	3rd Battery
IIc	I 6 c 42		
IIIc	I 5 d 10.10.		
IVc	I 6 c 37	night	

Identification Trace for use with Artillery Maps.

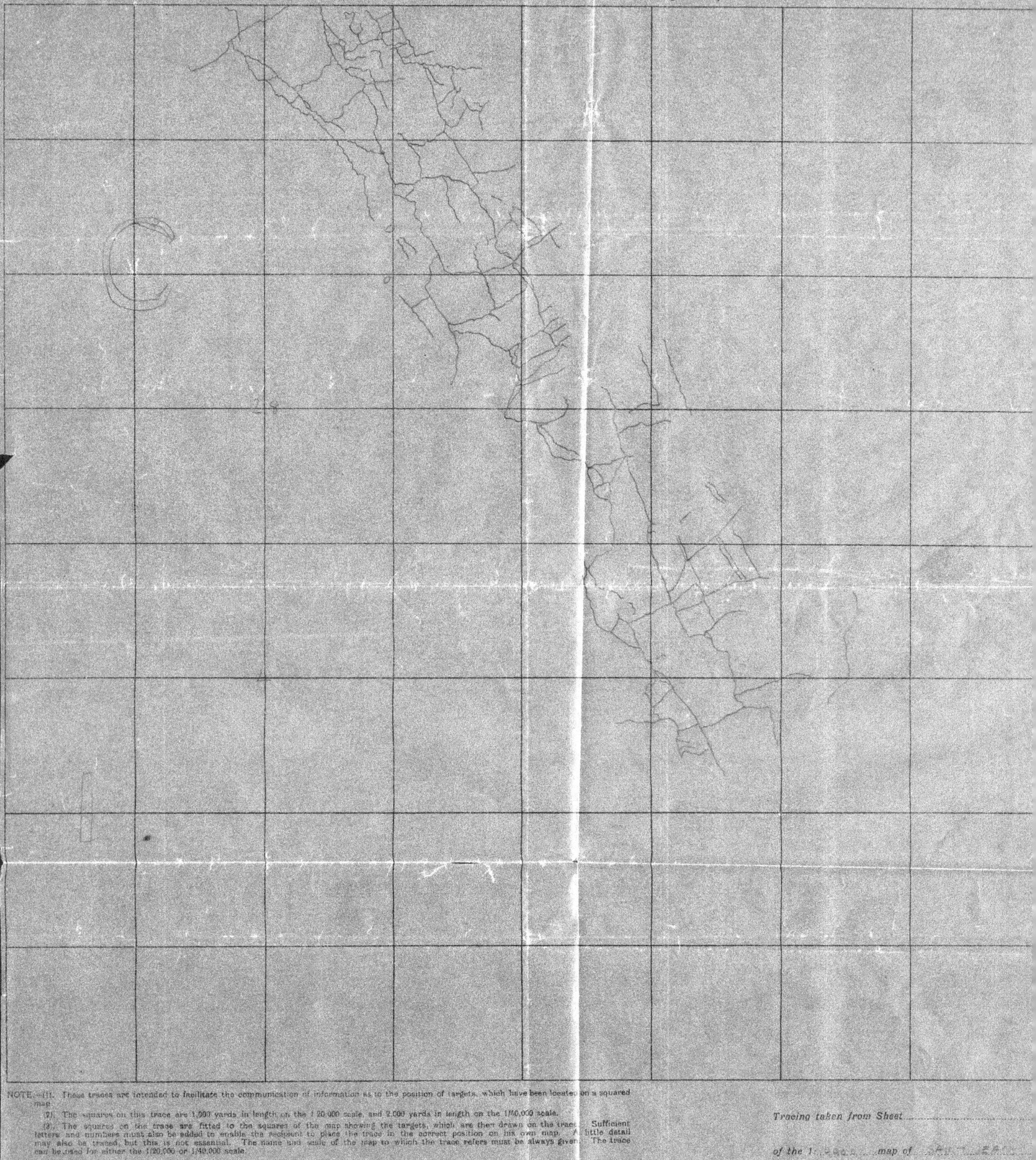

C

28

NOTE.—(1). These traces are intended to facilitate the communication of information as to the position of targets, which have been located on a squared map.

(2). The squares on this trace are 1,000 yards in length on the 1/20,000 scale, and 2,000 yards in length on the 1/40,000 scale.

(3). The squares on the trace are fitted to the squares of the map showing the targets, which are then drawn on the trace. Sufficient letters and numbers must also be added to enable the recipient to place the trace in the correct position on his own map. A little detail may also be traced, but this is not essential. The name and scale of the map to which the trace refers must be always given. The trace can be used for either the 1/20,000 or 1/40,000 scale.

G.S.G.S. 3023

German Trenches

Tracing taken from Sheet ....

of the 1: [illegible] *map of* [illegible]

Signature [illegible] *Date* [illegible]

50th Division

121/5931

1st Northumbrian Bde RFA

Vol II 7 – 30.6.15.

A2

A/6.

1st Northumbrian Bde RFA.
1.

Army Form C. 2118. /

Instructions regarding War Diaries and Intelligence Summaries are contained in F. S. Regs., Part II, and the Staff Manual respectively. Title page will be prepared in manuscript.

WAR DIARY
or
~~INTELLIGENCE SUMMARY.~~

(Erase heading not required.)

Hour, Date, Place.	Summary of Events and Information.	Remarks and references to Appendices
June 7-9.	Nothing of importance occurred Batteries refilled with amm and cleaned up.	[illegible]
June 10.	The O.C. and adjutant reconnoitred possible positions for the Brigade south of ZILLEBEKE. positions were difficult to find, chiefly owing to the open nature of the country and the difficulty of obtaining defilade from the south as well as the East. a bad position was eventually found in I27 a and b. near BLAUWPOORT FARM on the KLIETGAT BEEK. The position and nature of the ground would necessitate placing Batteries almost directly behind one another. The dampness of the ground makes little digging possible and a great deal of work would be necessary to provide cover for the guns. The approaches are bad, and it is doubtful if guns, having once got into the position, could be got out. The position is much too far forward.	

2 2

Instructions regarding War Diaries and Intelligence Summaries are contained in F. S. Regs., Part II, and the Staff Manual respectively. Title pages will be prepared in manuscript.

WAR DIARY

or

~~INTELLIGENCE SUMMARY.~~

(Erase heading not required.)

Army Form C. 2118.

Hour, Date, Place.	Summary of Events and Information.	Remarks and references to Appendices
June 10th (cont)	Very great difficulty has been experienced throughout the Brigade's sojourn on the Continent, in obtaining the stores from Ordnance, so much so that the Equipment of Batteries has never been complete, + many essential stores are still missing. This appeared of such grave importance that a strongly worded report was sent in to the C.R.A. on the subject. It is difficult to justify the sending of partially equipped troops into action against a powerful and well armed enemy. There is little doubt that the 15 pr B.L.C. Mk I is unequal to the strain of modern artillery fighting, and that even with the best of detachments it is unable successfully to oppose more modern + up to date Equipments. Battery Commanders have felt very keenly the impossibility of keeping their Batteries up to the mark owing to the non-provision of stores by Ordnance.	W.O.

Army Form C. 2118. 3

WAR DIARY

or

INTELLIGENCE SUMMARY.

(Erase heading not required.)

Instructions regarding War Diaries and Intelligence Summaries are contained in F. S. Regs., Part II, and the Staff Manual respectively. Title pages will be prepared in manuscript.

Hour, Date, Place.	Summary of Events and Information.	Remarks and references to Appendices
June 11 & 12th	Nothing of importance occurred.	[initials]
June 13th	Further reconnaissance of the positions at BLAUWPOORT FARM was made by Battery leaders, with a view to their possible occupation.	[initials]
June ~~13th~~ 14th [initials]	Orders were received at 8.30 pm. to move two Batteries to N.W. of YPRES to relieve two Belgian Batteries. (Major H.S. BELL D.S.O. assumed command of the Brigade in the absence of Lt. Colonel C. FENWICK who was admitted to hospital.) The O.C. and O.C. 2nd & 3rd Batteries went on to VLAMMERTINGHE CHATEAU and reported to C.R.A. VI Division, and were shown the positions of the Batteries. These were in I.C. The Batteries were placed under the command of O.C. 24 Bde R.F.A.	[initials]

4

Army Form C. 2118.

Instructions regarding War Diaries and Intelligence Summaries are contained in F. S. Regs., Part II, and the Staff Manual respectively. Title pages will be prepared in manuscript.

WAR DIARY
or
INTELLIGENCE SUMMARY.

(*Erase heading not required.*)

Hour, Date, Place.	Summary of Events and Information.	Remarks and references to Appendices
June ~~16~~th 15 CHO	The Belgian Batteries moved out at 1 am. the 2nd & 3rd Northumberland Batteries taking their places immediately. The positions were left in a very foul state. The Batteries were ready to open fire at 11 am. but nothing was done until the afternoon owing to presence of German observation balloons. 2nd Battery registered farm C 16. c. 8. 8. 3rd Battery " " C 22 b 8 8 and C 16 b 5 1 Orders were given to open fire at 3.45 am. the next morning (17th) as a demonstration in support of an attack near BELLEWAARDE	all ref. Sheet 28 N.W. CHO
June ~~17~~ 16th CHO	Fire was opened at 3.45 am. & maintained till 3.55 - 97 rounds being fired. Artillery bombardment on front attacked lasted till 4.15.	

5

Army Form C. 2118.

WAR DIARY

or

INTELLIGENCE SUMMARY.

(Erase heading not required.)

Instructions regarding War Diaries and Intelligence Summaries are contained in F. S. Regs., Part II, and the Staff Manual respectively. Title pages will be prepared in manuscript.

Hour, Date, Place.	Summary of Events and Information.	Remarks and references to Appendices
June ~~17~~ 16th Ap	2nd Battery fired successfully on working party C16a 8 8. Both Batteries searched for German Battery behind C16b which was firing on our Infantry trenches. The enemy's Battery ceased fire. Information was received of the success of the attack of the morning. The Bombardment re-opened about 7.30 pm for a short time but the Batteries of the Brigade did not take part. The night passed quietly.	Cl.O.
June 17th	2nd Battery fired on German working party at "farm 8" obtaining 4 direct hits. 3rd Battery fired on trenches near Shell trap farm. Both observation stations shelled. 2nd Lieut L. J. MILBURN wounded left arm. Night quiet.	Cl.O.

6

Army Form C. 2118.

Instructions regarding War Diaries and Intelligence Summaries are contained in F. S. Regs., Part II, and the Staff Manual respectively. Title pages will be prepared in manuscript.

WAR DIARY
or
INTELLIGENCE SUMMARY.

(Erase heading not required.)

Hour, Date, Place.	Summary of Events and Information.	Remarks and references to Appendices
June 18.	The day was quiet. Both Batteries fired on German trenches & working parties.	[illegible]
June 19.	The Batteries moved out of action at 8.30pm and returned to Billets.	[illegible]
June 20.	The O.C. & B.Cs. reconnoitred positions at KEMMEL occupied by 2nd NORTH MIDLAND Bde R.F.A. Headquarters at DRANOUTRE Batteries on KEMMEL HILL.	[illegible]
June 21	The Brigade moved to DRANOUTRE - 1 Section per Battery moved into action in the Evening.	[illegible]

Army Form C. 2118. 7

WAR DIARY

or

INTELLIGENCE SUMMARY.

(Erase heading not required.)

Instructions regarding War Diaries and Intelligence Summaries are contained in F. S. Regs., Part II, and the Staff Manual respectively. Title pages will be prepared in manuscript.

Hour, Date, Place.	Summary of Events and Information.	Remarks and references to Appendices
June ~~[illegible]~~ 22nd	The sections in action registered points in their zone. The remaining section came into position at 9.30 pm. the 2nd N. Midland Bde moving out.	[illegible]
June 23rd	Registration was continued. All remained quiet on the front covered by the Brigade	[illegible]
June 24th	2nd & 3rd Batteries registered points on the portions of the zone outside their own. The weather was misty & observation not so easy as on previous days.	[illegible]
June 25	12.30 am. report received that ~~[illegible]~~ Enemy were massing opposite centre of zone. Btys stood to arms till 3 am. Practically no firing was done. Weather very misty with heavy thunder storm in evening.	[illegible]

8

Army Form C. 2118.

WAR DIARY
or
INTELLIGENCE SUMMARY.
(Erase heading not required.)

Instructions regarding War Diaries and Intelligence Summaries are contained in F. S. Regs., Part II, and the Staff Manual respectively. Title pages will be prepared in manuscript.

Hour, Date, Place.	Summary of Events and Information.	Remarks and references to Appendices
June 26	Clear bright day. Observation Easy. Fire was, however, stopped at the request of ~~the~~ Infantry as the Enemy had retaliated on our trenches in answer to our howitzers' fire in the morning. Communications taken over from N. Midland Division proved very unsatisfactory & required much work to keep going – but were improved daily.	[initials]
June 27.	1st & 2nd Batteries continued registration. Reports were received as follows: 1st Battery reported a lamp signalling from hill 63 in U13-14 at 11.30 pm. on 26th. 2nd Battery reported Enemy wire much strengthened opposite F4 trench and	Sheet 28 S.W.

Instructions regarding War Diaries and Intelligence Summaries are contained in F. S. Regs., Part II, and the Staff Manual respectively. Title pages will be prepared in manuscript.

WAR DIARY

or

INTELLIGENCE SUMMARY.

(*Erase heading not required.*)

Army Form C. 2118. 9

Hour, Date, Place.	Summary of Events and Information.	Remarks and references to Appendices
June 27.	Hostile fire on Trench 15. 3rd Battery experimented with system of signalling from Infantry trenches at night. The positions of Batteries etc were – H.Q. – DRANOUTRE observation post KEMMEL HILL 1st Bty N33 a 8.8. wagon line DRANOUTRE observation Stn in front of Battery and KEMMEL HILL 2nd Bty N26 d 8.0. observation post KEMMEL HILL wagon line N31 a 8.8. 3rd Bty N32 d 2.6. observation post KEMMEL HILL wagon line WATERGAT Ammunition Column S9 b 6.5. Dump in DRANOUTRE	Sheet 28 S.W. [initials]
June 28	Quiet day. 3rd Battery registered LONE TREE FARM. Weather very misty	[initials]

- Instructions regarding War Diaries and Intelligence Summaries are contained in F. S. Regs., Part II, and the Staff Manual respectively. Title pages will be prepared in manuscript.

WAR DIARY

or

INTELLIGENCE SUMMARY.

(Erase heading not required.)

Army Form C. 2118. 10

Hour, Date, Place.	Summary of Events and Information.	Remarks and references to Appendices
June 29.	A new zone was allotted to the Brigade so as to cover the ground occupied by the 151 Infantry Brigade. Considerable difficulty was found in establishing communication with the trenches in the new zone owing to lack of wire. The Batteries registered points on the new zone.	[illegible]
June 30.	Batteries continued registration. 3rd Battery zone very difficult owing to trees obscuring the view + proximity of trenches to one another. Ordnance Stores still very difficult to get + now appear many complaints about rations	[illegible]

50th Division

121/6231

1st Northumbrian Bde RFA.

Vol III

1 - 31 - 7 - 15

1st NORTHUMBRIAN BDE R.F.A.T.

Army Form C. 2118.

WAR DIARY

or

~~INTELLIGENCE SUMMARY.~~

(Erase heading not required.)

Instructions regarding War Diaries and Intelligence Summaries are contained in F. S. Regs., Part II, and the Staff Manual respectively. Title pages will be prepared in manuscript.

Hour, Date, Place.	Summary of Events and Information.	Remarks and references to Appendices
July 1st 1915 – 2nd	The weather was very misty and no firing was done on either of these days, except registering the sights of the zone. The communications were improved throughout.	[initials]
July 3rd + 4th	Batteries continued registration. Reconnaissances for forward gun positions and for drumming positions were also carried out. Enemy's artillery displayed considerable activity – shelling NEUVE EGLISE and MONT KEMMEL.	[initials]

Army Form C. 2118.

WAR DIARY

or

~~INTELLIGENCE SUMMARY.~~

(Erase heading not required.)

Instructions regarding War Diaries and Intelligence Summaries are contained in F. S. Regs., Part II, and the Staff Manual respectively. Title pages will be prepared in manuscript.

Hour, Date, Place.	Summary of Events and Information.	Remarks and references to Appendices
July 6 & 7.	Batteries continued registration. Nothing of interest to report: Communications still require much improvement.	[illegible initials]
July 8.	German working parties observed in open. Fired at & dispersed. Red cross flag & small blue & white flag on German trenches. Batteries also registered several points on MESSINES ridge	[illegible initials]
July 9	Batteries only fired on night-lines.	[illegible initials]
July 10.	Enemy showed activity with trench howitzers & bombs. Fire of Batteries appeared to silence them. Further registration.	[illegible initials]

Instructions regarding War Diaries and Intelligence Summaries are contained in F. S. Regs., Part II, and the Staff Manual respectively. Title pages will be prepared in manuscript.

WAR DIARY

or

~~INTELLIGENCE SUMMARY.~~

(Erase heading not required.)

Army Form C. 2118.

Hour, Date, Place.	Summary of Events and Information.	Remarks and references to Appendices
July 11	Nothing of interest occurred. Positions to support G.H.Q. line were reorganised. Two of those prepared by North Midland Division were found impossible – one too exposed and high trees blocking the line of fire & the other behind a hill which could only be cleared at extreme range. Others more suitable were chosen.	[illegible]
July 12.	Enemy's artillery much more active. Several shells fell near LINDENHOEK and NEUVE EGLISE. During the night a good deal of bombing – which was three times stopped by 3rd Northumberland Battery.	[illegible]

Instructions regarding War Diaries and Intelligence Summaries are contained in F. S. Regs., Part II, and the Staff Manual respectively. Title pages will be prepared in manuscript.

WAR DIARY

or

~~INTELLIGENCE SUMMARY.~~

(Erase heading not required.)

Army Form C. 2118.

Hour, Date, Place.	Summary of Events and Information.	Remarks and references to Appendices
July 13.	Again activity displayed by Enemy's artillery at LINDENHOEK and MONT KEMMEL. At night heavy firing to North & South & a report of gas at 8.30 pm. All quiet again at 10 pm.	[initials]
July 14.	Warned for move to ARMENTIERES. C.R.A. 28th Division came to inspect positions with a view to taking over.	[initials]
July 15.	C.O. went to ARMENTIERES to inspect positions. 1st sections of relieving Batteries came in during night - ~~[illegible]~~ Our Sections moving out to position. Night very wet & dark.	[initials]

Instructions regarding War Diaries and Intelligence Summaries are contained in F. S. Regs., Part II, and the Staff Manual respectively. Title pages will be prepared in manuscript.

WAR DIARY

or

INTELLIGENCE SUMMARY.

(Erase heading not required.)

Army Form C. 2118.

Hour, Date, Place.	Summary of Events and Information.	Remarks and references to Appendices
July 16–19	Remaining sections moved to ARMENTIERES. Great congestion in the area. Though the town was supposed to be for 50th Division it appeared to be full of other troops who made no attempt to move out. 3rd Battery had to prepare its position near Hospice. After great labour was told the position must not be occupied for fear of drawing fire on infantry in hospice. Thus a very good position had to be abandoned in a country where positions are rare. The hospice can be seen by enemy & infantry should not be billetted on that side of town at all	

Army Form C. 2118.

Instructions regarding War Diaries and Intelligence Summaries are contained in F. S. Regs., Part II, and the Staff Manual respectively. Title pages will be prepared in manuscript.

WAR DIARY

or

~~INTELLIGENCE SUMMARY.~~

(Erase heading not required.)

Hour, Date, Place.	Summary of Events and Information.	Remarks and references to Appendices
	No headquarters available for Brigade. House next to infantry Brigadier occupied by Arty Bde of another Division, so Bde H.Q. had to find quarters on the other side of the town where they were quite out of touch with everybody. Reconnoitred for new position for 2nd B.G. There seems to be a considerable difference of opinion between 27th & 50th Divisions as to areas. Everybody here seems extraordinarily sleepy.	CW

Army Form C. 2118.

WAR DIARY

or

~~INTELLIGENCE SUMMARY.~~

(Erase heading not required.)

Instructions regarding War Diaries and Intelligence Summaries are contained in F. S. Regs., Part II, and the Staff Manual respectively. Title pages will be prepared in manuscript.

Hour, Date, Place.	Summary of Events and Information.	Remarks and references to Appendices
July 20.	3rd Battery still looking for fresh position. No billets or office for H.Q.s.	
21	Decided on a position for 3rd Battery. No headquarter communications can yet be laid out. The Staff appear to do nothing towards finding available place for office. Positions of batteries are as follows:- 1st I 8.b. 3.2. 2nd I 9.a. 7.8. 3rd C. 26.d. 5.5. 3rd Battery position requires to be carefully made - wooden huts from market gardens are being put over all the guns which are in the gardens.	
22.	The 3rd batt: put one gun into position - still working on others. No office or billets for Hdqrs fixed yet. Started a dugout in the garden of the Infantry Brigadier to make a telephone room.	
23.	Nothing of interest to report - dugout nearly finished.	
24	The Staff gave us a very small & dirty house near the Infantry Brigade Hdqrs for our headquarters - after much trouble made habitable - telephone lines laid to all three batteries - the infantry brigade & the brigade Hdqrs of the Artillery Brigade on our left. communications good.	

Instructions regarding War Diaries and Intelligence Summaries are contained in F. S. Regs., Part II, and the Staff Manual respectively. Title pages will be prepared in manuscript.

WAR DIARY

or

~~INTELLIGENCE SUMMARY.~~

(Erase heading not required.)

Army Form C. 2118.

Hour, Date, Place.	Summary of Events and Information.	Remarks and references to Appendices
	3rd Battery guns in position but not yet ready to fire – Some shell fell on 1st & 3rd Battery wagon lines – in former killed 2 chargers & wounded one man slightly.	
25 July – 29th	Nothing of interest to report. Our batteries fired chiefly on working parties in front of trenches & shelled PERENCHIES and WEZMACQUART in reply to the shelling of the Asylum & ARMENTIERES generally, by the enemy.	
30 July	The 3rd North'd Battery while registering found the range to the enemies trenches with a good burst & then verified. – The verifying round burst short though fired at the same elevation & with the same corrector. The head of the shell fell into a dug out in our trenches & killed a man. An examination of this part of the shell showed that the accident was due to a faulty shell for the case of the shell had expanded at the shoulder & slipped over the neck – the centre tube was not in one piece as it should have been & apparently had failed to support the head. The shell had not had a true flight but apparently a series of gyrations.	

Army Form C. 2118.

WAR DIARY

or

~~INTELLIGENCE SUMMARY.~~

(Erase heading not required.)

Instructions regarding War Diaries and Intelligence Summaries are contained in F. S. Regs., Part II, and the Staff Manual respectively. Title pages will be prepared in manuscript.

Hour, Date, Place.	Summary of Events and Information.	Remarks and references to Appendices
31 July.	The Brigade combined with the 2nd North[n] Brigade & 4th North[n] (How) Brigade, the Artillery of the 27th Div[n], and the 21st Trench Battery & the Infantry Trench Mortars in bombarding the German Trenches. Several large gaps were made providing good opportunities for machine guns. There was very little retaliation. The Bombardment lasted for about an hour.	

50th Division

121/6587

1st Northbn Bde R.F.A.

Vol IV.

From 1 - 31. 8. 15

Army Form C. 2118

Instructions regarding War Diaries and Intelligence Summaries are contained in F. S. Regs., Part. II. and the Staff Manual respectively. Title Pages will be prepared in manuscript.

WAR DIARY
or
~~INTELLIGENCE SUMMARY~~
(Erase heading not required.)

1st Northumbrian Brigade R.F.A.
50th Division.

Imp. Hav., 26/7 — 40.000

Place	Date	Hour	Summary of Events and Information	Remarks and references to Appendices
ARMENTIERES	August 1915			
	1-2		On this night the 149th Infantry Brigade relieved 151st on our front.	
	2.		The third battery again had a shell short + into our own trenches - fortunately it caused no casualties. - it was fired by the same gun as the previous one. All guns of the Brigade appear to be getting very worn. An aeroplane flew over from the German lines with no distinguishing marks on it - neither side fired at it.	
	3.		A report was sent to the C.R.A. on the state of the guns. 1 gun of 3rd Battery sent to I.O.M. + borrowed one from the 3rd North. Brigade	
	4.		The running-out gear of one of the 2nd Battery guns jammed - on being taken to pieces this was found to be due to a defective gland. This gun had just previously been to the I.O.M. to be overhauled + when it was there the work had been done by the battery fitter sergeant + limber gunner without any supervision + no one had examined the gun when it was taken down. A report has been sent to the C.R.A. + a suggestion made that such work in future be done at the battery position under the supervision of the battery officers.	
	5.		Received 10 more reinforcements + 1 returned sick.	
	6.		Received orders to move all wagon lines to the field where the 3rd Battery now are. The C.O. went to make the necessary arrangements but when he arrived he was told the move was cancelled.	

Army Form C. 2118

WAR DIARY
or
INTELLIGENCE SUMMARY
(Erase heading not required.)

Instructions regarding War Diaries and Intelligence Summaries are contained in F. S. Regs., Part. II. and the Staff Manual respectively. Title Pages will be prepared in manuscript.

Imp. Hav., 26/7 — 10.000

Place	Date	Hour	Summary of Events and Information	Remarks and references to Appendices
ARMENTIERES	August 1915 7		Received fresh orders as to moving wagon lines. Adjutant went with the Staff Captain to make the necessary arrangements. The 1st Battery moved to the same field as the 3rd Battery occupy + Headquarters and the 2nd Battery moved to a field at B.17.d.6.5. There is no cover whatever from aeroplane observation and no shelter for the men. Received fresh instructions as to forage allowances and classification of horses. The 2nd lot in 3 days. Received a long list of "amended requirements as to returns" the covering letter saying "much unnecessary correspondence is caused by inaccurate returns". On enquiry it turned out this list is inaccurate in many respects.	
	8.		Another letter giving instructions as to forage:-	
	8-9		This night there was very heavy firing to the North which went on for some time. The Brigade stood by from 3 a.m. to 7 but things on our front were quiet.	
	9.		Asked for instructions as to present forage regulations. The questions could not be answered + all the previous regulations are to be consolidated. A captain from the I.O.M made an inspection of guns of 1st + 2nd Batteries. His report was that the guns were not bad though one of the 2nd Battery guns is worn to as much as 3/100th of an inch, but the sights elevating gear + traversing gear are practically done.	
	10.		Received a further amended list of returns required. Five officers (one Lt. Col + 4 subalterns) from 2nd line units arrived for a course of instruction.	
	11.		The 1st battery registered on the zone of the 1st Brigade R.F.A. (27th Divn) on our right and caused a considerable fire behind the German lines. The 2nd + 3rd Batteries registered on the zone of the 2nd Northumbrian Brigade on our left. Some 4.2 H.E. how. shells fell very near Brigade Headquarters but fortunately did very little damage. The wheel of a bicycle was punctured. We were able to obtain the bearing of the battery.	
	12.		The 3rd Batt: shot over the German trenches in conjunction with the 5th Durham (How) battery + the enemy in reply shelled the North Riding Battery of the 2nd North: Brigade	

Instructions regarding War Diaries and Intelligence Summaries are contained in F. S. Regs., Part II. and the Staff Manual respectively. Title Pages will be prepared in manuscript.

WAR DIARY
or
INTELLIGENCE SUMMARY
(Erase heading not required.)

Army Form C. 2118

Imp. Hav., 26/7 — 10.000

Place	Date	Hour	Summary of Events and Information	Remarks and references to Appendices
ARMENTIERES	August 1915 12.		Some more H.E. shells fell just over Brigade Headquarters apparently from the same battery.	
	13.		Nothing of interest to report.	
	14		Some cavalry were sent to dig a switch line of trenches passing through the 3rd Battery position - this is in full view of German observation stations & is sure to cause trouble.	
			Major H.S. Bell D.S.O. Gazetted Lt. Col. to date from 27 July	
	15.		The 2nd battery position was shelled probably owing to the new line of trenches - three 15 cm. shell fell within 5 yards of one gun but no damage was done except to the house used by the officers. fortunately they had moved to another yesterday. All telephone lines were cut. One 15 cm shell fell into a cellar but did not explode. The inhabitant appeared 2 mins. later carrying it on his shoulder. The battery took charge of it.	
			Col. Bell went on leave & Major Johnston assumed command of the Brigade.	
			Heavy thundershowers & some hail.	
	16.		Major General Wilkinson (G.O.C. division) visited the Brigade Headquarters & 1st Battery. More thundershowers.	
	17.		Some trouble has been caused lately as to who has to decide when support should be given by retaliating for fire over our trenches. Up to the present it has been left to the decision of the artillery officer in the trenches but a new battalion was in front of us & when a few shells only came over they rang up their headquarters & asked for	

Instructions regarding War Diaries and Intelligence Summaries are contained in F. S. Regs., Part. II. and the Staff Manual respectively. Title Pages will be prepared in manuscript.

WAR DIARY
or
INTELLIGENCE SUMMARY
(Erase heading not required.)

Army Form C. 2118

Imp. Hav., 26/7 — 10.000

Place	Date	Hour	Summary of Events and Information	Remarks and references to Appendices
			artillery support - They did not ask the F.O.O. & did not ring up the battery direct although there were 3 direct lines from their particular trenches to the battery supporting them. The message went right round by Div^nl Hdqrs & so to CRA & then to this brigade Hdqrs. It was then too late. The F.O.O. reported that he had not told his battery to fire as he did not consider it necessary owing to the small number of shells arriving - there were only about 20 & those over our trenches - it turned out that the trench commander was a young subaltern who was going on leave the next day & consequently rather nervous. It has now been decided that the F.O.O. has no discretion but fire must be given whenever any infantry officer asks for it - it will probably lead to a great waste of ammunition. Probably no trouble would ever have arisen if the infantry would trouble to learn something about the telephone lines - no officer knows or cares anything about instruments or lines yet it is their business to keep the lines to the batteries in repair in the trench zone.	
		18.	Sent in to C.R.A. a report on the telephone system asking for help from the infantry to make lines safer & for proper dug outs to be prepared for artillery telephonists at the end of the communicating trenches - such dug outs should be an R.E. service - nothing seems likely to be done.	

Instructions regarding War Diaries and Intelligence Summaries are contained in F. S. Regs., Part. II. and the Staff Manual respectively. Title Pages will be prepared in manuscript.

WAR DIARY
or
INTELLIGENCE SUMMARY
(Erase heading not required.)

Army Form C. 2118

Imp. Hav., 26/7 — 10.000

Place	Date	Hour	Summary of Events and Information	Remarks and references to Appendices
		19.	Sent a letter to CRA asking for proper dug outs to be prepared for F.O.Os. The Germans appear to be preparing a gun emplacement about 600x behind their trenches & we are watching it. It has now been proved by our seeing cables ~~[illegible]~~ on insulators on posts that the Germans are using electricity in their trenches. This has long been suspected owing to a hum heard in our trench telephones & to experiment made whereby the current was picked up into a telephone & the hum read as that caused by an alternating current of 50 which is the periodicity of the LILLE system. They seem to be using this for pumps & other machinery. Very little firing has been done by us lately - the light has been bad.	
		20	Nothing of interest to report.	
		21	The Brigade fired 45 rounds of gun fire at the gun emplacement mentioned on the 19th - all shots seemed well placed but result ~~[illegible]~~ could not be ascertained.	
		22.	~~[illegible]~~ Col. Bell was to have returned from leave but did not arrive & all sorts of rumours did. It afterwards turned out that a collier had sunk in Boulogne harbour & all traffic been stopped	
		23.	Col: Bell returned & assumed command.	
		24.	Nothing of interest to report.	
		25.	Sir John French, C-in-C, visited the 3rd Battery while he was inspecting the new trenches dug by the cavalry, The 151st Inf. Brigade relieved the 150th.	
		26.	Not a single round was fired by the Brigade & no hostile shell fell anywhere near us. We have been told to economise ammunition as much as possible. A demand has been received from Ministry of Munitions for the services of Lieut. W.S. Walker.	

Army Form C. 2118

Instructions regarding War Diaries and Intelligence Summaries are contained in F. S. Regs., Part. II. and the Staff Manual respectively. Title Pages will be prepared in manuscript.

WAR DIARY
or
INTELLIGENCE SUMMARY

(Erase heading not required.)

Imp. Hav., 26/7 — 40.000

Place	Date 1915	Hour	Summary of Events and Information	Remarks and references to Appendices
ARMENTIERES	Aug 27		The 1st Battery fired at the enemy's transport in conjunction with infantry & 27th Div. Arty on one night at 10.5 pm.	
	28.		Lt. W. C. Walker returned to civil employment.	
	29-30		Nothing of interest to report.	

50th Division

121/6930

1st North'n Bde RFA.

Vol V

Sept. 15

Army Form C. 2118

Instructions regarding War Diaries and Intelligence Summaries are contained in F. S. Regs., Part. II. and the Staff Manual respectively. Title Pages will be prepared in manuscript.

WAR DIARY

1st Northumbrian Brigade R.F.A.

~~INTELLIGENCE SUMMARY~~

(Erase heading not required.)

Imp. Hav., 26/7 — 10.000

Place	Date	Hour	Summary of Events and Information	Remarks and references to Appendices
ARMENTIERES	1915 Sept 1-3		Nothing of interest to report.	
	4.		There was a rehearsal of what would happen in the case of a German attack. All headquarters moved to advance stations on receipt of a message from Divisional Hdqrs. Imaginary orders + messages were sent each being prefixed "scheme aaa". So far as this Brigade was concerned everything moved well only one or two minor defects being found, but probably new arrangements will be made for C.R.A + Divisional headquarters.	
			The rain of the last few days has had a serious effect on telephone communication with the trenches. The lines of 1st + 2nd Battery have been weak + those of the third battery which are much longer have failed altogether. The lines are pinned to the side of the communicating trenches + the insulation of the D 3 wire does not appear to be strong enough to resist the wet. Each line of the 1st + 2nd batteries is probably 2 or 2½ miles long + those of the 3rd 3½ - 4.	
	6.		A fair amount of activity among the civil population, all west of the railway to HOUPLINES being under orders to clear out by night. The Bosch with quite a number of well timed shots livened up the removal operations + somewhat quickened the pace of the old chaps taking loads of bricks from CHAPELLE D'ARMENTIERES for horse standings in the wagon lines. A party of Infantry (27th Div.) showed	

WAR DIARY
or
INTELLIGENCE SUMMARY
(Erase heading not required.)

Instructions regarding War Diaries and Intelligence Summaries are contained in F. S. Regs., Part. II. and the Staff Manual respectively. Title Pages will be prepared in manuscript.

Army Form C. 2118

Imp. Hav., 26/7 — 10.000

Place	Date	Hour	Summary of Events and Information	Remarks and references to Appendices
			Great bravery by advancing towards LILLE in fours regardless of being in full view of a somewhat watchful enemy. Total bag 1 killed 10 wounded just beside 1st North Battery position. It was regrettable that our quack was unable to attend to these but he was at 'that Belial' (Bailleul) procuring medical & other comforts with the mess cart	
	7.		Not quite all the civilians got away last night & the Bosch again disturbed the peaceful serenity of the neighbourhood & hurried proceedings some. One old woman was passing Brigade headquarters carrying a basket full of glass when a shell arrived in the street & result to contents of basket disastrous & old woman took shelter in the office - after about 10 minutes she proceeded on her way with a basket full of broken glass & (judging by the state of the floor) a damp pair of underclothing. One item of interest noticed was the strength of the native "articles de chambre". A hand cart full of a labourers household goods was suddenly increased in speed by a rude shell & one of these articles fell on to the cobbles but was replaced unbroken	
	8.		A fairly quiet day on the whole. Brick leading much curtailed as traffic is now only allowed on the road between 5 PM & 9 am.	
	9.		One shell passed through 1st Battery O.P. The gunner look out was covered with brick dust but came out shook himself & continued till relieved.	

Instructions regarding War Diaries and Intelligence Summaries are contained in F. S. Regs., Part. II. and the Staff Manual respectively. Title Pages will be prepared in manuscript.

WAR DIARY
or
INTELLIGENCE SUMMARY
(Erase heading not required.)

Army Form C. 2118

Imp. Hav., 26/7 — 10.000

Place	Date	Hour	Summary of Events and Information	Remarks and references to Appendices
			Another was a direct hit in a gun emplacement. The nose got through the sandbags + lodged in the front part of a waggon body. The steel plates fitted before leaving England no doubt saved the whole being blown up. The Staff Captain 50th Div. Artʸ was called from his dinner to be told what we thought of his telephone staff.	
	10+11		Nothing of interest occurred.	
	12.		The 27th divⁿ are experimenting with a new H.E. ammunition + fired 2300 rounds from 2 batteries. No reply from the enemy	
	13.		The enemy replied to the hate of 27th Divⁿ + did not confine it to them. They started at 4.30 am + continued at intervals throughout the day. They killed two horses + hit the house of the 149th Infantry Brigade Headquarters, next to this Brigade headquarters. The 27th Divⁿ continued their experiment. Two horses attached to the limber of a G.S. wagon galloped down the road without any driver. They showed considerable skill in keeping on their legs + off other traffic being probably considerably helped by the absence of the driver.	
	14		A few more shells but nothing important.	
	15		A very quiet day. 1st Battery did some registration ~~by~~ with an aeroplane observer + wireless but the light was bad.	
	16		The Brigade had a shoot over trench 70 but 48 rounds elicited no reply from the enemy	

Army Form C. 2118

Instructions regarding War Diaries and Intelligence Summaries are contained in F. S. Regs., Part. II. and the Staff Manual respectively. Title Pages will be prepared in manuscript.

WAR DIARY
or
INTELLIGENCE SUMMARY
(Erase heading not required.)

Imp. Hav., 26/7 — 10.000

Place	Date	Hour	Summary of Events and Information	Remarks and references to Appendices
	17.		A quiet day - told to economise ammunition as much as possible although 2 days ago we were told two days ago there was no need for economy. Leave boat stopped - nobody returned but it didn't affect any of our fellows going away.	
	18.		2nd Battery registered two targets with aeroplane - some trouble with 2nd target as jamming breech made it impossible to shoot just as observer was ready. Enemy killed 3 rats in our trenches	
	19		The enemy put a lot of shell behind + into our trenches between 5+6 am. The infantry kept repeatedly calling for support + "asked for more" - As a result we fired 98 rounds but nothing seemed to happen on either side. Our infantry had one man killed + one wounded. Several fuzes have been received with the gas vents unscaled - If any of these get into shells without being checked + are fired, they are certain to cause prematures. One of the batteries of 3rd Brigade fired 3 prematures into our 2nd Batt. yesterday within 15 mins - fortunately they wounded no one - We can get no front + rear discs for obturating pads with the result the pads are wearing quickly + the supply of them is <u>very</u> limited.	
	20.		There was a bombardment of The Black Redoubt in the enemy trenches. The whole of the Divisional artillery took part also machine guns + rifle batteries. Considerable damage was done to the enemy's works and there was very little reply from him. The bombardment last 5 minutes + everything was over ½ an hour. Our batteries fired 88 rounds between them.	

Army Form C. 2118

Instructions regarding War Diaries and Intelligence Summaries are contained in F. S. Regs., Part. II. and the Staff Manual respectively. Title Pages will be prepared in manuscript.

WAR DIARY
or
INTELLIGENCE SUMMARY
(Erase heading not required.)

Imp. Hav., 26/7 — 10.000

Place	Date 1915	Hour	Summary of Events and Information	Remarks and references to Appendices
	Sept. 21		A quiet day on the whole. A few shells near Brigade Hdqrs in the early morning - one piece of a H.E. came through the window on to the breakfast table but did no damage.	
	22		A good deal of shelling in the evening - one came through the house of 1st Battery & Capt Shiel & Qr. Stewart who were on the stairs at the time had marvellous escapes.	
	23		The bombardment in the South is now creeping north & is just on our right. It has been going on for some days & looks as if we were preparing to attack. It has produced a certain amount of activity in our front - bombardment very heavy about 4.30 pm. We have been ordered to send all our baggage wagons to A.S.C. - it is not known why they want them but now have no means of getting meals & the necessary R.E. stores for work on gun positions & wagon lines. Div Arty. Hdqrs will not apparently help us to resist the demand.	
	24		All units of the division moved forward to battle headquarters & we went down to our cellar preparatory for a bombardment tomorrow morning. This Army is to hold the enemy to his front & attack if opportunity offers. This division is going to use smoke if the wind is favourable in the hopes that the enemy will think it is gas & get a panic.	

Instructions regarding War Diaries and Intelligence Summaries are contained in F. S. Regs., Part. II. and the Staff Manual respectively. Title Pages will be prepared in manuscript.

WAR DIARY
or
INTELLIGENCE SUMMARY
(Erase heading not required.)

Army Form C. 2118

Imp. Hav., 26/7 — 10.000

Place	1915 Date	Hour	Summary of Events and Information	Remarks and references to Appendices
ARMENTIERES	Sept 25.		The scheme so far as this front is concerned was a fiasco. The Germans could not possibly have thought we intended to attack. The orders as to lighting the straw were altered too late apparently for the information to reach the front trenches - it was lighted at different times (varying at 4.a.m. to 6 a.m.) all along the line + most of it blew back across our own parapet. To artillery observation stations it did not look like anything but smoke from bonfires + the enemy asked if we thought it was 5th Novr. We opened with a bombardment of 7 rounds per gun from 5.0 to 5.5 a.m. then spread 9 rounds per gun over from 5.5 to 6.a.m. + repeated the bombardment from 6.0 to 6.5. The points bombarded were behind the German fire trenches - being mostly in the support line + main communicating trenches were also ~~bombarded~~ enfiladed. There was a thick mist + observation was impossible. For the most part the Infantry showed very little activity - brigade headquarters sleeping peacefully right through. After 6.5 am things were extremely quiet from the artillery point of view though their snipers were active. During the afternoon there were isolated artillery duels of short duration + the enemy continued firing their big guns from some way back at intervals of 20 to 30 minutes throughout the night. The North Riding Battery (2nd Northn Brigade) has been temporarily attached to this Brigade.	
	26. to 30.		Things very quiet on the whole, though some fairly big shells (including an old 9 cm + what is probably a captured French 12 cm) have been sent over us into the town daily. Hugh Ryles Capt + Adjt.	

50th Division

121/7368

1st Northumbrian Bde RFA

Vol VI

Oct 15

Army Form C. 2118

Instructions regarding War Diaries and Intelligence Summaries are contained in F. S. Regs., Part. II. and the Staff Manual respectively. Title Pages will be prepared in manuscript.

WAR DIARY

1st Northumbrian Brigade R.F.A.

or ~~INTELLIGENCE SUMMARY~~

(Erase heading not required.)

Imp. Hav., 26/7 — 10.000

Place	Date 1915	Hour	Summary of Events and Information	Remarks and references to Appendices
ARMENTIERES.	Oct. 1 to 6		Nothing of any interest to report. Things very quiet on our front. Arrangements are being made with the 23rd Div. on our right for mutual support in case of attack. On the evening of the 6th was told the ammunition allowance for the Division for the week was NIL. On the afternoon of the 6th we received orders that the Brigade will be relieved tomorrow night. No further particulars at present.	
	7.		The relieving of the Brigade by the 96th Brigade R.F.A. began – one section of each battery being moved – when the relief is completed the North Riding Battery will return to its own Brigade – our sections are to march tonight to near St. JANS CAPPELL & move tomorrow to billets ~~near HONDEGHEM~~ between HAZEBROUCK & St. SYLVESTRE CAPPELL.	
	8.		The first sections of A,B,&C, batteries 96th Brigade registered over trenches.	
	9		On the night of 9/10 the relief was completed.	
	10		The remainder of the Brigade arrived at its billets. Headquarters being in the village of LA KREULE.	
	11.		Received orders from C.R.A. 21st Div. to move to new billets tomorrow	

Army Form C. 2118

Instructions regarding War Diaries and Intelligence Summaries are contained in F. S. Regs., Part. II. and the Staff Manual respectively. Title Pages will be prepared in manuscript.

WAR DIARY
or
INTELLIGENCE SUMMARY
(Erase heading not required.)

Imp. Hav., 26/7 — 10.000

Place	Date	Hour	Summary of Events and Information	Remarks and references to Appendices
			although we have no orders that we are under his command. an inspection of the area given to us shows that there not sufficient billets in it for the Brigade. Subsequently received orders that the move is cancelled owing to the presence of foot & mouth disease in the area.	
	12.		Received information that we are under the orders of C.R.A. 21st Divn & attached to them for administration.	
	14		21st Divn say we are still under 50th Divn for administration – result we only make such returns as we think advisable.	
	16.		We held a Brigade Horse Show + riding + driving competitions – all went very well.	
	17.		Lt. J.V.G. Elliot who died last night was buried in HAZEBROUCK. His horse bolted with him on the 14th + fell + he fractured the base of his skull + had since been lying in hospital unconscious.	
	31.		The Brigade remained in its rest billets for the remainder of the month. Training continued daily in quick action drill gun drill signalling (lamps & telephones) fuze setting etc. C.R.A. 50th Div. + the remainder of the Div. arty returned to this area on the 24th.	W. [illegible] Capt. R.A. Adjt.

50th Division

121/7636

1/1 Northumbrian Bde R.F.A.

Nov. 1915

Vol VII

Army Form C. 2118

Instructions regarding War Diaries and Intelligence Summaries are contained in F. S. Regs., Part. II. and the Staff Manual respectively. Title Pages will be prepared in manuscript.

WAR DIARY

or

~~INTELLIGENCE SUMMARY~~

1st Northumbrian Brigade R.F.A.

(Erase heading not required.)

Imp. Hav., 26/7 — 10.000

Place	Date	Hour	Summary of Events and Information	Remarks and references to Appendices
HAZEBROUCK	1915 November			
LA KREULE	1		The Brigade remained in its rest billets as before – the weather at the beginning of the month was vile. On the 6th The Officers played the Officers of the 2nd Northumbrian Brigade at Association football & beat them 3-1.	
	9.		The Brigade moved to new billets at BORRE and were told to make them ready for winter occupation – material is to be supplied shortly.	
	16th		The 2nd & 3rd Batteries each received a mark IV gun to replace condemned guns but they will not fit the Mk I carriage which we have.	
	28.		The amount of material supplied so far is for 2 harness sheds per battery & column 1 cook house per unit (including headquarters) 15000 bricks for the Brigade. The various shelters have been delivered short – we have carted sand from MONT NOIR but can get no cement or timber edging for bricks. On the 23rd we received 18 pdr. equipment for 1½ batteries & 6 limbered ammunition waggons for the column and on the 25th a similar quantity thus completing the brigade. Many important stores were not delivered. The equipment is all very stiff & a lot of work will be necessary before it is in good working order. The equipment was drawn from rail at HAZEBROUCK. The train was very late and the work done in the dark in vile weather. The batteries put their 15 pdr. carriages on to the same train.	

Army Form C. 2118

Instructions regarding War Diaries and Intelligence Summaries are contained in F. S. Regs., Part. II. and the Staff Manual respectively. Title Pages will be prepared in manuscript.

WAR DIARY

or

~~INTELLIGENCE SUMMARY~~

(Erase heading not required.)

Imp. Hav., 26/7 — 10.000

Place	Date	Hour	Summary of Events and Information	Remarks and references to Appendices
	November 1915			
	30		The Brigade with the other units of the Divisional Artillery "marched past" the G.O.C. 2nd Army near STRAZEELE. A very hard frost had "given" in the afternoon of yesterday + last night was very wet. Consequently it was impossible to make either horses or vehicles as clean as they should have been.	
			Hugh [illegible] Capt + Adjt. 1st North^n Bgde R.F.A. 30/XI/15.	

1/1 Northumbrian Bde R.F.A.

Dec 1915

Vol. VIII

50

Army Form C. 2118

Instructions regarding War Diaries and Intelligence Summaries are contained in F. S. Regs., Part. II. and the Staff Manual respectively. Title Pages will be prepared in manuscript.

WAR DIARY

1st Northumbrian Brigade R.F.A

~~INTELLIGENCE SUMMARY~~

(Erase heading not required.)

Imp. Hav., 26/7 — 10.000

Place	Date	Hour	Summary of Events and Information	Remarks and references to Appendices
	1915 December			
MILLAM.	6.		The Brigade moved from its billets at BORRE on the night of 5th 6th. We had to arrive here on the 6th and it was made a night march at the request of Battery Commanders so that they might arrive in daylight + have time to settle down before dark. The experiment does not seem to have been successful because we started at 9 p.m. and arrived at 6 a.m. (the distance being about 22 miles) and it was not light till 7 am. and the whole Brigade slept all the morning instead of settling in - an inspection of billets at 11 produced nothing but snores. This place ~~of~~ is part of WATTEN artillery training camp N of ST. OMER. Certain fields are put apart for training in but a great deal has to be imagined + all the fields are waterlogged. We are to stay here 10 days - The billets for men seem good but the horse lines are atrocious. Lt Col Bell did not move with the Brigade but stayed behind at BORRE as he was unwell.	
	7.		We are told we have not to use the training fields at present as they are too wet - We have been sent here to do driving drill + brigade + divisional artillery manoeuvres - apparently all to be done on the roads. Three 2nd battery horses had to be dug out this morning + scarcely any knees or hocks can now be seen in the 3rd Battery lines. It should have been mentioned yesterday that the march here last night went very well although the road was unknown to us as the 3 Battery Captains came on in the morning + posted orderlies at all turnings + the scheme worked excellently. The night was warm + very little rain though a chilly wind got up about 3.30 am. The Brigade	

Army Form C. 2118

Instructions regarding War Diaries and Intelligence Summaries are contained in F. S. Regs., Part. II. and the Staff Manual respectively. Title Pages will be prepared in manuscript.

WAR DIARY
or
INTELLIGENCE SUMMARY
(Erase heading not required.)

Imp. Hav., 26/7 — 40.000

Place	Date	Hour	Summary of Events and Information	Remarks and references to Appendices
			Orderly Officer (Lieut: Chapman) had been motored through in the morning + had taken over the billets from the 24th Brigade R.F.A. who had been the first artillery to use the training camp + had left, after 10 days stay, on the 5th	
		8.	Lt. Col. Bell arrived. All the batteries got through some training - Gun drill appears to be badly needed.	
		9.	Lt. Gen. Wilkinson, G.O.C. 50th Divn inspected the Brigade at work. He was 50 minutes late + everybody was kept waiting in a very cold rain. He saw a very fair sample of what the drivers have to contend with.	
		10.	We attempted a Brigade tactical exercise with skeleton batteries but it rained so hard that no messages could be written + the thing was abandoned.	
		11.	All gun parks + horse lines were moved on to roads.	
		12	We had a voluntary church parade in a school but very few men turned up	
		13.	Maj. Gen. Plumer G.O.C 2nd Army inspected the Brigade. He was accompanied by Maj. Gen. Headlam (M.G.R.A. 2nd Army). He saw the 1st Battery come into action on a road, the 2nd Battery come out of action off a road + the 3rd Battery doing Gun drill + stables. The G.O.C. arrived more than an hour late but seemed pleased with all he saw. The day was fine. Such inspections + the weather have effectively prevented anything in the way of mobile training being done in this "training" area.	

Instructions regarding War Diaries and Intelligence Summaries are contained in F. S. Regs., Part. II. and the Staff Manual respectively. Title Pages will be prepared in manuscript.

WAR DIARY
or
INTELLIGENCE SUMMARY
(Erase heading not required.)

Army Form C. 2118

Imp. Hav., 26/7 — 10.000

Place	Date	Hour	Summary of Events and Information	Remarks and references to Appendices
	17		The Brigade left the training camp + returned to its former billets at BORRE. The march began at 8.15 a.m. + the batteries + brigade headquarters arrived about 2.15 pm. The baggage wagons + water carts marched as a separate convoy and did not arrive till 5.30. It was a dull misty day with a lot of rain ~~fo~~ later on, but it was quicker + better than marching at night. Lt Col. Bell who had been seedy all the stay at WATTEN went to HAZEBROUCK to hospital by a motor ambulance.	
	18.		Major J G D Johnston (as O.C. Brigade) and the Adjutant visited the H.Q. of the 50th Brigade RFA. (9th Div.) at KRUISTRAAT. We are to relieve the 50th Brigade when the 50th Div. relieves the 9th. This Div. is to be transferred to the 5th Corps. The 50th Bgde H.Q. had been abandoned about a week ago + were then in the H.Q. of the 53rd Brigade owing to hostile shelling + the water in the dug outs being beyond the capacity of the pumps. As the 4th Northn Bgde are relieving the 53rd Bgde. we had to look for new H.Q. – it was eventually decided to use what was left of the old ones.	
	19.		The Brigade Ammunition Column moved to its new wagon lines near BUSSEBOOM – Sheet 28 G. 22 central. The battery commanders + brigade orderly officer also moved to the new wagon lines so as to have longer time to take over positions telephone lines etc. They moved up to the positions the next morning. The H.Q. ~~was to~~ marched at 8.15 but were soon stopped + sent back as there had been a gas attack ~~last~~ the night previous + the move was temporarily stopped but the move was on again at 12 noon.	

Instructions regarding War Diaries and Intelligence Summaries are contained in F. S. Regs., Part. II. and the Staff Manual respectively. Title Pages will be prepared in manuscript.

WAR DIARY
or
INTELLIGENCE SUMMARY
(Erase heading not required.)

Army Form C. 2118

Imp. Hav., 26/7 — 10.000

Place	Date	Hour	Summary of Events and Information	Remarks and references to Appendices
	20. -22		Brigade Hdqrs and 3 batteries left their billets at BORRE and marching VIA CAESTRE, GODEWAERSVELDE, BOESCHEPE, WESTOUTRE, + RENINGHELST came to their new wagon lines in or near OUDERDOM as follows:- 1st Battery G.30.c.1.7. 2nd Batt. + HQ G.29.c.5.5. 3rd Batt. G.30.c.5.7. The 2nd + 1st Batteries took up the personnel of one section that evening + the 3rd batt. the next morning. The HQ also moved up the next morning. The march to the wagon lines was very slow as the Brigade marched behind the 3rd North'n Bgde who frequently blocked the road for traffic both ways + left vehicles behind and finally took the wrong road in RENINGHELST. The relief was completed on the morning of the 22nd and O.C. Brigade took over at 12 noon. The officers of the 1st Group 9th Divn gave us every possible help in the handing over but as usual a good deal of difficulty is being experienced over telephone lines. The C.R.A. came up to see Brigade Commanders and told us he is going to 15th Corps as B.G.R.A + is to be succeeded in this division by Brig. Gen. Robinson.	
KRUISTRAAT.	23		The C.R.A. came up + went round batteries. Batteries registered yesterday but it was really only checking the registration of our predecessors as we have taken over their guns. There are about 200 rounds of ammunition per gun at the positions + no vehicles except the gun carriages. The battery wagons + limbers are full but the Brigade A.C. has only 2 rounds per gun + the D.A.C. is I believe empty but are to fill up battery wagon lines as required, so that the batteries would be complete in the case of a move. The gun positions of batteries are as follows - 1st Battery I.15.b.5.5. 2nd Battery I.27.a.6.7. 3rd Batt. I.26.c.7.3. and Headquarters are round about the KRUISTRAAT corner in H.24.a.	

Army Form C. 2118

Instructions regarding War Diaries and Intelligence Summaries are contained in F. S. Regs., Part. II. and the Staff Manual respectively. Title Pages will be prepared in manuscript.

WAR DIARY
or
INTELLIGENCE SUMMARY
(Erase heading not required.)

Imp. Hav., 26/7 — 10.000

Place	Date	Hour	Summary of Events and Information	Remarks and references to Appendices
KRUISTRAAT.	24		The C.R.A. brought up the new C.R.A. and went round some of the batteries. The batteries continued to verify some of our predecessors registrations. The telephone lines to batteries & from batteries to trenches seem to need a lot of work & as usual the plans handed over are not much help but nobody ever yet thought a telephone system he took over to be a good one. The new C.R.A. is Brig. Gen. Robinson.	
	25.		We tried to give the men a good Christmas dinner. Lt. Col. Bell (who went on sick leave from the hospital yesterday) had given each B.C. a sum of to be spent on extra food etc & a good many things had been purchased from the Expeditionary Force Canteen but cooking was not easy. There was a certain amount of shooting done and none of the fraternising of last years Christmas Day.	
	26.		It appears the ammunition allowance is all to be spent in breaching the enemy's parapets and if any retaliation is asked for, ammunition required will be additional to the weekly allowance.	
	27 – 28.		Nothing of importance occurred. A certain amount of artillery activity on both sides.	
	29.		There was a good deal of artillery activity on both sides from noon onwards. This Brigade and the 2nd Northumbrian Brigade had a	

Army Form C. 2118

Instructions regarding War Diaries and Intelligence Summaries are contained in F. S. Regs., Part. II. and the Staff Manual respectively. Title Pages will be prepared in manuscript.

WAR DIARY
or
INTELLIGENCE SUMMARY
(Erase heading not required.)

Imp. Hav., 26/7 — 10.000

Place	Date	Hour	Summary of Events and Information	Remarks and references to Appendices
KRUISTRAAT.			Combined shoot on the German trenches in I 29 d. near Hill 60. The enemy apparently thought we were going to attack and replied by creating a barrage with gas shells along the canal + the LILLE Rd. In the evening the enemy had a "strafe" against our transport putting gas shells + coal boxes over many roads + causing a deal of trouble with telephone lines. Many shells fell near Headquarters + the office window was blown in but only a portion of the roof was broken.	Lieut. M. Mi[illegible] was wounded in the trenches.
	30.		A quiet day on the whole. Mi[illegible] died on the ambulance train.	
	31.		O.C. Brigade and the Adjutant spent the day looking for suitable O.P's. Ruskin House + Battersea Farm were found to be suitable for portions of the zone covered by the Brigade but both have been heavily shelled and a lot of work must be done by night before they are usable.	
	31-1/1/16	mid night	Some of the batteries near Brigade Headquarters fired for 5 minutes on the zone on our right but apparently produced no reply.	

Hugh [illegible]
Capt & Adjt
1st Northumbrian Brigade
R.F.A.

50

8

1st. Northumbrian Bde RFA

Jan 1916

Vol IX

Army Form C. 2118

WAR DIARY
1st Northumbrian Brigade RFA.
or
~~INTELLIGENCE SUMMARY~~

(Erase heading not required.)

Instructions regarding War Diaries and Intelligence Summaries are contained in F. S. Regs., Part. II. and the Staff Manual respectively. Title Pages will be prepared in manuscript.

Imp. Hav., 26/7 — 10.000

Place	Date	Hour	Summary of Events and Information	Remarks and references to Appendices
KRUISTRAAT	1/1/16		A quiet day on the whole with nothing of interest to report.	
	2.		During the morning the 1st Battery had a very successful shoot breaching the enemy's parapets. H.E. with 85 fuze was used + found to be much more suitable than 100 fuze which frequently bursts after ricochet and does no harm to the parapet. Between 1 + 2.30 p.m. the trenches and battalion headquarters were heavily bombarded with 7.7 cm. + hand grenades + also 10.5 cm. The 3rd Battery had to fire 340 and the 2nd Battery 90 rounds before the enemy quieted down. The 5" how: + 8" also helped.	
	3.		A quiet day on the whole nothing of interest to report.	
	4.		The 3rd North'd. Battery received a severe "strafing" from 1.30 to 2.30 p.m. At least 2 direct hits on emplacements. 2 guns slightly damaged but not out of action. 1 Sergeant (Gibson) wounded and Gr. [illegible] killed. The position has evidently been spotted. The flashes are probably visible from WYTSCHAETE Ridge and an enemy aeroplane flew over the position very low a few days ago.	
	5.		Two of the guns of 3rd Battery were removed from their position + taken into the buildings of LANKHOF Fm close by. It is intended to make a new position in these buildings. The other two guns are left in their old position to be used in an emergency only + two guns of the 1st Battery are covering the 3rd Battery zone. The infantry say they will not ask for fire unless absolutely necessary.	
	6.		Several possible positions for 3rd Battery were reconnoitred but that in the farm seems best. One other possible one might be useful as an alternative if put into repair by a fatigue party from the Column. [illegible]	

Army Form C. 2118

Instructions regarding War Diaries and Intelligence Summaries are contained in F. S. Regs., Part II. and the Staff Manual respectively. Title Pages will be prepared in manuscript.

WAR DIARY
or
INTELLIGENCE SUMMARY
(Erase heading not required.)

Imp. Hav., 26/7 — 10.000

Place	Date	Hour	Summary of Events and Information	Remarks and references to Appendices
	6.		Experience confirms that fuze 85 is better than fuze 100 with H.E. for breaking parapets as 100 fuze too many blinds after recoil. We are told the enemy transport mostly comes up & reliefs take place in the early morning so all likely spots are sprayed with shrapnel at intervals between 5 & 8 a.m. Capt. N. Fairbairn was wounded with a stray rifle bullet when near the battery billets & Lieut A.O. Pyke wounded by a whizzbang when acting as F.O.O.	
	7.		Lt. Col. H.S. Bell returned & resumed command of the Brigade. Nothing of interest happened.	
	8.		The 1st + 2nd Batteries practised creating a barrage on the "gas barrage zone" of the 2nd battery. Each battery was allowed 50 rounds T.S. The shooting was good but it was fired at section fire 15 seconds. This seems too slow a rate of fire for an effective barrage and it is suggested that, as a faster rate could not be maintained for long owing to the quantity of ammunition that would be used, it would be better to fire in bursts of quick fire - say section fire 10 seconds - with intervals of say battery fire 30 seconds.	
	9. -14.		Nothing of interest to report - a lot of retaliation has been asked for + given - The 1st Battery are still keeping one section to help over the 3rd Battery zone. The 3rd Battery have left the two guns in their old position + have shot from them occasionally without drawing fire	

Instructions regarding War Diaries and Intelligence Summaries are contained in F. S. Regs., Part. II. and the Staff Manual respectively. Title Pages will be prepared in manuscript.

WAR DIARY
or
INTELLIGENCE SUMMARY
(Erase heading not required.)

Army Form C. 2118

Imp. Hav., 26/7 — 10.000

Place	Date	Hour	Summary of Events and Information	Remarks and references to Appendices
			but they have not yet shot from the new one. On the 14th The Duke of Northumberland & Capt. Napier (president & secretary of the T.F. Assoc^n of the County of Northumberland) visited the wagon lines. Unfortunately they had no time to come to the gun positions though they wished to.	
	15.		A stray shell fell on one of the emplacements in the old position of the 3rd Battery. Ammunition was scattered & 3 men slightly wounded in the leg - the gun was not damaged. The emplacement has been mended & the gun remains in action in the same place.	
	16.		The 1st Battery was to have registered with an aeroplane but it failed to turn up. A very quiet day.	
	17.		There was a combined divisional shoot on communication trenches in I.30.d. in which the 2nd & 3rd Batteries took part. Other calibres firing were 9.2", 8", 6", 5" how, 60pdrs, 4.7". Aeroplane observation reports that the fire of the field guns was very successful & much damage was done to the German trenches. The enemy retaliated to some extent & all batteries had to counter-retaliate. This further damaged their front line but they destroyed some of our communication trenches, damaged a part of our front line & severely strafed the Batt^n H.Q. of the 5th D.L.I. They also shelled the new position	

Army Form C. 2118

Instructions regarding War Diaries and Intelligence Summaries are contained in F. S. Regs., Part. II. and the Staff Manual respectively. Title Pages will be prepared in manuscript.

WAR DIARY
or
INTELLIGENCE SUMMARY
(Erase heading not required.)

Imp. Hav., 26/7 — 10.000

Place	Date	Hour	Summary of Events and Information	Remarks and references to Appendices
			of the right section of the 3rd Battery but did not touch the old position where the left section remains. The new position is evidently a difficult position to range on. There was one direct hit with a 10.5 cm H on the barn where the guns are but it was a dud. The officers cook house was destroyed and all their crockery etc + some boots destroyed, also their bath tubs. Fortunately no casualties + only one telescope sight broken. The battery is not to shoot again until the new emplacements are made strong enough to stand anything but direct hits from big guns. The 24th Div: batteries just in front of the 2nd Battery got shelled with gas shells + the gas made some of the 2nd Battery violently sick but otherwise did no harm.	
	18.		The 3rd Battery got a permit from the Town Major of YPRES and replenished their crockery + furniture etc. A dull wet day quiet on the whole.	
	19.		The enemy began an organised strafe on our sector about 9.15 am till 11.30. It appeared to be in retaliation for our bombardment of the 17th. A lot of heavy stuff was fired. The first + 2nd Batteries shot practically continuously from 9.20 to 11.40 + got rid of a lot of ammunition + had the last say but in the afternoon the 2nd Battery was ranged on by a battery of 15 cm probably from HOLLEBEKE and received a severe doing. They had to leave the position while it was going on but went back about 4.30. Two of our	

Instructions regarding War Diaries and Intelligence Summaries are contained in F. S. Regs., Part. II. and the Staff Manual respectively. Title Pages will be prepared in manuscript.

WAR DIARY
or
INTELLIGENCE SUMMARY
(Erase heading not required.)

Army Form C. 2118

Imp. Hav., 26/7 — 10.000

Place	Date	Hour	Summary of Events and Information	Remarks and references to Appendices
			aeroplanes are supposed to have gone up to drive away the observer but it was apparently too late. No guns were damaged - one 15 cm shell buried itself under the mess but did not explode. One corporal was killed. The position was put in order again & communications restored about 9 p.m. It appears that when the any battery makes itself much felt by the enemy they promptly find it & give it a severe doing with heavy stuff from all sides. They appear to have any amount of it & use it unsparingly in one place at a time. One wonders if our heavies ever strafe any of their batteries in the same way - at any rate they never seem to fire 200 shells on end at one place like the Bosche does. We haven't nearly enough artillery - especially heavies - for this place. We are now told the greatest economy is necessary in ammunition especially shrapnel. We have already (Wednesday) fired 3½ times as much as we are now told is our allowance for the week.	
	20.		A very quiet day. Adjutant went on leave.	
	21.		A very quiet day: none of our batteries fired - lack of ammunition - 2nd Battery started preparing dug outs for a new position which is well forward & will enfilade the enemy trenches well.	
	22.		Quiet day - no steel shelters available for 2nd Batt: as infantry want same for reserve trenches.	

Army Form C. 2118

Instructions regarding War Diaries and Intelligence Summaries are contained in F. S. Regs., Part. II. and the Staff Manual respectively. Title Pages will be prepared in manuscript.

WAR DIARY
or
INTELLIGENCE SUMMARY
(Erase heading not required.)

Imp. Hav., 26/7 — 10.000

Place	Date	Hour	Summary of Events and Information	Remarks and references to Appendices
	23.		A quiet day. Capt. Shiel returned from a fortnights course at the Artillery School at BERTHEN which he says is very good. Capt. Law went on a similar course. Div. H.Q. send hourly wires as to direction of wind.	
	24.		A fairly quiet day. 3rd Battery received some attention from 10.5 cm & 7.7 cm but no harm done. 1st Battery stood by for 1½ hours waiting for an aeroplane to come & register but it did not come	
	25.		1st Battery registered 2 targets with an aeroplane quite successfully. G.O.C. 149th Inf. Brigade objected to new position for 2nd Batt: as it is about 300x from some reserve infantry dug outs which are 30° out of the line of their fire. Infantry must think gunners exceptionally brave as they appear to think a battery always draws a hail of shells, but I believe we are no worse off than other divisions in this respect.	
	26.		Quiet day – sent in a certificate that all earth fires 200x back from trenches for 3rd time since we came here. Still hourly wires re wind.	
	27.		Quiet. D.R. 2nd Army cart – for the 3rd time of asking. The horse that bolted with & killed Elliot in ~~Dece~~ October & has bolted every time anybody has ridden it since. H.Q. now ask us to supply saddlers & shoemakers. If such men are wanted why trouble to train them as gunners first. C.R.A. unable to overcome prejudices of G.O.C. Div.n against the new 2nd Batt: position.	

Army Form C. 2118

Instructions regarding War Diaries and Intelligence Summaries are contained in F. S. Regs., Part. II. and the Staff Manual respectively. Title Pages will be prepared in manuscript.

WAR DIARY
or
INTELLIGENCE SUMMARY

(Erase heading not required.)

Imp. Hav., 26/7 — 10.000

Place	Date	Hour	Summary of Events and Information	Remarks and references to Appendices
	28.		Draft of 10 reinforcements arrived – 3 telephonists. The 8" Hows spent a merry afternoon sniping our own infantry with "Duds". It is rumoured that out of 20 shells fired one burst said 97.	
	29.		Signal Co: sent us a 12 line telephone exchange – one important internal connection had been left out but we were able to put it in + it appears to be the first satisfactory government field exchange that we have seen – As a matter of fact our own 17 line one (home made) had been working very satisfactorily. 2/Lt. T. Sample arrived as a reinforcement.	
	30.		Quiet nothing of interest happened.	
	31.		Quiet at 6pm. the division of the whole artillery of the Division into 2 groups took effect. The O.C. of the two flank brigades took command so that O.C. of this Brigade has nothing to do with his batteries except for administrative purposes. The right group consists of 2nd North[n] Bgde – 1st + 3rd North[n] Batt[s] (from this Bgde) + 5th Div: (How) Battery. The left group consists of 3rd North[n] Bgde 2nd North[n] Batt (from this Bgde) + 4th Div: (How:) Battery. This change is due to the fact that we now have only 2 infantry Brigades in at a time + one whole Brigade in reserve. The Adjutant returned from leave.	[illegible signature] Adjt 1st Northn Bgde RFA

Instructions regarding War Diaries and Intelligence Summaries are contained in F. S. Regs., Part. II. and the Staff Manual respectively. Title Pages will be prepared in manuscript.

WAR DIARY

Army Form C. 2118

1st Northumbrian Brigade R.F.A.

~~INTELLIGENCE SUMMARY~~

(Erase heading not required.)

Imp. Hav., 26/7 — 10.000

Place	Date	Hour	Summary of Events and Information	Remarks and references to Appendices
KRUISSTRAAT	1916 Feb. 1.		One gun of the 2nd Battery has been put forward into a hedge at I.28.C.½ 8½ and a position being prepared for another along side it.	
	2		The gun of the 2nd Battery registered + a possible position chosen for the other section. 3 of the guns are still in the old position + have shot a little so far without further damage but it is not considered safe to leave them there if they have to shoot much. The infantry are being asked if they object to our going to this new position.	
	3.		Very quiet.	
	4.		3rd Battery right section was shelled with 10.5 cm + the bath room blown in but no other damage done.	
	6.		The 2nd + 3rd Batteries each experienced a certain of strafing but nothing very serious.	
	7		The same as yesterday with the addition that the 1st Battery also got some shells among them in the evening.	
	8.		Shells from a 10 CM. gun came all round Brigade H.Q. at fairly long intervals all day. No damage was done. The 1st Battery yesterday recovered a complete "dud" round from what appears to be a new 10.5 cm. gun. It is this that has been causing a good deal of trouble lately. The enemy appear to have got some very effective means of hiding flashes. [Army eventually decided from marks on the fuze that the new gun was a Russian one]	

Instructions regarding War Diaries and Intelligence Summaries are contained in F. S. Regs., Part. II. and the Staff Manual respectively. Title Pages will be prepared in manuscript.

WAR DIARY
or
INTELLIGENCE SUMMARY
(Erase heading not required.)

Army Form C. 2118

Imp. Hav., 26/7 — 10.000

Place	Date	Hour	Summary of Events and Information	Remarks and references to Appendices
	9.		The Mess + part of Brigade Headquarters moved to another billet about 400x further West as the old billet was too near frequent shells. The office will be moved later when a place has been made. Nothing of interest happened.	
	10.		Three guns of 2nd Battery were moved to a new position in I.26.b.4.9 without mishap. They had a shoot before leaving their old position. One gun is still forward.	
	11.		A wet cold day with rain + snow. Nothing of interest happened. Enemy Artillery very active.	
	12.		Starting about 2.0 p.m. there was very heavy artillery firing to the north. this lasted till about 4.30 + then gradually subsided. We received a message that the enemy were making a gas attack on the front of the Corps to our left. We received orders to stand by but these were cancelled to "a state of vigilance" about 8 p.m. When we received the report as to gas the wind was blowing from us to the enemy, though it had been N.E. previously.	
	13.		All the roads in the neighbourhood of KRUISTRAAT were shelled at intervals throughout the night by high velocity guns of at least 2 calibres 10 cm + 13 cm. It now appears that the shelling yesterday arose as follows:- The previous night during a ~~Divisional~~ relief of one Division by another the enemy occupied part of our trenches but were driven out again at once - but yesterday tried to attack again with considerable artillery support and a smoke barrage (not gas). The attack was repulsed by our artillery fire with	

Army Form C. 2118

Instructions regarding War Diaries and Intelligence Summaries are contained in F. S. Regs., Part. II. and the Staff Manual respectively. Title Pages will be prepared in manuscript.

WAR DIARY
or
INTELLIGENCE SUMMARY
(*Erase heading not required.*)

Imp. Hav., 26/7 — 10.000

Place	Date	Hour	Summary of Events and Information	Remarks and references to Appendices
			Small loss to ourselves but apparently considerable loss to them as their trenches were heavily manned at the time. The trenches of the Division to our left (in front of HOOGE) were heavily shelled this afternoon with apparently very little reply from their own divisional artillery though our batteries fired on several enemy batteries with apparently good results.	
	14.		Fairly quiet until about 3.0 pm. Then very heavy shelling both to North + South of us + heavy on our front. Our batteries were kept busy till about 7.30. It appears that the enemy attacked + took 6 trenches from the 17th Divn on our right but 2 of them were at once retaken. The enemy also sprung two mines on our front + attacked + he also attacked the 24th Divn front on our left but both these attacks were repulsed. The enemy also shelled all transport roads until about 1 am. + caused 3 fires in our area with incendiary shells – one of them being a bomb store in the R.E. dump at KRUISTRAAT. Four men were wounded in the 2nd battery position one gun emplacement received two direct hits + the officers mess two. Both emplacements of the left section of the 3rd Battery were destroyed but no guns were damaged. 3 men at the 3rd Battery position were wounded. The 17th Divn made unsuccessful counterattacks at 11.30 pm + 3 am. which meant a lot of more heavy firing but not much on our front.	

Army Form C. 2118

Instructions regarding War Diaries and Intelligence Summaries are contained in F. S. Regs., Part. II. and the Staff Manual respectively. Title Pages will be prepared in manuscript.

WAR DIARY
or
INTELLIGENCE SUMMARY
(Erase heading not required.)

Imp. Hav., 26/7 — 10.000

Place	Date	Hour	Summary of Events and Information	Remarks and references to Appendices
	15.		A new position was looked for the left section of 3rd Northumberland Battery - perhaps one may be found at I.27.a.1.3 - about 800x from the position of the right section.	
	16.		A very windy day + quiet except for whizzbangs near the 3rd Battery.	
	17.		A bombardment of the trenches recently lost took place at 5 am but apparently no attack followed. Otherwise a quiet day - Some of the 3rd Battery officers would prefer a position at I.26.d.4½.9 for their left section as the other position is so far from that ~~way~~ of the right section. This position had already been considered but thought not so suitable as the other as it is on the top of the ridge. Further inspections are to be made.	
	18.		A further bombardment of the lost trenches took place for ½ hour at 4.22 pm but otherwise a quiet day - Our batteries did not take part in the bombardment.	
	19.		An uneventful day. 3rd Battery are to put 1 gun at I.26.d.4½.9 + the other is either to be put beside it or into LANKHOF Fm with their right section.	
	20.		Aeroplanes very active in the morning. An uneventful day.	
	21.		A large number of gas shells arrived in KRUISTRAAT + I.15.b. in the morning - a great deal of weeping was caused but no casualties. The 1st battery also got some more in the afternoon and evening + linesmen had a bad time of it	

Army Form C. 2118

Instructions regarding War Diaries and Intelligence Summaries are contained in F. S. Regs., Part. II. and the Staff Manual respectively. Title Pages will be prepared in manuscript.

WAR DIARY
or
INTELLIGENCE SUMMARY
(*Erase heading not required.*)

Imp. Hav., 26/7 — 40.000

Place	Date	Hour	Summary of Events and Information	Remarks and references to Appendices
	22.		A lot of heavy firing to the North of us in the afternoon. The enemy fired a great many smoke and gas shells all over our area + made a very good smoke barrage across KRUISTRAAT. The 1st Battery also had a very nasty time of it.	
	23.		A good deal of snow last night, very cold with heavy clouds. an uneventful day.	
	24		Still very cold but clearer - aeroplanes very active over 1st Battery, neither our planes nor our anti aircraft guns seem to do anything to abate the nuisance. It renders our artillery useless without the enemy having to fire a shot - it prevents us getting artillery superiority + we most certainly have not got "mastery of the air."	
	25.		A good deal of snow last night which made things very difficult for batteries. no work could be done near a position. a quiet day.	
	26.		A lot of firing on the 17th Div: front on our right towards evening otherwise quiet.	
	27.		A quiet day on the whole.	
	28.		A lot of shells fell all round Brigade H.Qrs at 1 am - many of them gas. it appeared to be a transport strafe but no harm done. Brigade office was moved to OUDERDOM in the morning, the Orderly Officer remaining at KRUISTRAAT with the telephone portion of H.Q.S.	
	29.		nothing to report so far as this Brigade is concerned.	

Hugh Bly[illegible]
Capt & Adjt
1st [illegible] Brigade RFA

50

o/c Northbrn Bde R.F.A.

Vol XI

Instructions regarding War Diaries and Intelligence Summaries are contained in F. S. Regs., Part. II. and the Staff Manual respectively. Title Pages will be prepared in manuscript.

WAR DIARY

or

1st Northumbrian Brigade R.F.A.

~~INTELLIGENCE SUMMARY~~

(Erase heading not required.)

Army Form C. 2118

Imp. Hav., 26/7 — 10.000

Place	Date	Hour	Summary of Events and Information	Remarks and references to Appendices
	March 1916 1-3		During these days there was great activity on our front - Owing to the grouping system definite detailed information cannot be given by the Headquarters of this Brigade but all the batteries took part - At 4.30 pm on 1st there was a violent bombardment for 30 minutes of the enemy's lines both on our right and our own front. The enemy's wire had been cut for 40 yards on our front by systematic Shrapnel bombardments during the previous 48 hours and at the close of our bombardment on the 1st our infantry opposite to this cheered & opened rapid rifle fire at 5pm. This made the enemy thickly man his trenches and open crossing machine gun fire into No Man's Land - evidently he expected an attack & gave away all the battle positions of his front line machine guns - The bombardment was not renewed after a 5 minutes interval which might have been done with advantage - At 4.30 am on the 2nd the infantry of the division on our right attacked successfully & retook the trenches recently lost. The artillery bombardment started at 4.32 am on our front & both sides but that on the left soon subsided as the enemy apparently soon knew nothing was doing there & switched the greater part of his guns southwards. No attack was made on our front but the artillery barrages throughout were so successful that apparently no enemy reinforcements could be got up. The infantry on our right not	

Army Form C. 2118

Instructions regarding War Diaries and Intelligence Summaries are contained in F. S. Regs., Part. II. and the Staff Manual respectively. Title Pages will be prepared in manuscript.

WAR DIARY
or
INTELLIGENCE SUMMARY
(Erase heading not required.)

Imp. Hav., 26/7 — 10.000

Place	Date	Hour	Summary of Events and Information	Remarks and references to Appendices
			only retook their trenches but penetrated in some places to the German 3rd or 4th line but were subsequently withdrawn (after blowing up these lines) so as to keep our own old line + a line of theirs + so improved the position considerably. Our artillery fire had been so successful + intense that they could work practically unmolested at this point all day + consolidated the position. Severe counter attacks were made after midday but were all repulsed - portions of the infantry of this division had to go to reinforce the Division on our right as there was difficulty in getting their reinforcements up. There was continual artillery activity on the 2nd but things quietened down on the 3rd. A noteworthy thing was that enemy artillery from the north created a barrage on the LILLE Road outside YPRES which barrage had previously always been created by artillery much further South. The infantry say the artillery of this division was magnificent.	
	4-6.		All troops remained on a battle footing but nothing of importance occurred. It might perhaps have been mentioned that ammunition for all batteries was replenished during daylight on the 3rd without a casualty.	
	7-8.		Things slightly easier + nothing occurred.	
	9-11.		The left group was relieved by 24th Div: Artillery (a section at a time) on the nights of 9/10 + 10/11 + the 24th Div: infantry also took over the left sector about this	

Instructions regarding War Diaries and Intelligence Summaries are contained in F. S. Regs., Part. II. and the Staff Manual respectively. Title Pages will be prepared in manuscript.

WAR DIARY
or
INTELLIGENCE SUMMARY
(Erase heading not required.)

Army Form C. 2118

Imp. Hav., 26/7 — 10.000

Place	Date	Hour	Summary of Events and Information	Remarks and references to Appendices
			~~[illegible]~~ time - The 24th Div: merely extended their front southwards to do this. The result (so far as this Brigade is concerned) is that the 2nd North'd Battery is now of action + resting at their wagon lines in OUDERDOM.	
			Lieut: Victor Parker came out of the trenches on the morning of 4th where he had been acting as F.O.O. for the 1st North'd Battery - he was then seedy + went to hospital on the 5th but died from pneumonia before he arrived there.	
	12 -		Verbal Instructions were received from C.R.A. that we are to form another Battery to be called "4th Northumberland Battery" - There was a meeting of Battery Commanders and each battery and the Ammunition Column named 20 N.C.O.s + men to be handed to the 4th Battery when the formation is made. A good nucleus is thus obtained + the necessary personnel to complete this battery and to refill the other batteries and the Ammunition Column is to be demanded from Base Depot. Captain A. H. LAW is to command the new battery and Lieut G. CHAPMAN is to be captain. The other officers will be decided on later.	
	15.		Lieut R.P.B.B. BLUETT (R.A.M.C.) (now attached to this Brigade in the place of Surg: Maj: WREFORD who has returned home to do X Ray	

Army Form C. 2118

Instructions regarding War Diaries and Intelligence Summaries are contained in F. S. Regs., Part. II. and the Staff Manual respectively. Title Pages will be prepared in manuscript.

WAR DIARY
or
INTELLIGENCE SUMMARY
(Erase heading not required.)

Imp. Hav., 26/7 — 10.000

Place	Date	Hour	Summary of Events and Information	Remarks and references to Appendices
			work) was awarded the Military Cross for work done when he was attached to the D.L.I. before coming to us.	
	21-22		This night one section of 2nd North'd Battery took over 2 guns of 3rd Div'n in SANCTUARY WOOD. These guns only fire on an emergency. There is thus only one section of the Brigade + Headquarters out.	
	23.		Major Johnston left for England to undergo a course of shooting at a practice camp at LARK HILL (an appropriate place for a battery commander who has been shooting every day for some months to go to for a course) - but it is presumably handling a battery in the open that is to be practised.	
			Nothing of interest happened during the rest of the month.	
			Hugh Bruce [?] Capt. + Adjt.	

Instructions regarding War Diaries and Intelligence Summaries are contained in F. S. Regs., Part. II. and the Staff Manual respectively. Title Pages will be prepared in manuscript.

Army Form C. 2118

WAR DIARY or INTELLIGENCE SUMMARY

1st Northumbrian Brigade R.F.A.

(Erase heading not required.)

Imp. Hav., 26/7 — 10.000

Place	Date	Hour	Summary of Events and Information	Remarks and references to Appendices
OUDERDOM	2.10.16		Officers visited the positions of 5th Brigade 2nd Canadian Div: Art'y between DICKEBUSCH and KEMMEL. This brigade is to relieve that one in the near future. One gun of 1st Northumberland Battery got a piece of shell through the [illegible] + was sent to I.O.M.	
	3.		Major Johnston returned from LARKHILL - the course was a farce - no manoeuvring with a mounted battery - guns already in position - he fired series at 3 [illegible], simple targets - 20 rounds in all.	
EECKE.	4 to 6.		The 1st + 3rd Northumberland Batteries + the section of the 2nd Northumberland Battery were relieved by artillery of 1st Canadian Division on the nights of 4th/5th + 5th/6th and the Brigade marched to rest billets near EECKE. All ammunition brought back was dumped.	
MILLEKRUIS.	7-9.		The Brigade marched to the new area + took over from the 5th Canadian Brigade on the nights of 7/8th + 8th/9th. The relief went off smoothly + the handing over was good.	
	9-12		Great artillery activity on both sides particularly on the left of our zone + to the north - recent mining activity having produced heavy fighting round ST. ELOI. Enemy appear to have plenty of guns + ammunition + to be registering + practising barrages. We can get no heavy artillery support at all. The gun of 1st North'd Battery received back on a new carriage.	
	13.		Not so much artillery fire but still a good deal. Two guns of 3rd North'd Battery sent to I.O.M. The inner spring case having stretched in length + got narrower so that the piston rod cannot run up properly.	

Army Form C. 2118

Instructions regarding War Diaries and Intelligence Summaries are contained in F. S. Regs., Part. II. and the Staff Manual respectively. Title Pages will be prepared in manuscript.

WAR DIARY
or
INTELLIGENCE SUMMARY
(Erase heading not required.)

Imp. Hav., 26/7 — 10.000

Place	Date	Hour	Summary of Events and Information	Remarks and references to Appendices
	14-16		A good deal of artillery activity on both sides, ours being mostly retaliation. One gun of the 3rd battery received back from I.O.M on 15th + the other on 19th. One gun of 1st Battery went to I.O.M. on 15th + came back on 23rd the ~~inner spring case of this having also scratched~~ ½" piston rod having seized on recoil + the whole running out apparatus having become damaged.	
	16.		3 subalterns + 134 other ranks arrived for D battery. There is no where to put them + for the time being they are accomodated at 2nd battery wagon lines. Most of the N.C.Os were promoted only a week ago + have temporary rank but the full numbers are there. It is intended that they should practically all revert to gunner and driver and work their way up again. Some of the men are medically unfit for service abroad and none have had sufficient training - there are no signallers and a man has been sent out as farrier sergeant who cannot ride and cannot cold shoe - no fitters and a wheeler whose only qualification is that he has been a cabinet maker. Officers who have recently come out as reinforcements from the training depot at RIPON where these men have come from tell us that the best men are kept there and that at least 100 men there have had training as signallers - Are they kept so that those in charge can make a good show at inspections?	
	19.		The G.O.C 149th Infantry Brigade complained that he was not getting enough retaliation though the Brigade has fired 4600 rounds during the 10 days it has been in and it has nearly all been in retaliation, + the battery covering the trenches particularly complained of has today fired 357 rounds in retaliation. He says	

Instructions regarding War Diaries and Intelligence Summaries are contained in F. S. Regs., Part. II. and the Staff Manual respectively. Title Pages will be prepared in manuscript.

Army Form C. 2118

WAR DIARY
or
INTELLIGENCE SUMMARY
(Erase heading not required.)

Imp. Hav., 26/7 — 10.000

Place	Date	Hour	Summary of Events and Information	Remarks and references to Appendices
			he requires our batteries to shoot whenever the Germans do and to shoot more than they do without waiting for our infantry to ask for retaliation & irrespective of what nature of gun the enemy use. It was suggested to him that this was a great waste of ammunition & could not be done on the present allowance, that the enemy goes through his programme no matter what we do and that the best way to retaliate is to take time and organise a counterstraafe with as many guns as possible on some soft spot.	
	20.		A message was received from G.O.C. I Bgde that he was very pleased with the promptness and accuracy of the retaliation today. his requirements have been considerably modified since the question of ammunition supply has been further explained to him. A few rounds were fired round the 3rd Battery position in the evening.	
	21.		The enemy did a great deal of counterbattery work starting at 7 am registering the 3rd Battery position with an aeroplane. The men had to leave the position several times during the day but no casualties were suffered. The enemy used 15, 10.5 & 7.7 cm	
	22.		A quiet day on the whole but 500 rounds fired in retaliation between 4 & 6.30 pm.	
	23.		3rd Battery again shelled but not so heavily as on 21st.	
	24.		Much quieter. Early this morning the enemy blew up a portion of his own front line by a small ~~his~~ mine - the infantry could not give us the exact map location and most of the damage was repaired by daylight.	

Army Form C. 2118

Instructions regarding War Diaries and Intelligence Summaries are contained in F. S. Regs., Part. II. and the Staff Manual respectively. Title Pages will be prepared in manuscript.

WAR DIARY
or
INTELLIGENCE SUMMARY
(Erase heading not required.)

Imp. Hav., 26/7 — 10.000

Place	Date	Hour	Summary of Events and Information	Remarks and references to Appendices
			The Infantry in the left subsector were much bothered by a trench mortar. It is known where it is but they are not willing to clear their front line to enable the howitzers abate the nuisance but frequently called on us for retaliation — a useless proceeding	
	24.		A gun of 2nd Battery had to go to I.O.M the front end of the inner spring case having broken right away — also one of 1st Battery the inner spring case having stretched ½"	
	25.		Officers of the batteries of the 3rd Divn who are to relieve us came to reconnoitre the positions.	
	26.		During the shelling of the trenches this afternoon the telephone dug out of 2nd Battery was destroyed — 1 telephonist killed + 2 badly wounded + 2 telephones broken. The Battery lines have now been run into the infantry dug out + are being operated by them — During last night the 149th Infantry Brigade on our front were relieved + replaced by the 9th Brigade 3rd Divn. At 10.35 pm heavy firing on our left began. At first it seemed to be a bombardment by enemy field guns + then the guns on our left began. The 1st Battery received Gas S.O.S. from the right battalion + began to barrage within 1 second of receiving the call. 2nd + 3rd Batteries reported all quiet on their front — after further enquiries it appeared all was quiet on 1st Battery front too but not till 92 rounds had been fired — There does not appear to have been any justification for the Gas S.O.S. signal which originated with the trench commander of K.1	

Instructions regarding War Diaries and Intelligence Summaries are contained in F. S. Regs., Part. II. and the Staff Manual respectively. Title Pages will be prepared in manuscript.

WAR DIARY
or
INTELLIGENCE SUMMARY
(Erase heading not required.)

Army Form C. 2118

Imp. Hav., 26/7 — 10.000

Place	Date	Hour	Summary of Events and Information	Remarks and references to Appendices
	28.		At 4.10 am. the first battery again received "gas S.O.S." from K1 trench. all batteries stood to but fire was not opened – again no justification for the call can be made out as everything on the front was quiet at the time.	
	29.		Information was received from a deserter at 9.30pm that the enemy intended to make a gas attack tonight on the front of the Brigade on our right and later that it would take place about 1am.	
	30.		At 12.45 am heavy firing broke out on our right and a gas S.O.S. signal was received from the Infantry Brigade Headquarters on our front through C.R.A's office (since the relief this Brigade has cut out the direct line from them to us without telling us & it was found out by our linesmen going over the line which is their duty to keep up – their excuse was they had too many lines for their switch board). The Battalion headquarters at this time reported no gas and all normal on our front. The 1st & 2nd batteries opened fire shortly after 1am. as the enemy shelling opened up to our front but it never became really heavy and the left of our zone remained quiet. Our batteries ceased fire at about 2.30 am and ammunition was replenished. It appears gas was let off opposite the F trenches (to the right of our zone) and attack made & a footing obtained in the BULL RING (E1) opposite SPANBROEK MOLEN, but the enemy were promptly driven out by a counter bombing attack. By 3.10 am, all field guns near us had ceased firing and only a few heavies kept it up by occasional shells	

Instructions regarding War Diaries and Intelligence Summaries are contained in F. S. Regs., Part. II. and the Staff Manual respectively. Title Pages will be prepared in manuscript.

WAR DIARY
or
INTELLIGENCE SUMMARY
(Erase heading not required.)

Army Form C. 2118

Imp. Hav., 26/7 — 10.000

Place	Date	Hour	Summary of Events and Information	Remarks and references to Appendices
	30 (continued)		At 8pm the relief of one section of each battery began. All reliefs reported complete by 9.45. At 9.50 a gas horn was heard to the South. Then shortly afterwards to the North. No definite information could be obtained as to where the gas was but the battalions reported all quiet on our front. At 10.10pm orders were received from C.R.A. to open fire as if there was a gas attack on our front. This was done although all was quiet on our front. These orders were cancelled at 10.27. It is not clear to us why they were given. At 11.0pm a report was received that gas had been let off on the right of the 76th Inf. Brigade on our right but it had blown back over the enemy lines. All quiet by 12 midnight. Hugh [illegible] Capt & Adjt	

Instructions regarding War Diaries and Intelligence Summaries are contained in F. S. Regs., Part. II. and the Staff Manual respectively. Title Pages will be prepared in manuscript.

WAR DIARY or INTELLIGENCE SUMMARY

1st Northumbrian Brigade R.F.A.

(Erase heading not required.)

Army Form C. 2118

250 Bde R.F.A. late 1/1 Nbn. Bde

Vol 13

Imp. Hav. 26/7 — 10.000

Place	Date 1916	Hour	Summary of Events and Information	Remarks and references to Appendices
	May 1		The position of the 2nd Battery was heavily shelled in the morning and intermittently all day – a direct hit was obtained in the telephone dug out and all wires destroyed – Casualties one gunner wounded. The farm was burnt & several pigs cows & farm horses destroyed – one horse of the relieving battery was destroyed. The battery relieving the 1st battery had 2 guns still with the I.O.M so these guns were taken by 1st Battery & 2 left in position. The 3rd Battery broke a trail-eye on the journey out. The Brigade headquarters were relieved at noon by a group of 3rd Div: Arty. D battery marched to the new area on foot and the AC also moved by day.	
	2		All units arrived during the night in the rest area near EECKE and occupied their former billets.	
			The first week in the rest area was spent in overhauling stores etc and from 8-18 May in training under Battery Commanders & from 19-27 training on similar lines was continued ~~on similar lines~~ under the supervision of the Brigade Commander. All guns were sent to I.O.M for a thorough overhaul & repainting of all vehicles done though this work was much hampered by the difficulty of obtaining paint from Ordnance.	
			From 14-17 a company commander from 4th 5th & 6th Battns of Northumberland Fusiliers was attached respectively to 1st 2nd & 3rd Batteries so that they might get to know something about the limits of the capabilities of our guns and of the work entailed in working a battery & maintaining the ammunition supply.	
			On 9th May 4 guns & 8 ammunition wagons were received for D battery. 3 of the guns had range drums for Mk I shrapnel & 1 for Mk IV shrapnel – an exchange	

Army Form C. 2118

Instructions regarding War Diaries and Intelligence Summaries are contained in F. S. Regs., Part. II. and the Staff Manual respectively. Title Pages will be prepared in manuscript.

WAR DIARY
or
INTELLIGENCE SUMMARY
(Erase heading not required.)

Imp. Hav., 26/7 — 10.000

Place	Date	Hour	Summary of Events and Information	Remarks and references to Appendices
			was arranged with D battery of the 3rd Northumbrian Brigade so that our battery had 2 of each sort so that the battery can be shot by sections if necessary. Leave has been asked to indent for 2 more range drums for Mk IV shrapnel.	
			On the 10th instructions were received that horses + personnel necessary to complete D battery + the other batteries to establishment were to be drawn from the Brigade Ammunition Column and the remainder of the B.A.C. handed over to the D.A.C. All B.A.C.s are to be abolished and the D.A.C. slightly increased + divided into 2 echelons. A to do the work formerly done by the B.A.C.s + B to do the work formerly done by the D.A.C. the result being a large saving in each Division in officers other ranks and horses but a sacrifice of 104 rounds per 18 pdr. gun carried in field echelons in front of Park. In this Division the 3 sections of the D.A.C form echelon A (each section having the same establishment as an old 18 pdr. B.A.C.) and the 4 B.A.C.s together form echelon B + the surplus disposed of in sundry ways (trench mortars for this + other Divisions + some sent to the base to be drawn on as future reinforcements). Our B.A.C. has practically all been absorbed into echelon B so has not been broken up so much as might have happened.	
			The same result could have been arrived at had the 3 B.A.C.s been formed into the 3 sections of echelon A + the D.A.C formed into echelon B. This would have meant less splitting up of units + have meant that echelon A was formed of persons who knew the work instead of having people entirely new to it as is	

Army Form C. 2118

Instructions regarding War Diaries and Intelligence Summaries are contained in F. S. Regs., Part. II. and the Staff Manual respectively. Title Pages will be prepared in manuscript.

WAR DIARY
or
INTELLIGENCE SUMMARY
(Erase heading not required.)

Imp. Hav., 26/7 — 10.000

Place	Date	Hour	Summary of Events and Information	Remarks and references to Appendices
			now the case	
			On the 15th all the new D batteries of the 3 18pdr brigades started to march to WISSANT between CALAIS & BOULOGNE for training.	
			On the 16th all the 3 new D batteries were transferred to a new brigade under the HQ staff of the 4th Northumbrian Brigade and each of the 1st 2nd & 3rd Northumbrian Brigades (18pdr) had transferred to them a howitzer (4.5) battery from the 4th Northumbrian Brigade & the titles of units changed. The 4th Durham Howitzer Battery was sent to this Brigade.	
			OLD TITLE. — NEW TITLE.	
			1st Northumbrian Brigade RFA — 250th (Northumbrian) Brigade R.F.A.	
			1st Northumberland Battery — A Battery 250th (Northumbrian) Bgde R.F.A.	
			2nd — B " "	
			3rd — C " "	
			4th Durham Howitzer Battery — D " "	
			D Battery 1st Northumbrian Bgde — A " 253rd "	
			On 17th Capt. N. SOUTHERN returned to England to take over a 2nd line battery. Two other officers were sent from the Divisional Artillery for the same purpose.	

Army Form C. 2118

Instructions regarding War Diaries and Intelligence Summaries are contained in F. S. Regs., Part. II. and the Staff Manual respectively. Title Pages will be prepared in manuscript.

WAR DIARY
or
INTELLIGENCE SUMMARY
(Erase heading not required.)

Imp. Hav., 26/7 — 10.000

Place	Date	Hour	Summary of Events and Information	Remarks and references to Appendices
	23.		O.C. + Adjutant + on 24th O.C. B battery + on 25th O.C. A C + D batteries visited our old positions near MILLEKRUIS to which we are to go back on 29/30 + 30/31 to arrange details of relief. A new 4 gun position is being built to replace that of C battery which has been still more heavily shelled since we left. The position of B battery was vacated the night after we left + has not been shot from or at since. A copy of the Brigade Operation order for this relief is attached.	
	30.		A communication was received that Capt. R.H. BREMNER of 3rd line 4th Lowland Brigade R.F.A. + Capt E.H. CAWSTON of 3rd line 1st WESSEX. Brigade R.F.A. have been posted to this unit - Presumably they have been sent to replace Capt. SOUTHERN + Capt. CHAPMAN (from what is now D battery of this Brigade) who were sent to England to take over 2nd line units. Nothing is yet known of the service of these officers or what position they are to take in this Brigade.	
			Hugh Sykes Capt Adjt 250th (Northumbrian) Brigade R.F.A.	

Copy No..1.....

250TH (NORTHUMBRIAN) BRIGADE R.F.A.

OPERATION ORDER NO.3

ISSUED BY LT.COL."H.S.BELL D.S.O.,COMMANDING.

Reference Sheet 27 S.E.(Second Edition) and 28 S.W.(Edition 3B) 1/20,000.

1. The Brigade will relieve the centre group,3rd Divisional Artillery on the nights of 29/30 and 30/31 May.
   Details of reliefs to be arranged between Battery Commanders.
2. The first sectioms will march to the new area on 29th.,and the remainder on the 30th.,under Battery arrangements.
   Route via FLETRE - METEREN - BAILLEUL. Sections will go into action as soon as possible after dark.
3. Positions in action ZONES and wagon lines are shown in the schedule hereunder written.
4. Command of Brigade will pass ~~xx~~ at Noon 30th. Command of Batteries will pass on completion of relief. Completion of relief to be reported to Brigade Headquarters by wire.
5. 50th Divisional Artillery will be responsible for Ammunition supply after 10.30a.m. on 30th. 50th Divisional Artillery will move into new area with Echelons full. Approximately 200 rounds per gun and 100 rounds per howitzer will be taken over,dumped, at the positions. Os.C.,Batteries,50th Divisional Artillery will be responsible for return of all ammunition expended by both Divisions after Noon 30th.
6. All Water troughs must be left in present area.
7. Certificates and receipts for transfer of all tents and other camp equipment,and also certificates that owners of vacated billets have no claim against the unit,will be rendered to Brigade Office by Noon 31st.
8. Rations for consumption on 30th will be delivered in this area on 29th. The portions required for personnel moving on 30th will be taken off the wagons, and the remainder taken to new area in Supply wagons which will march with units.
9. Acknowledge.

S C H E D U L E

	Position.	Zones.		Wagon Lines.
Brigade H.Q.	N.8.b.2.2.			M.16.d.1.7.
"A" Battery.	N.14.a.7.9.	N.24.d.0.6.) N.24.a.9.5.)	Trenches G.4 to J.3	M.21.b.8.3.
"B" Battery.	N.9.b.5.5.	N.24.a.9.5.) N.18.d.2.2.)	J.2 to K2b.	M.12.b.0.3.
"C" Battery.	N.10.c.0.9.	N.18.d.2.2.) N.18.b.0.7.)	K2a to L5.5	M.12.c.6.3-4.
"D" Battery.	N.14.c.9.9.	N.24.d.0.6.) N.18.b.0.7.)		M.11.d.3.7.
No.1 Section,50th D.A.C.				M.8.c.8.1.

Issued at 6.0p.m.,27. 5. 16.   By orderly.

Hugh Ellis.

Captain,
Adjutant 250th (North'bn) Brigade RFA.

Copy No.1 O.C.,Brigade.
Copy No.2 O.C.,"A" Battery.
Copy No.3 O.C.,"B"Battery.
Copy No.4 O.C.,"C" Battery.
Copy No.5 O.C.,"D" Battery.
Copy No.6 Spare.

Instructions regarding War Diaries and Intelligence Summaries are contained in F. S. Regs., Part. II. and the Staff Manual respectively. Title Pages will be prepared in manuscript.

Army Form C. 2118

50

WAR DIARY
or
INTELLIGENCE SUMMARY

250th (Northumbrian) Brigade RFA

(Erase heading not required.)

Vol 14

Imp. Hav., 26/7 — 10.000

Place	Date 1916	Hour	Summary of Events and Information	Remarks and references to Appendices
	1 June		A quiet day – all batteries did a lot of registering – Capt BREMNER arrived – he appears to have had no training and to be totally unfitted to be a captain in this brigade – a report has been sent to CRA	
	2.		During the afternoon our trench mortars had a mild strafe. The enemy retaliated with TMs & our infantry called for 18pdr support – they got it and the enemy added field guns to his retaliation – counter retaliation became necessary & in the end a lot of shooting became necessary –	
			Capt. CAWSTON arrived at C battery – nothing is yet known as to his capabilities –	
			An emergency call was received by the wireless attached to us that 2 guns were firing at O.14.d 8.5 – This is one of our selected squares – It was a dangerous light to shoot in but B battery gave it 2 salvoes.	
			A lot of heavy firing both in the morning & evening to the north of our zone – probably about HOOGE	
	3.		Brigade Headquarters were moved to N.13.a.3.0. – This place is not nearly so convenient for us as it is far further from batteries & there exists at present practically no accomodation	

Army Form C. 2118

Instructions regarding War Diaries and Intelligence Summaries are contained in F. S. Regs., Part. II. and the Staff Manual respectively. Title Pages will be prepared in manuscript.

WAR DIARY
or
INTELLIGENCE SUMMARY
(Erase heading not required.)

Imp. Hav., 26/7 — 10.000

Place	Date	Hour	Summary of Events and Information	Remarks and references to Appendices
			but it is nearer to the Headquarters of the G.O.C. 49th Infantry who likes to have his artillery commander in his pocket if possible.	
			Captains Bremner & Cawston went to be interviewed by C.R.A. & orders are now received that these officers are to be regarded as attached for instruction only until further orders & not to be posted to us.	
	4.		At 12.30 am a minor enterprise was carried out in conjunction with [illegible] Div. on our right. The operation orders are attached. The enemy retaliated to a certain extent but all was quiet by 1.15.	"A"
			Major Johnson was awarded the D.S.O in the Honours List of the Kings Birthday and Sergt. Major MORRISS (D battery) & Corpl BURNETT (H.Q.S) the Military Medal	
	5.		A high wind all day – a certain amount of retaliation required for Trench Mortars in the afternoon but otherwise an uneventful day.	
	6.		Still a very high wind and rain. An uneventful day except for the usual Trench Mortar Strafe in afternoon.	
	7.		A very quiet day, a few Trench Mortars in the morning otherwise nothing to report.	
	8.		At 3.30 am a bombardment by our Trench Mortars, 18 prs & 4.5 How took place; the Operation Orders are attached. There was very little retaliation, and the object, the damaging of enemy works appeared to be very successfully achieved.	"B"

Army Form C. 2118

Instructions regarding War Diaries and Intelligence Summaries are contained in F. S. Regs., Part. II. and the Staff Manual respectively. Title Pages will be prepared in manuscript.

WAR DIARY
or
INTELLIGENCE SUMMARY
(Erase heading not required.)

Imp. Hav., 26/7 — 10.000

Place	Date	Hour	Summary of Events and Information	Remarks and references to Appendices
	9		Very little of interest to report, except Trench Mortar Activity.	
	10		At 6 am enemy sprang 2 mines simultaneously in front of Petit Bois no damage was done to our trenches. The Bosch occupied the Craters. Later on in the day the Craters were taken on by TMs Stokes gun &c.	
	11		A quiet day, The New Craters were Strafed by 6" Howitzers and a lot of damage done.	
	12		A good deal of Artillery Straf but mostly on our Left.	
	13		Much TM Strafe on both sides but nothing else of interest	
	14		Our heavies Strafed the New Craters in Petit Bois & Hollandchesschuur which caused a good deal of retaliation from the Bosch & counter retaliation on our part.	
	15		Usual Trench Mortar Straf	
	16		Very quiet day, ~~on the~~ at night however great activity on the part of enemy machine guns & rifles on our Front. At 11.15 a very heavy Strafe up in the Salient which lasted till 12.30 am. At 12.30 am a gas attack & heavy Strafe on the Right of our Divisional area, this lasted to about 1.30 am & then ceased, and another Straf started in Salient. None of our Batteries were engaged.	
	17		A very quiet day, practically nothing on our front. Major Johnston & Bomb M F Scott (A) mentioned in Dispatches.	

Army Form C. 2118

Instructions regarding War Diaries and Intelligence Summaries are contained in F. S. Regs., Part. II. and the Staff Manual respectively. Title Pages will be prepared in manuscript.

WAR DIARY
or
INTELLIGENCE SUMMARY
(Erase heading not required.)

Imp. Hav., 26/7 — 10.000

Place	Date	Hour	Summary of Events and Information	Remarks and references to Appendices
	18.		376 rounds fired in retaliation between 12 & 4 otherwise quiet – Gas was sent over in two clouds on the front of the Division on our right during the night 18/19 but no infantry attack took place – all quiet on our front.	
	19.		A quiet day – misty & some rain – accurate observation impossible except during short intervals. D battery blew up the ammunition store of a trench mortar at N.18.d.2.9 which had been particularly troublesome of late	
	20		A lot of retaliation required all day starting at 8·30 am.	
	21.		Orders received that ammunition expenditure is to be cut down as much as possible	
	22.		A quiet day – no shooting done at all.	
	23.		One round fired only – to stop rifle fire at one of our aeroplanes flying low over the trenches.	
	24.		This was "A" day referred to in the attached Brigade operation order No 5.	"C"
			A full report on the shooting which extended into the 25th is attached	"D"
	25		A very quiet day.	
	26.		This was B day of the operations but the tasks were postponed till what was really "C" day viz 27th as they did not start till 1·30 am on the instructions of C.R.A. so that not very much firing was done though a certain amount of retaliation for T.M.s was necessitated.	

Army Form C. 2118

Instructions regarding War Diaries and Intelligence Summaries are contained in F. S. Regs., Part. II. and the Staff Manual respectively. Title Pages will be prepared in manuscript.

WAR DIARY
or
INTELLIGENCE SUMMARY
(Erase heading not required.)

Imp. Hav., 26/7 — 10.000

Place	Date	Hour	Summary of Events and Information	Remarks and references to Appendices
	27.		This was C day of the operations and a very great deal of shooting was done between 1.30 am & 6 pm. X hours C night was at 10.30 pm. A full report of the operations B day, B night & C day is attached all really taking place on 27th. During all this time, as well as all this shooting, a tremendous lot of work is being done on OPs & new gun positions further forward for all batteries. All of them have to be proof against 15 cm shells. It is very hard work all batteries being below establishment & have several men sick, attached to T.Ms for training, working for R.E. on brick laying etc. Reinforcements have been asked for	"E"
	28.		This was D day of the operations. A full report of the shooting on night 27-28 & 28th is attached	"F"
	29.		This day formed no part of the set scheme of operations but C Battery in particular did some very useful straafing & all batteries were called on for retaliation particularly late at night when the Division ~~[illegible]~~ on our right appeared to have a shoot on & the enemy retaliation spread up to our zone. Several guns including some 15 cm hows were shooting on this zone which have not done so for some time, as no new registrations were observed it may be that the same guns have been brought back & are using their old registrations or perhaps they have only switched over further south & have now been switched back.	

Army Form C. 2118

WAR DIARY
or
INTELLIGENCE SUMMARY
(Erase heading not required.)

Instructions regarding War Diaries and Intelligence Summaries are contained in F. S. Regs., Part. II. and the Staff Manual respectively. Title Pages will be prepared in manuscript.

Imp. Hav., 26/7 — 10.000

Place	Date	Hour	Summary of Events and Information	Remarks and references to Appendices
	30.		This was E day of the operations. a detailed report of the days shooting is attached. In addition D/250 did considerable damage to communication trenches & has provided good exposure points as targets for shrapnel & machineguns. It was again found that cordite + fuze 85 was the best for cutting wire. N.C.T is far too erratic & 85 fuze seems to have more powerful burst that fuze 80.	"G"
			2/Lt. S.J.C. SMITH from C/250 was posted to 50th D.A.C. & 2/Lt. I. McKinnon from 50th D.A.C. was posted to C/250.	
			Hugh [illegible] Capt R.F.A. Adjutant 250th (North.) Bde R.F.A.	

SECRET.

"A"

B.M. 1273/

O.C.,
250th (Northumbrian) Brigade R.F.A.

---

1. A minor enterprise will take place on the 72nd I.B. front (24th Division) on the night 3rd/4th June. The hour of zero time will be notified later.

2. The 24th Div. Arty., and 50th Div. Arty., and the Heavy Arty. V. Corps will co-operate and demonstrate on selected places along the V. Corps front.

3. The official time will be telephoned from this Office at 9.10p.m. on 3rd June.

4. Groups will carry out programme as per table attached.

5. At 0.15' Strombos horns will be sounded somewhere on the 24th Division front as a signal for the withdrawal of a raiding party. Care must be taken not to mistake this for a gas signal.

6. At 0.3' our aeroplanes will drop signals behind enemy's lines. These signals will be answered from our line by red and green Very lights.

7. The utmost care will be taken to ensure that the enemy are kept in ignorance of the enterprise, and only the necessary information issued beforehand to those concerned.

8. Please acknowledge.

F. Brown

Major R.A.,
B.M. 50th D.A.

3. 6. 16.

Ref: Map WYTSCHAETE, 28
S.W. 2. Edition 3 B.

SECRET.

TIME TABLE FOR 50th D.A.

Time.	No. of guns.	Nature.	OBJECTIVE.	Remarks.
1st Phase. Oh-0' to Oh.15'	12 4	Right (18-pdrs. (4.5" Hows.	Bombardment :- Front Line N.30.a.3½.1½ to N.30.a.4½.3½.	
	12 4	Centre (18-pdrs. (4.5" Hows.	Front line N.18.c.8.0. to N.18.c.9¾.1.	
	12 4	Left (18-pdrs. (4.5" Hows.	Front line N.18.b.1¾.5½ to N.18.b.2.9.	
2nd Phase. Oh.15' to Oh.20'	As in 1st Phase.		Barrage (N.30.a.3½.1½. (N.30.a.4½.1½. (N.30.a.5.2½. (N.30.a.5¾.3¾. Barrage (N.24.a.8½.9½. (N.24.b.½.9¾. (N. 18.d.1⅓.1½. Barrage (N.18.b.3½.5. (N.18.b.4½.7½. (N.18.b.6.9½. (N.12.d.5½.0.	Ammunition allotted :- 4.5" Hows. 160.) Per 18-pdrs 600.) Group. Average rate of fire 2 rounds per gun per minute for 1st 15 minutes. 1 Round per gun per minute for 2nd 5 minutes. 2 rounds per gun per minute for 3rd 10 minutes.
3rd Phase. Oh.20' to Oh.30'.	As in 1st Phase.		As in 1st Phase.	Howitzers rather slower rate for all Phases. Bombardment. 18-pdrs. fire 75% H.E. Barrage. 18-pdrs. fire 75% Shrapnel.

SECRET.

B.M. 1273/1.

O.C., 250th (Northbn) Bde. R.F.A.

With reference to my B.M. 1273 sent you this morning, will you please note the following :-

1. Zero time will be at 12.30a.m.
2. Signal for withdrawal (at 0.15 min) will be a "G" on the bugle and NOT short blast on STROMBOS HORNS as previously arranged. 0 15 F.B.
3. Signals to be dropped from an aeroplane at 0.3 mins. will be :-

(a) One red and one greem Very Light, followed at one minute by

(b) One green foll•wed by one green Very light.

Please acknowledge by wire.

F. Bronson

6.0p.m.
3. 6. 16.

Major R.A.,
B.M. 50th D.A.

"B" SECRET. Copy No. 6

250TH (NORTHUMBRIAN) BRIGADE R.F.A.

OPERATION ORDER NO. 4

Reference Map
Sheet 28 S.W.
1/10,000.

7th June 1916.

(1) The 250th (Northumbrian) Brigade R.F.A., and X50 Trench Mortar Battery, will undertake a bombardment of the enemy's position on THURSDAY morning, 8th June, the object being to do as much damage as possible to the craters in front of K.1. trench and the works in progress behind them.

(2) The bombardment will commence at 3.30 a.m., and will be kept up for 30 minutes. Intervals at discretion of Battery Commanders.

(3) The Batteries will fire on targets as follows :-

"A" 1 gun on LONE TREE N.24.d.7.7.
1 gun on BRICK PILE O.13.c.6.1.
2 guns on HOSPICE.
Allowance for this 60 A.X., 80 A.

"B" 2 guns on trenches N.24.b.4½.9½. to N.24.b.3.3.
2 guns on trenches N.18.c.9.0. to N.24.a.7.8.
Allowance for this 100 A.X., 40 A.

"C" 1 gun on RED CHATEAU (O.P.).
1 gun on trench N.18.d.6.3½. to N.18.d.10.3.
Allowance for this 100 A.X., 20 A.

"D" 1 gun on BRICK PILE. O.13.c.6.1.
3 guns on trench N.24.b.4½.9½. to N.24.b.3.3.
Allowance for this 30 B., 80 B.X.

(4) Retaliation if required must be forthcoming, and any enemy trench motter positions known or observed during the bombardment, must be taken on.
Expenditure of ammunition for this must be at Battery Commanders' discretion, but must be very moderate.

(5) The 2" Trench Mortars will open fire at 3.32 a.m., and concentrate their fire on the craters in front of K.1., and the works behind. They will fire about 150 bombs.

(6) K.1. and J.3. trenches will be cleared for these operations.

(7) Acknowledge.

Issued at by orderly.

Lt.Col.
250th (Northumbrian) Brigade R.F.A.

"C"

COPY NO...I....

250TH (NORTHUMBRIAN) BRIGADE R.F.A.

OPERATION ORDER NO.5

ISSUED BY

LT.COL.H.S.BELL D.S.O., COMMANDING.

---

1. An operation will be carried out with the objects :-
   (a) To make the enemy think we are going to attack on this zone.
   (b) To worry and fatigue him as much as possible.
2. Detailed schemes of firing are laid down in the attached table which must be adhered to.
   The ammunition allotted for the operation is, each 18-pdr., Battery - 1666 A and 1333 A.X., for the 4.5" (How) Battery, 1250 B.X., and/for the T.M., Battery 500 rounds, No.107 fuze.
   The ammunition allotted in the table does not exhaust this allotment for 18-pdr.Batteries, and the balance is to be used as Battery Commanders may think advisable, either to enable them to better carry out the allotted tasks or to worry the enemy, e.g., by firing on roads at night, or to meet the extra counter-retaliation which it is expected will be required.
   The amount shewn in the table for the 4.5" (How) Battery exceeds this allotment. The balance must be made up from the ordinary daily allowance.
   The T.M., ammunition will be allotted between the mortars as the O.C., T.M.Battery may think advisable.
3. "A" day is 24th June 1916. Notification will be sent from time to time as to what days are represented by B, C, D and E.
4. Acknowledge.

Issued at ~~10.0p.m.~~ 1 am. on ~~23rd~~ 24 June 1916 by Orderly. Copies 2.3.4 & 5

8 am 24 6.7 & 8

8.50 24 personally 9.

A = 24th B = 26th C = 27th D = 28th E 30th

Day.	Hour.	Battery.	Task.	Ammunition allotted
A.	To be arranged between B.C. & O.C. T.M. battery.	A.	Spray Trenches to prevent observation while T.Ms cut wire between N.18.c.9.1 & N.18.d.2.2.	150 A. 50 AX.
	at B.Cs convenience	B.	Cut wire from N.24.a.9½.6. to 9½.5.	370 A.
	"	C	Cut wire from N.18.b.2.2. to d 2.8 2.4.	300 A.
	"	D.	Destroy C.Ts in N.18.b. south of the main road	100 BX.
	as necessary, see above.	T.M.	1 will help C Battery. 1 will help B battery. 2 will cut wire from N.18.c.9.1.-N.18.d.2.2.	80.
A night.		A.	Prevent the mending of wire cut by B battery.	~~60~~ 40 A.
		B.		
		C	Prevent the mending of wire cut by itself	40 A.
	0. 1-30. 3-0.	A and D.	Bombard O.13.a.5½.1¼. Zero time will be notified later. The ammunition allotted will be divided between the three bombardments each of which last 15 minutes & be accompanied by bursts of T.S. from A battery about 30 seconds after D has fired	BX. 200. AX 100 A. 170.
		T.M.	Shell craters in N.24.a.	15.
B	0. to 0.40	A.	Create a barrage behind PETIT BOIS so as to isolate that salient in the enemy's lines ~~and~~	150 A. 200 AX
	0. to 0.10	B.	with 2 guns open fire on front line N.18.c.9.1 – N.18.d.2.2 with 2 guns open fire on front line N.24.a.9½.6 – 9½.5.	120 AX.
	0. to 0.10	C	Open fire on front line N.18.b.2.4 – 2.6.	100 AX.
	0 to 0.40	D	stop all reinforcements coming down C.T's in O.19.a.	~~300~~ BX. 200
	0.10 to 0.30	B & C	Lift their fire and barrage so far as possible all C.T.s leading to the front line they have bombarded. each battery	60 A. 100 AX.
	0.30 to 0.40.	B & C.	Renew task started at 0. o'clock but at a slower rate each battery	80 AX
	0 to 0.40	T.M.	Shell craters in N.24.a.	50.

Day.	Hour.	Battery.	Task.	Ammunition allotted.
B night.		A.	Prevent the mending of wire cut by B battery.	40 A.
	0.0.	B.	Barrage N.24.c.8½.6 to N.24.d.6.3	100 A. 100 AX.
		C.	Prevent the mending of wire cut by itself.	40 A.
		D	Help B battery in their task of barraging N.24.c.8½.6 – N.24.d.6.3	50 BX
		T.M.		
C.	0. to 0.30.	A.	Barrage N.18.c.9.1 to N.18.d.2.2.	52 A. 60 AX.
		B.	Barrage N.24.a.9½.6. to N.24.b.2.3.	52 A. 60 AX.
		C.	Barrage N.18.b.2.2. to N.18.b.2~~1~~.6.	52 A. 60 AX.
		D	Fire on N.18.b.9.1 & neighbourhood. 0.19.c.2.8 to 0.19.a.5.1. 0.19.b.1.5. 0.19.b.3.2.	100 BX.
		T.M.	2 will help A battery. 1 will help B battery. 1 will help C Battery.	60.
	1.30 approx	A.B.C. D & T.M.	Retaliation on a point or points to be detailed later. each 18 pdr Batt: / 4.5 H. Battery / T.M.	30 A. 60 AX. / 60 BX. / ~~40~~ 20
	to be arranged between B.C. & T.M. Batt:	A.	Shell trenches to prevent observation while T.Ms cut wire from N.18.c.9.1 to N.18.d.2.2.	150 A. 100 AX.
		T.M.	2 will continue to cut wire N.18.c.9.1 – N.18.d.2.2. 1 will help B battery. 1 will help C Battery	80.
	at B.C.'s conveni-ence	B.	cut wire from N.24.a.9½.5 to N.24.b.1.3½.	300 A.
		C	cut wire at N.18.b.2.6. (on road)	250 A.
		D	bombard N.18.b.2.6. (machine gun)	30 BX.
C night.	~~A.~~	A.	Prevent the mending of wire cut by B battery on A & C days	50 A.
		B		
		C	Prevent the mending of wire cut by itself on A & C days	50 A.
	X.0 / X+1 hr. / X+2 hr.	A & D.	Bombard 0.19.b.1½.6½. Time represented by X hours will be notified later. The ammunition allotted will be divided between the three bombardments each of which will last 10 minutes, & be accompanied by bursts of T.S. from A battery.	~~150~~ BX 100 / 100 AX. / 170 A.
		T.M.	Shell craters in N.24.a.	15.

Day	Hour	Battery	Task	Ammunition allotted.
D	To be arranged between B.C. & O.C. T.M. battery at B.Cs convenience.	A.	Shell trenches ~~which~~ to prevent observation while T.Ms cut wire between N.18.c.9.1 & N.18.d.2.2.	150 A. 100 AX.
		T.M.	2 will cut wire N.18.c.9.1. to N.18.d.2.2. 1 will help B battery. 1 will help C battery	80.
		B.	Cut wire from N.24.b.1.3½ to N.24.b.2.3.	300 A.
		C.	Cut wire from N.18.b.2.6 to N.18.b.2.8.	300 A.
		D.		
D night.		A.	Prevent the mending of wire cut by B battery on A C & D days	20 A. 20 AX.
		B.		
		C.	Prevent the mending of wire cut by itself on A C & D days	20 A. 20 AX.
	Y. Y+1hr.30 Y+2hrs.	D and A.	Bombard O.19.a.5.1½. Time represented by Y hours will be notified later. The ammunition allotted will be divided between the three bombardments each of which will last 15 minutes, & be accompanied by bursts of T.S. from A battery.	~~200~~ BX. 100 ~~100~~ AX. 200 170 A.
		T.M.		
E.	To be arranged between B.C. & O.C. T.M. battery	A	Shell trenches to prevent observation while T.Ms cut wire from N.18.c.9.1. to N.18.d.2.2.	100 150 ~~150~~ A. ~~100~~ AX.
		T.M.	2 will complete destruction of wire N.18.c.9.1 - N.18.d.2.2. 1 will help B battery, ~~1 will help C battery~~ & bombard the front line behind. 1 will help C battery & bombard the front line behind	100
		B	Complete the destruction of wire between ~~N.18.b.2.2.~~ N.24.a.9½.6 ~~to~~ and N.24.b.2.3 & widen the gap if possible	400 A. 400
		C	Complete the destruction of wire between N.18.b.2.2 & N.18.b.2.8 & widen the gap if possible	400 A. 400
		D.	Destroy C.Ts & supports all over zone.	~~300~~ BX. 150

Capt.& Adjt.
250th(Northumbrian)Brigade R.F.A.

Copy No. 1 to O.C.,Brigade.
" 2 O.C. A/250.
" 3 O.C. B/250.
" 4 O.C. C/250.
" 5 O.C. D/250.
" 6 C.R.A.,50th Division.
" 7 149th Infantry Brigade.
" 8 O.C.,T.M.,Brigade,50th Division.
" 9 O.C.,Z/50 T.M.Battery.
" 10 Retained.

Copy No. 5

SECRET.

149th INFANTRY BRIGADE OPERATION ORDER NO. 89.

Reference Map
Sheet 28 S.W.
1/10,000.

5th June 1916.

The 250th (N) Brigade R.F.A. and X.50 Medium Trench Mortar Battery will undertake a bombardment of the enemy's position on Thursday morning, the 8th June, 1916. The object being to do as much damage as possible to the craters in front of K.1. trench and the works in progress behind them.

ARTILLERY. The Howitzer Battery will open fire at 3-30 a.m. on the enemy's observation posts, and continue for 30 minutes.

The 18 pdrs. Batteries, R.F.A. will open fire at 3-30 a.m. on the enemy's support line from about N.24.b.3.3. to N.18.c.9.1. and continue for 30 minutes.

MEDIUM TRENCH MORTARS. Light 2" Trench Mortars will open fire at 3-32 a.m. and concentrate their fire on the craters in front of K.1. and the works in progress behind them. They will fire about 150 bombs.

LIGHT TRENCH MORTAR BATTERIES. The Stokes Guns will assist the 2" trench mortars and will open fire at 3-32 a.m. on the enemy's front line and support trenches opposite their positions, and fire intermittently during the 30 minutes bombardment.

REGISTRATION by MEDIUM TRENCH MORTARS. The Medium Trench Mortars will register on the craters and works behind them in front of K.1. trench, under cover of artillery fire at 2-0 p.m. on Tuesday, 6th June, and at 4-0 p.m. on Wednesday, 7th June.

It will not be necessary for O.C. Right Sub-sector to clear any trenches on account of Registration.

CLEARING OF TRENCHES. On Thursday, 8th June, O.C. Right Sub-Sector will have K.1. and J.3. trenches cleared, except for necessary posts, before dawn, taking care that the enemy do not see or hear the withdrawel, and that the trenches are judiciously re-occupied by two or three men at a time in the course of the morning.

Acknowledge as understood.

[signature] Hill
Captain,
for Brigade Major,
149th Infantry Brigade.

Issued at 8-0 p.m.
through Signals.

Copy No.1 to WAR DIARY.
No.2 - Filed.
No.3. - 4th N.F.
No.4. - 7th N.F.
No.5. - 250th (N) Bde. R.F.A.
No.6. - X50 Medium T.M. Battery.
No.7. - 149/1 & 149/2 Light T.M. Batteries.

Instructions regarding War Diaries and Intelligence Summaries are contained in F. S. Regs., Part II. and the Staff Manual respectively. Title Pages will be prepared in manuscript.

WAR DIARY
250th (NORTHUMBRIAN) BRIGADE R.F.A.
INTELLIGENCE SUMMARY

(Erase heading not required.)

Army Form C. 2118

JULY 1916 50

Vol 15 VOL No ~~XVI~~

Imp. Hav., 26/7 – 10.000

Place	Date	Hour	Summary of Events and Information	Remarks and references to Appendices
	July 1916 1 - 4		On the whole quiet days except for Trench Mortars - though it is evident the enemy have increased the number of guns covering this front. They have brought up a heavy minenwerfer (24.5 cm) + arrangements have been made for us to get retaliation for it from our 12" Howitzers. On the 3rd the enemy put up a strong barrage on the road used by B.C + D batteries taking material to their new gun positions.	
			On the nights ~~of 2/3 & 3/4~~ of 1/2 the 24th Division extended their line northwards & took over part of our zone (up to J32) + relieved part of the 149th Infantry Brigade but this front is still covered by 50th Divnl artillery. The 251st Brigade on our right has been attached to 24th Div Arty for some time + now A/250 is attached for tactical purposes to that group. On the nights of 2/3 + 3/4 the 149th Infantry Brigade on our front was relieved by 150th Infantry Brigade.	
	4 - 5		On the night of the 4/5 C/253 Battery was placed under the orders of O.C. this Brigade for tactical purposes. Two of the guns of C/253 were placed in the new emplacements of C/250 at N.10.a.2½ 4¼ and handed over to C/250. C/253 placed two guns in the vacant emplacements of the right section of C/250 + took over this position + the one gun of C/250 now there. The fourth gun of C/250 when it comes back from I.O.M will also be handed over to C/253. A fair amount of retaliation required chiefly for trench mortars.	
			All our wagon lines have been moved up into a much smaller area as many new troops are being brought on to this front, work on the new positions continues. Owing to the new + smaller zone + the attachment of A/250 to the brigade on our right + the attachment of C/253 to us all barrage and other arrangements have been altered.	

Army Form C. 2118

Instructions regarding War Diaries and Intelligence Summaries are contained in F. S. Regs., Part. II. and the Staff Manual respectively. Title Pages will be prepared in manuscript.

WAR DIARY
or
INTELLIGENCE SUMMARY
(Erase heading not required.)

Imp. Hav., 26/7 — 10.000

Place	Date	Hour	Summary of Events and Information	Remarks and references to Appendices
			On the night 6/7 one section of the right group including A/250 was relieved + returned to their wagon lines. The relief was postponed from night 5/6.	
			On the 6th Lieut J.L. Priestman rejoined the Brigade from Headquarters 17th Corps + was posted to B/250. On the 7th one gun of C/250 was returned from I.O.M. + handed over to C/253. The gun has come back with the sights + elevating gear rather more loose than when they went.	
			On the night 7/8 the relief of second sections of right group was cancelled as it was in process of taking place + the sections that went out last night came in again.	
			On the 8th another gun of C/250 now handed to C/253 was sent to I.O.M.	
			On the night of 8th the 150 Infantry Brigade took over some more line to the South from the 24th Divn. The following batteries were handed over to this Brigade on completion of relief at midnight A/250, A/251 + B/251 + this group has also a call on D/107 how. battery of 24th Divn for help if necessary. The front now covered by this group extends from trenches G1 left to L5 inclusive + the group comprises the following batteries A/250, B/250, C/250, D/250, A/251 B/250 C/253. The whole of the defensive arrangements have again to be altered.	
			On the 8th 2/Lt A. SCOTT was posted to A/250.	
	10		At 1.15 am 10th the 150 Infantry Brigade made a raid on one ~~new~~ of the new craters in front of the PETIT BOIS. All batteries of the group stood by ready to put up a strong barrage if required so as to stop any enemy reinforcements coming up but every thing went off very successfully + the batteries were not called on to fire. The rest of the Day saw a lot of retaliation chiefly for heavy trench mortars but was devoid of interest on this front.	

Instructions regarding War Diaries and Intelligence Summaries are contained in F. S. Regs., Part. II. and the Staff Manual respectively. Title Pages will be prepared in manuscript.

WAR DIARY
or
INTELLIGENCE SUMMARY
(Erase heading not required.)

Army Form C. 2118

Imp. Hav., 26/7 — 10.000

Place	Date	Hour	Summary of Events and Information	Remarks and references to Appendices
	11.		At 12.45 am all batteries stood by ready to put up a barrage behind PECKHAM Fm & for retaliation if necessary as the 24th Division on our right were going to make a raid there at 12.55. We have heard nothing as to the success or otherwise of the raid officially nor even if it was made but at 1.24 the infantry commander asked for the barrage which was put up by A/251, B/251 A/250 & D/250. It lasted for 15 minutes & was section fire 10 seconds. A lot of retaliation still required the group firing 1706 rounds in 24 hours ending 5 pm.	
	12 & 13.		Considerable retaliation chiefly for trench mortars but otherwise quiet days.	
	14.		Rather more quiet till 3 pm. The Corps heavy artillery were supposed to bombard the front trench on the PETIT BOIS SALIENT at 4 pm and our batteries were to cooperate but nobody could tell when the heavies were shooting as their bursts seemed to be no bigger than a 4.5 how - the cooperation was rather a disjointed affair	
	15.		Wire cutting operations on various parts of the Brigade front were begun with a view to being a counter attraction to what is going on in the South & also preparation for a contemplated raid. The usual retaliation required in the afternoon.	
	16.		Wire cutting continued. B/251 helped in a shoot by the 6" How: which was called a bombardment but was not a very serious affair.	
	17.		Wire cutting continued - retaliation as usual. At 11 pm B/251 helped in a barrage for 24th Divn & two other batteries stood by. The 24th Divn were to make a raid but from information available (which is not much) they do not seem to have been very energetic about it,	
	~~18~~			
	18.		B/251 continued to cut wire also T.M.S but this is preparation for an operation to come & not part of the scheme started on 15th. On the night 18/19 A/250 moved two guns to a new position further South with a view to getting an enfilade for future operations, B/251 taking over the normal zone of A/250.	

Army Form C. 2118

Instructions regarding War Diaries and Intelligence Summaries are contained in F. S. Regs., Part. II. and the Staff Manual respectively. Title Pages will be prepared in manuscript.

WAR DIARY
or
INTELLIGENCE SUMMARY
(Erase heading not required.)

Imp. Hav., 26/7 — 10.000

Place	Date	Hour	Summary of Events and Information	Remarks and references to Appendices
	19.		At 1. am. the first bombardment mentioned in the attached operation "A" took place. A very much quieter day – a little retaliation required in the afternoon but no Brigade one. At 11. pm the bombardments detailed for C night in the attached operation "A" commenced	
	19-20		There was practically no retaliation to the 1st bombardment, very little to the second & none to the 3rd. The enemy did not seem in the least put out or to expect an attack – from the smaller amount of very lights & rifle fire he probably evacuated the area at any rate the first signs of the bombardment.	
	20.		Quiet in the morning: wire cutting continued – some of that previously cut has again been mended. D night in operation A attached cancelled. On night 20/21 A/250 moved his remaining two guns to the new forward 4 gun position which is in process of being made. Received instructions that the strictest economy must be practised as to ammunition. A/250 registered his right section being covered during the process by A/251 + B/251. about 8.30pm B/250 received a direct hit on one of their guns which	
	#		was damaged beyond repair – Lt. HOPWOOD had just left the gun emplacement when it occurred having removed the dial sight – about 70 rounds of ammunition were destroyed. & a fire occurred which was gallantly put out by Lt. HOPWOOD. No casualties. The battery removed with its remaining three guns to the new position which was practically ready.	
	21.		B/250 registered from its new position – very little shooting done – no 4.5" How	

Instructions regarding War Diaries and Intelligence Summaries are contained in F. S. Regs., Part. II. and the Staff Manual respectively. Title Pages will be prepared in manuscript.

WAR DIARY
or
INTELLIGENCE SUMMARY
(Erase heading not required.)

Army Form C. 2118

Imp. Hav., 26/7 — 10.000

Place	Date	Hour	Summary of Events and Information	Remarks and references to Appendices
			ammunition may be expended without authority of C.R.A. – In the evening A/253 battery moves into the old position of A/250 + became tactically attached to this Group.	
	22.		A/253 registered. TMs very active in afternoon also much noise during the night. C/253 was shelled during the day.	
	23		C/253 was shelled again, but no damage done. Another very noisy night & lots of bombing.	
	24.		Hopwood was recommended for Military Cross. Chapman's C/253 was shelled again. Lt A.H. LEATHART B/250 was wounded by bullet in the side. Very quiet night.	
	25.		Lt CHAPMAN C/253 was ordered to move to Major JOHNSTON'S Left Xn position & C/250 to occupy all their new positions. TM's a great nuisance; also several more Batteries appear to have arrived on the scenes and have been making themselves objectionable. Some Mines were sprung to the North during the night.	
	26.		Quiet day till about 6 pm when TMs started a Strafe. At about 7.30 pm the Bosch Craters on our front were Strafed by 9.2s very successfully. Another very peaceful night.	
	27.		A very quiet day & not so many TMs as usual. LT. HORNSBY A/253 fell down a ladder at their O.P. and broke some ribs.	
	28.		The quietest day for weeks. Not a single TM and only about ½ a doz shells all day.	

Army Form C. 2118

Instructions regarding War Diaries and Intelligence Summaries are contained in F. S. Regs., Part. II. and the Staff Manual respectively. Title Pages will be prepared in manuscript.

WAR DIARY
or
INTELLIGENCE SUMMARY
(Erase heading not required.)

Imp. Hav., 26/7 — 10.000

Place	Date	Hour	Summary of Events and Information	Remarks and references to Appendices
	29.		More changes. We are losing 2 more Batteries from the Group ie A/253 & C/253 and after tomorrow night will only have the Batteries of our own Brigade and A/251. The order of Battle will then be as follows:- North to South. 2nd CANADIANS 250 FAB Group with 151st Infantry Bde. 251 FAB Group & 150th Bde 252 FAB Group & 149th Infantry Bde. A very quiet day.	
	30		Another very quiet day. It looks as if a relief had taken place on our front. or that the enemy is short of Ammunition	
	31.		No shells or TMs all day.	

H.C. Bell Lt-Col.
C.C. 250th Bde. R.F.A.

Instructions regarding War Diaries and Intelligence Summaries are contained in F. S. Regs., Part. II. and the Staff Manual respectively. Title Pages will be prepared in manuscript.

WAR DIARY

~~or~~

~~INTELLIGENCE SUMMARY~~

(Erase heading not required.)

Army Form C. 2118

250 (N) BRIGADE RFA(T)

50 Div

AUGUST 1916

VOL No. ~~XVII~~ Vol 16

Imp. Hav., 26/7 — 10.000

Place	Date	Hour	Summary of Events and Information	Remarks and references to Appendices
	1.		Another very quiet day. The BOCHE are working hard at their trenches all along our Zone.	
	2.		More TMs today but mostly to the Right of our Zone. Capt PYBUS Adjutant went to Hospital on the 28th with jaundice and has now gone to CALAIS. GRAHAM Orderly Officer in bed with same sort of complaint. More changes in Battery positions. B/250 is now Rt Battery in A/250's old position, C/253 is centre Battery & C/250 Left as before. A/250 has moved a Section still further forward and has a roving commission.	
	3.		A very quiet day, but heavy Straf in Salient at night. SHIEL A/Adj out of action with toothache, Staff reduced to Colonel and 2nd Lt EARLE A/Orderly Officer. GRAHAM went Hospital also the Colonel's henchman Br. LAWSON.	
	4.		A very quiet day. A Bombardment near KRUISTRAAT CAB.T was carried out in the afternoon but brought forth very little response.	
	5.		2nd Lieut HOPWOOD was awarded the MILITARY CROSS. Very quiet in our Zone.	
	6.		A particularly quiet day, but great Aeroplane activity.	
	7.		Orders received that we will be relieved by the 19th DIVISION on the nights of 8th/9th & 9th/10th August and proceed to EECKE to commence entraining for ? on the afternoon of the 11th. This order was not entirely unexpected. A copy of Operation Orders will be attached to Duplicate Copy.	
	8.		Quiet day. First half of Relief carried out. Gas attack to North of Salient about 11 pm.	

Army Form C. 2118

Instructions regarding War Diaries and Intelligence Summaries are contained in F. S. Regs., Part. II. and the Staff Manual respectively. Title Pages will be prepared in manuscript.

WAR DIARY

~~or~~

~~INTELLIGENCE SUMMARY~~

(Erase heading not required.)

Imp. Hav., 26/7 — 10.000

Place	Date	Hour	Summary of Events and Information	Remarks and references to Appendices
	9		Second half of Relief carried out very quietly	
	10		A quiet day spent at EECKE.	
	11		Batteries commenced entraining at BAILLEUL MAIN at 6.30 pm A Battery first followed by the others at 3 hours interval during the night No untoward incidents occurred	
	12		Batteries arrived DOULLENS NORTH during the morning after a 5 hours journey, and after watering marched direct to Billets in the neighbourhood of OCCOCHES about a 5 miles march. Hd Qrs, entrained at GODESWARVELDE and left at 10.53 am arriving FIENVILLERS CANDAS at about 4.50 pm, they then marched to OCCOCHES a distance of about 9 miles. Very nice billets for everyone here but D Battery had 4 miles to go each way to water.	
	13.		A pleasant & quiet day spent chiefly in resting.	
	14.		D Battery moved nearer the water & went into the same field as B & C Rest of the day spent in inspections &c	
	15.		Marched out of OCCOCHES as a Brigade at 4 am and via MONTRELET & HALLOY to BOURDON a distance of about 20 miles, arriving about 1 pm A pleasant march, but one casualty. Gr MAHON of A Battery falling off a wagon & being run over, & probably having some ribs smashed.	
	16		Left BOURDON at 1.15 am in heavy rain and marched to FRECHENCOURT via VIGNACOURT & VILLERS BOCAGE about an 18 mile march, fortunately the rain soon ceased and it was a very successful and rapid march, we arrived at	

Army Form C. 2118

Instructions regarding War Diaries and Intelligence Summaries are contained in F. S. Regs., Part. II. and the Staff Manual respectively. Title Pages will be prepared in manuscript.

WAR DIARY
or
~~INTELLIGENCE SUMMARY~~
(Erase heading not required.)

Imp. Hav., 26/7 — 10.000

Place	Date	Hour	Summary of Events and Information	Remarks and references to Appendices
	16 cont		our destination at about 8 am. Everyone very tired, as no one had had more than an hour or two's sleep the night before. On arrival we found our billeting officer Lt HUTCHINSON in despair as his area after all his arrangements had been made had been changed and given to the DAC. So there were no billets ready for us. By midday however we had fixed up accommodation and the rest of the day was spent by most in slumber. This village is about the worst we have ever been in for squalor & dirt & there is not a single shop.	
	17		Orders having been received that we are to relieve the 34th DIV Artillery on the 18th & 19th the Col & Orderly Officer have gone forward to inspect & the first half Brigade will leave here tomorrow. The Col returned in the afternoon to say the orders were cancelled and we were not to move, but had to take over the positions of the 160th Bde Col WARBURTON.	
	18		Officers from each Battery were sent up with telephonists and the Orderly Officer from Hd Quarters to look after the positions. These positions were good ones & most of them had excellent dugouts, made by the Bosche in the chalk up to 30 feet deep. They were situated in SAUSAGE VALLEY. The whole countryside presents a most extraordinary spectacle, with hundreds of all types of guns.	
	19 to 22.		Brigade remained at FRECHENCOURT and was able to do a certain amount of useful training. Orders were received on 21st to prepare a scheme for Brigade training for period 25th 31st. On 22nd orders were received that we had to relieve the 70th Brigade 15th DIVISION on 24th & 25th.	
	23.		The Colonel, Major JOHNSTON & the Adjutant went up to see the positions. Head Qrs is in CONTALMAISON and the Batteries between that place & BAZENTIN LE PETIT	

Instructions regarding War Diaries and Intelligence Summaries are contained in F. S. Regs., Part. II. and the Staff Manual respectively. Title Pages will be prepared in manuscript.

WAR DIARY

~~or~~

~~INTELLIGENCE SUMMARY~~

(Erase heading not required.)

Army Form C. 2118

Imp. Hav., 26/7 — 10.000

Place	Date	Hour	Summary of Events and Information	Remarks and references to Appendices
			It is an even more shell strewn area than SAUSAGE VALLEY.	
	24		One Section of each Battery went into action, leaving FRECHENCOURT at 5.45 am & being in action by about 11 am. All relieving & supply of ammunition so far as possible is done by day, on account of roads being barraged at nights.	
	25		The Second Sections and Hd Qrs went up at 5.45 am & got into action safely at about 11 am. C Battery were very unfortunate during the night of 24th 25th and had 3 men & 9 horses killed and 4 men and 2 horses wounded, also 2 horses missing. This happened in CONTALMAISON when they were bringing ammunition up. A & B Batteries had a bad night with gas shells. Hd Qrs have already had a dose of 5.9s but no damage done. A B & C Batteries commenced at 5.25 pm firing a Barrage on SWITCH-LINE at the rate of 100 rounds per ~~Battery~~ per hour to be kept up till ordered to stop. The Relief on the whole was carried through easily, but information given to Hd Qrs scant and many important items forgotten. Copy of O.P. Orders re relief are attached to duplicate copy. One Hd Qr telephonist wounded during the afternoon.	
	26		A bad night after a long day. The 18 prs were engaged on a Barrage taking it in turn, there appeared to be counter attacks and attacks all night. C Battery again had bad luck during the night 25/26 CONTALMAISON was shelled and a dug out of theirs blown in, 2 men were killed & 4 wounded. During the day we were told to move the whole Bde & be in action again under the 1st DIVISION by that night. This was ultimately changed to C & D moving & A & B remaining but altering their ~~positions~~ emplacements.	

Instructions regarding War Diaries and Intelligence Summaries are contained in F. S. Regs., Part. II. and the Staff Manual respectively. Title Pages will be prepared in manuscript.

WAR DIARY

~~or~~

~~INTELLIGENCE SUMMARY~~

(Erase heading not required.)

Army Form C. 2118

Imp. Hav.. 26/7 — 40.000

Place	Date	Hour	Summary of Events and Information	Remarks and references to Appendices
	27		Most of Hd Qrs Staff moved to new position on night of 26th but the rest and C & D Batteries moved at daylight 27th. Hd Qrs had a very bad place but finally fixed up in some saps on the side of a road and have now very good Head Quarters & incidentally safe. A & B Batteries were very heavily shelled during the afternoon and one would imagine must be wiped out, but had actually no damage done except a few dugouts blown in 2nd Lt SAMPLE and 2 gunners were partly buried but extricated unhurt. In the evening C Battery again had bad luck and had 3 casualties. Sergt HEARTY being killed also Br BUMFREY and Br CHIVERTON buried, but he was got out alive and had a wonderful escape. B Battery had one man slightly wounded during the afternoon. Batteries registered and did some night firing.	
	28		Batteries continued registering, which is very difficult as no one seems to know exactly how the line runs and with so many Batteries on a small front if complaints of short shooting are made it is difficult to determine who is responsible. 2 slight casualties today. A & B Batteries firing by programme at night.	
	29		Things getting easier and more workable. A & B Batteries registered and heavily shelled with 8". Dugouts blown in but no damage to personnel or important equipment. Their Office was also blown in. In the shelling on the 27th B Batteries Office was blown in & 1000 francs blown away, this was found next day some distance away. It was expected that certain operations would be carried out tonight by our front but these have been put off.	

Army Form C. 2118

Instructions regarding War Diaries and Intelligence Summaries are contained in F. S. Regs., Part. II. and the Staff Manual respectively. Title Pages will be prepared in manuscript.

WAR DIARY
~~or~~
~~INTELLIGENCE SUMMARY~~

(Erase heading not required.)

Imp. Hav., 26/7 — 10.000

Place	Date	Hour	Summary of Events and Information	Remarks and references to Appendices
	30		No items of very great interest. A shockingly wet day, observation almost impossible. 24th DIV relieved 33rd DIV on our Right.	
	31		A very fine day and consequently much shelling and aerial activity, C Battery again were unlucky, they were deluged with gas shells and had during the course of the day, One man killed, 2 wounded and Sergt CHAPMAN gassed, At about 1.30 pm the Huns attacked the Left Battalion of the DIVISION on our right and retook TEA TRENCH which was captured by the 33rd DIV about 5 days ago. We were kept busy Barraging and it was during this time that C had their Casualties. The 24th DIV are now preparing to Counter attack.	
			H. C. Bell Lieut-Col. C. C. 250th (NM) Bde. R.F.A.	

250th. BRIGADE R. F. A.

50th. DIVISIONAL ARTILLERY

S E P T E M B E R 1 9 1 6.

SEPT 1916

Instructions regarding War Diaries and Intelligence Summaries are contained in F. S. Regs., Part. II. and the Staff Manual respectively. Title Pages will be prepared in manuscript.

WAR DIARY
or
INTELLIGENCE SUMMARY
(Erase heading not required.)

250th (N) BRIGADE RFA (T)

Army Form C. 2118

VOL 17

Imp. Hav., 26/7 — 10.000

Place	Date	Hour	Summary of Events and Information	Remarks and references to Appendices
	1.		The Attack on WOOD LANE and HIGH WOOD has been postponed once more, and there is nothing much doing except Barrages. The Batteries are still having a bad time with gas shells, especially C & D who have been kept up all night for several nights.	
	2.		The Attack definitely settled for the 3rd inst. Operation Orders are attached to the duplicate copy. The preliminary bombardment by the Heavies has been kept up all day today.	
	3.		The attack took place at 12 noon and appeared to be successful, but unfortunately our men were driven out by the Counter Attack and the position is now as before. The Attack on the Left portion of HIGH WOOD was not successful owing to our Infantry having so many casualties before the Zero hour.	
	4.		Nothing has been heard of the attack by 24th DIVISION. Our Infantry position appears to be just the same as it was prior to the 3rd inst. Today the Heavies are Bombarding HIGH WOOD and WOOD LANE which will be followed by a CHINESE ATTACK.	
	5.		A dull wet day, very quiet on our front, we retaliated in afternoon on WOOD LANE for shelling of our trenches. Col HANSON is staying at Head Quarters as he may be taking over from our Brigade in a few days time.	
	6.		Another very quiet day. A good many aeroplane fights but nothing else of interest.	
	7		A quiet day except for shelling in the vicinity of Head Quarters which was unpleasant. Several mules, horses & men being strewn about. It was however only an occasional short round which worried us, when the Bosch had settled on his objective. O.P. Orders for an attack to take place on 8th sent out.	

Instructions regarding War Diaries and Intelligence Summaries are contained in F. S. Regs., Part. II. and the Staff Manual respectively. Title Pages will be prepared in manuscript.

WAR DIARY
or
INTELLIGENCE SUMMARY
(Erase heading not required.)

Imp. Hav., 26/7 — 10.000

Place	Date	Hour	Summary of Events and Information	Remarks and references to Appendices
—	8	—	The attack which was on the WESTERN portion of HIGH WOOD took place at 6 pm. It was not entirely successful. The Glosters who had the left portion failed and retired, but the 2nd WELCH got in and are holding on to their bit. About 30 prisoners taken. We had many casualties. 2nd Lts LYNN and McCALLUM were in the trenches. Lt LYNN was buried by a shell but was not much worse. McCALLUM sent back useful information.	—
—	9	—	Tonight 9th inst a further attack is to take place. The attack was only partly successful, the trench in HIGH WOOD proving a very serious obstacle. We however now hold about $\frac{3}{4}$ of WOOD LANE the trench running SE from HIGH WOOD. About 60 prisoners were taken. 2nd Lt McCALLUM and 2 telephonists were buried with 9 others of whom 4 were killed but fortunately our men got off with shock only. The Operation Orders and diary of the attack are attached to the Duplicate Copy.	—
—	10	—	A quiet day except for a report that the enemy were massing for a Counter Attack. We put up a barrage and then went to bursts of fire on our Area. 2nd Lt McCALLUM recommended for MILITARY CROSS and Gunner SAMBROOKS J for MILITARY MEDAL both of D/250. & both for gallant conduct in keeping up communication and sending information on the 8th inst.	—
—	11	—	Another quiet day. Parties were sent forward from each Battery and Head Quarters to BAVELINCOURT as we had received orders that we were to be relieved by the 253rd Bde on the 12th.	—

Army Form C. 2118

Instructions regarding War Diaries and Intelligence Summaries are contained in F. S. Regs., Part. II. and the Staff Manual respectively. Title Pages will be prepared in manuscript.

WAR DIARY
or
INTELLIGENCE SUMMARY
(Erase heading not required.)

Imp. Hav., 26/7 — 10.000

Place	Date	Hour	Summary of Events and Information	Remarks and references to Appendices
	12		At 2 am we received orders to proceed to the Wagon Lines only instead of BAVELINCOURT. This was done and all the reliefs were carried out without unusual incidents. A/250 was relieved by MAJOR PARMETER, B/250 by Capt LAW and C/250 by Capt HILLENS. D/250 remained in. In the afternoon orders were received that all the Batteries had to go in to action again the next day with the 251, 252 & 253 Brigades. Head Quarters have therefore no command. It is very hard on all the Officers & men but everyone got one good nights rest.	
	13		B. Cs went forward and reconnoitred and the Batteries went up in the afternoon. They have all gone into [illegible] positions without a vestige of cover. A/250 is attached to 252 Bde B to 253 & C to 251.	
	14		D/250 apparently have had a bad time and had one gun knocked out & the sights of another destroyed. The ammunition burnt furiously but was eventually put out. Sergt LAING Dr MARTIN & Gr DOYLE distinguished themselves by their gallantry & their names have gone forward for Awards. The Battery unfortunately had 7 casualties but none very serious. At 5.30 pm heavy Strafe started towards THIEPVAL. Our DIVISION is now in the line and holds a line from WEST of HIGH WOOD to nearly opposite MARTINPUICH.	
	15		Our Show started at 6.20 and appears to have been a great success. The 47th on the right were held up by HIGH WOOD for a time but the 50th soon reached all their objectives. They were compelled to retire again to their second objective later on in the day but progress was good and COURCELETTE, MARTINPUICH & FLERS remain in our hands as well as HIGH WOOD. The Land Ships were used for the first time and thoroughly put the wind up the Bosch, they were very successful.	
	16		Infantry consolidating & trying to join up on the flanks. D/250 moved in front of BAZENTIN LE PETIT. Lots of work for BCs finding new OPs &c. Lt BROWELL	

Instructions regarding War Diaries and Intelligence Summaries are contained in F. S. Regs., Part. II. and the Staff Manual respectively. Title Pages will be prepared in manuscript.

Army Form C. 2118

WAR DIARY
or
INTELLIGENCE SUMMARY
(Erase heading not required.)

Imp. Hav., 26/7 — 10.000

Place	Date	Hour	Summary of Events and Information	Remarks and references to Appendices
	16		was slightly wounded in the back on the 15th but is still "at duty"	
	17		A/250 moved and other Batteries prepared to move to near HIGH WOOD. The problem of roads is very serious as the whole area is terribly cut up. The question of ammunition supply is also serious as the Batteries are getting so far away. Many wagon lines have already moved and CATERPILLAR VALLEY and neighbourhood which was a few days ago a most unhealthy spot is now crammed with horses. The Cavalry are waiting for a chance to get through. The Batteries are not getting shelled at all the Boche evidently being too busy moving guns.	
	18		The weather has changed and is vile & raining hard, this if it continues will play havoc with transport.	
	19		Still raining, this has practically put a stop to all operations	
	20		A/250 moved forward to HIGH WOOD on the 18th and the Wagon lines of A/C moved forward today to near BOTTOM WOOD. The weather is still vile and we have no news, but the Germans appear to be Counter attacking heavily.	
	21		Still cold & damp. Lieut BROWELL & Lieut DARLINGS names sent in for MILITARY CROSS for good work done as FOO's on Sep 15th.	
	22		A fine day but cold. 2nd Lieut EARLE wounded in shoulder in the trenches	
	23		A fine warm day. Very quiet. 2nd Lieut McCALLUM awarded MILITARY CROSS	

Instructions regarding War Diaries and Intelligence Summaries are contained in F. S. Regs., Part. II. and the Staff Manual respectively. Title Pages will be prepared in manuscript.

WAR DIARY
or
INTELLIGENCE SUMMARY
(Erase heading not required.)

Army Form C. 2118

Imp. Hav., 26/7 — 10.000

Place	Date	Hour	Summary of Events and Information	Remarks and references to Appendices
	24		No special items of interest.	
	25		The French & Corps on our right attacked from FLERS to the South, no news yet to hand as to results. Lt SAMPLE posted to this Brigade as Orderly Officer.	
	26		The Reserve Army attacked and took THIEPVAL. No reliable news can be obtained yet, but all rumours point to a considerable success.	
	27		No news	
	28		Orders received that our Batteries personnel only will be relieved on 28th & 29th by 1st DIVISION. They will only go to their own Wagon Lines	
	29		A B & C Batteries relieved by Batteries of 1st DIV	
	30		Nothing of interest, except Lieut DARLING wounded	

J R A Shiel Capt
a/Adj
250th (N) Bde RFA (T)

Instructions regarding War Diaries and Intelligence Summaries are contained in F. S. Regs., Part. II. and the Staff Manual respectively. Title Pages will be prepared in manuscript.

WAR DIARY
or
INTELLIGENCE SUMMARY
(Erase heading not required.)

Army Form C. 2118

250th (NORTHUMBRIAN) BRIGADE R.F.A.(T.)
October 1916
VOL XIX

Imp. Hav., 26/7 — 10,000

Vol 18

Place	Date	Hour	Summary of Events and Information	Remarks and references to Appendices
	1 Oct 1916		A B & C Batteries moved their wagon lines down near Head Quarters. A lovely day. Portions of the FLERS line & LE SARS & EAUCOURT L'ABBAYE attacked by our Corps.	
	2		A very wet miserable day. D/250 now has 2 guns in MARTINPUICH and 2 near BAZENTIN-LE-PETIT. The former is a smelly and unhealthy place. Sergt LAING D/250 awarded the DCM.	
	3		A damp warm day. No news excepting that our CRA has now gone back to MILLENCOURT and the Brigades of this Division which are still in action are now under CRA 23rd DIVISION. Major WILKINSON & 2nd Lieut RICHARDSON went on leave	
	4		A wet day. Batteries cleaning up & doing Signalling & Rangefinding. We have no guns at now so cannot do any Gun Drill	
	5 7		Nothing to Report	
	8		Orders received that AB&C Batteries will relieve AB&C 251 Bde; relief to be complete by 12 noon 10th. D/250 is not to be relieved, they had several casualties in the 7th and Lieut WEDDELL was so severely wounded that he has since died, he will be a great loss to the Battery.	
	9		Brigade + Battery Commanders went to see H.Q + positions of 251 Bde RFA Capt Shiel commanding C/250 in place of Major Johnston sick + LT DICKINSON acting Adjutant. Arrangements made with 251 Bde that batteries should relieve as early as possible.	

Army Form C. 2118

Instructions regarding War Diaries and Intelligence Summaries are contained in F. S. Regs., Part. II. and the Staff Manual respectively. Title Pages will be prepared in manuscript.

WAR DIARY
or
INTELLIGENCE SUMMARY
(Erase heading not required.)

250 (Northumbrian) Bde RFA (T)

Vol ~~XIX~~ (cont)

Imp. Hav., 26/7 — 10.000

Place	Date	Hour	Summary of Events and Information	Remarks and references to Appendices
	10th Oct 1916		A, B, & C Batteries relieve 18 pr Batts of 251 Bde; reliefs completed before noon. D/251 came under command of 250 Bde for tactical purposes. All Batteries very short of Officers & men owing to difficulty in obtaining reinforcements. A/250 have three officers, B/250, 3 officers, C/250 three an D/251 four officers.	
			Map references of Battery positions, ~~A/250~~ Reference Sheet 57 C. S.W.	
			A/250 S3B8.5½, B/250 S3a½½, C/250 S3B7½.6 D/251 S3a42.	
			Orders were received from 15th D.A. (whose infantry the Bde is supporting) that the 15th Div would probably attack GALLWITZ LINE in M10 on 14th or 15th Oct; forward positions for batteries to support this attack to be reconnoitred. Divisions on flanks are going to push up alongside 15th Divs whose line M15A57 to M16B34 & thence southwards to a post at M22B58 is in the nature of a sharp salient.	
			Orders were then received to cut wire in front of GALLWITZ TRENCH from M10D05 to M10C6¾6¾. The intention being to give the enemy the impression that the next attack would be on this front.	
			During the night 10/11th a barrage was kept up by 18 pdrs on line M16B4½8 – M16A99. D/250 continued bombarding M10C26 – M9D76	
	11th		Wire cutting & Bombardment of GALLWITZ TRENCH continued. At 3.15 to 3.35 "Chinese" attack was made with object of finding where enemy would put up his barrages.	

Army Form C. 2118

Instructions regarding War Diaries and Intelligence Summaries are contained in F. S. Regs., Part. II. and the Staff Manual respectively. Title Pages will be prepared in manuscript.

WAR DIARY
or
INTELLIGENCE SUMMARY
(Erase heading not required.)

250 (Northumbrian) Bde RFA (T)
Vol XIX

Imp. Hav., 26/7 — 10.000

Place	Date	Hour	Summary of Events and Information	Remarks and references to Appendices
	11th Oct cont.		The enemy barrages were heaviest in M.22 B + at EAUCOURT L'ABBAYE. During the day LTs PRIESTMAN + RENNIE became ill leaving only one officer 2/Lt HOPWOOD fit for duty with B/250. This battery had one gun put out of action by shell fire, one man killed + 5 wounded.	
			During night 11/12 same barrage as previous night.	
	12th		Wire cutting + bombardment of same target as previous day. Orders received that 250 Bde was to find Liaison Officer with Rt Battalion 15th Div. A line was laid from Battalion H.Q. to B Battery exchange. 2/Lt SCOTT went forward for 24 hours. Orders were received to fire on area M17 C 04, M17 C 34, M16 B 97, M17 a 37 in support of attack by 9th Div. on GIRD TRENCH in M 17 A + B + to put up barrage on line M11 C 43 - M10 d 9-2. D/251 Bombarded trenches M10 C 28 - M9 D 7.6 on the 15th Div front. The attack by 9th Division failed to gain its objectives.	
	13th		A quiet day. The wire cutting + bombardment was continued as on previous days. During the afternoon, the enemy's artillery became active on our front + to the right + at 4.30 S.O.S was seen by batteries + fire opened. Message received from Liaison officer that no attack had developed. Normal night firing resumed. Lieut BROWELL awarded Military Cross	

Instructions regarding War Diaries and Intelligence Summaries are contained in F. S. Regs., Part. II. and the Staff Manual respectively. Title Pages will be prepared in manuscript.

WAR DIARY
or
INTELLIGENCE SUMMARY
(Erase heading not required.)

Army Form C. 2118

250 (Northumbrian) Bde RFA (T)

Vol XIX

Imp. Hav., 26/7 — 10.000

Place	Date	Hour	Summary of Events and Information	Remarks and references to Appendices
	14th		Wire cutting + bombardment continued. At 2.5 to 2.10 pm an aeroplane was to observe effect of this fire, but was prevented by bad weather + light conditions; which also interfered with observation. Little enemy shelling. Night firing at same target.	
	15th		Aeroplane shoot repeated 9.5 to 9.10 AM 18 pounders + 9.20 – 9.25 4.5 Hows again unobserved. All 4.5 How batteries of the Group concentrated an intense fire on 7.7 cm battery at M10D8.8. from 11.0 – 11.5 AM. Reports received of short shooting but nothing could be traced. Light became very good in afternoon. 2/Lt TROTTER + 2/Lt WALBANK were posted to the Brigade, both had been out before. Night firing as usual when further reports of short shooting were received.	
	16th		Wire cutting + bombardment continued. Another attempt to with aeroplane was successful as regards Howitzers, but it was unable to observe 18 pdrs. A/250 had 1 Dr killed 2 wounded + 4 horses killed while bringing up ammunition. Light good + considerable enemy movement reported + fired on. Orders received for Bde H.Q to move forward to H.Q at present occupied by 252 Bde who are going out of action. Night firing as usual.	
	17th		Fresh orders received as to day + night targets for normal firing and fresh S.O.S. lines. Day Target for 18 pdrs wire cutting M10D04 to M10C 5½ 6½. Road M10a06 to M10B 3.4½. Hows Front + support trench where 18 pdrs fire. Night Barrage M9C82 to M9C86.	

Army Form C. 2118

Instructions regarding War Diaries and Intelligence Summaries are contained in F. S. Regs., Part. II. and the Staff Manual respectively. Title Pages will be prepared in manuscript.

WAR DIARY
or
INTELLIGENCE SUMMARY
(Erase heading not required.)

250th (Northumbrian) Bde RFA (T)

Vol XIX

Imp. Hav., 26/7 — 10.000

Place	Date	Hour	Summary of Events and Information	Remarks and references to Appendices
	17th Oct (cont)		S.O.S lines for 18 pdrs M9C82 to M9C86 For Hows M9C82 to M9D08 Orders received for firing on 9th Div front on 18th in support on an attack by them on ~~Snag~~ SNAGTRENCH in front of BUTTE DE WARLENCOURT, ~~[illegible]~~ attack to take place at 3.40 A.M. 18 pdrs assisting by barraging. Night firing as usual	
	18th		3.40 A.M. 18 pdrs open fire at rate of 4 rounds per gun per minute on triangle M17C44 – M16B92 – M17a 3½.2. This rate of fire was kept up for 1 minute after when 2 rounds per gun per minute were fired on same objective until ~~the~~ infantry signalled by means of 2 red Very lights that they were establishing blocks at M17a 8.0 and M 17c 1.8. at 4.10 AM Fire was then lifted to ~~[illegible]~~ 200 yards North of these blocks + maintained at 2 rds per gun per minute till 5.30 AM when rate was reduced ~~[illegible]~~ by half. Normal day programme resumed at 9.20 AM. 3.40 AM. Hows barrage on 15th Div front M10C 7½ 6½ M10C 2½ 6½ at slow rate until 7.20 when they resumed normal. No information received from infantry till 10 A.M when vague message was sent, from this + later messages it appeared that left of 9th Div. had failed to attain their objective in M17c; to right of this the attack was reported to have succeeded, but in view of later reports this does not seem to be the case. From 2.30 to 3.35 D/251 fired on LOUPART WOOD in conjunction with heavies. Night firing as usual.	

Army Form C. 2118

Instructions regarding War Diaries and Intelligence Summaries are contained in F. S. Regs., Part. II. and the Staff Manual respectively. Title Pages will be prepared in manuscript.

WAR DIARY
or
INTELLIGENCE SUMMARY
(Erase heading not required.)

250th (Northumbrian) Bde RFA (T)

Imp. Hav., 26/7 — 10.000

Place	Date	Hour	Summary of Events and Information	Remarks and references to Appendices
	19th		Orders received to register trenches in M14a to support an attack by II Corps during the afternoon. A + C Batteries only could get round to this + only by altering emplacements so that the guns fired almost over the top of each other. From this (the extreme left point on which these batteries have fired on front line) to the BUTTE (the extreme right) is over 3000 yards. Extreme left of 9th Div bombed out of trench at M17C44; batteries ordered to bombard C.T running N.W. of this point. This was done during the day + at 4 p.m. the South Africans attacked this trench + took it up to M17C2.8. The 9th Div commented on accuracy of fire on the C.T. by 18 pdr Batteries. Attack by II Corps postponed owing to weather. Rain continuous all day, causing great discomfort to Batteries, who find it difficult to comply with orders as to ammunition racks, owing to shortage of R.E material + difficulty of obtaining what is available.	
	20th		A + C Batteries register trenches in M14a. B Battery continues on day programme. D/Battery takes part in 3 hourly bombardments of enemy battery positions, each lasting for five minutes rate of fire intense, also in two bombardments of LOUPART WOOD, one with Gas shell. The TAIL M17C44 was reported retaken by enemy + was consequently shelled by A + C batteries up to 4 pm when attack took place and fire was lifted gradually to a line just south of BUTTE	

Instructions regarding War Diaries and Intelligence Summaries are contained in F. S. Regs., Part. II. and the Staff Manual respectively. Title Pages will be prepared in manuscript.

WAR DIARY
or
INTELLIGENCE SUMMARY
(Erase heading not required.)

250th (Northumbrian) Bde
RFA (T)

Vol XIX

Army Form C. 2118

Imp. Hav., 26/7 — 10.000

Place	Date	Hour	Summary of Events and Information	Remarks and references to Appendices
	20th Oct 1916 cont.		Report received following morning that TAIL from M17C44 & M17C28 had been retaken.	
			At 9.15 a.m. a German aeroplane was brought down within 100 yards of B/250. Major WILKINSON was present & recovered papers, & personal belongings from the pilot who died very soon after reaching the ground.	
			Orders received that batteries had to reconnoitre new positions further forward to support impending attack. This was done, and arrangements made to have R.E. material ready & for work to begin at once	
			Night firing as usual.	
	21st		New positions for batteries further reconnoitred & the following finally selected & approved by 15th D.A. A/250 M28A18 B/250 M27B44 C/250 M27C6.3. Work to be pushed forward as fast as possible.	
			At 12.6 pm A & C batteries fire on REGINA TRENCH in M14A in support of attack by II Corps; this attack reported successful later in the day.	
			Firing continued on usual targets & on movement observed on roads.	
			News received that the TAIL on which we have fired so much during the last few days has been captured.	

Instructions regarding War Diaries and Intelligence Summaries are contained in F. S. Regs., Part. II. and the Staff Manual respectively. Title Pages will be prepared in manuscript.

WAR DIARY
or
INTELLIGENCE SUMMARY
(Erase heading not required.)

~~#~~ 250 (Northumbrian) Bde RFA (T)

Vol XIX

Army Form C. 2118

Imp. Hav., 26/7 — 10.000

Place	Date	Hour	Summary of Events and Information	Remarks and references to Appendices
	22 Oct 1916		Work continued on New positions where B/250 had 1 man killed during the morning.	
			A British aeroplane came down close to MARTINPUICH as result of gunfire, the occupants were unharmed.	
			Firing continued on usual targets D/250 took part in two Howitzer shoots one on LOUPART WOOD and one on Battery position in G 33 c.	
			Orders received that on the day of the attack each battery is to have an F.O.O with infantry. We will be supporting the left of the attack, consequently arrangements are being made to change Liaison Officer from Right Battalion to Left Battalion.	
	23rd		A very foggy day, during the morning nothing could be done owing to the fog in the way of observation. However it had the effect of allowing Batteries to move their ammunition etc up to the new positions during day light, which would otherwise have been impossible. Rate of fire on wire cutting increased, as reports were received that enemy were putting out more wire under cover of fog.	
			At dusk 1 Gun from A, 2 from B + 2 from C were moved to forward positions; by this time fog had changed to rain, making the change more difficult + uncomfortable.	

Army Form C. 2118

Instructions regarding War Diaries and Intelligence Summaries are contained in F. S. Regs., Part. II. and the Staff Manual respectively. Title Pages will be prepared in manuscript.

WAR DIARY
or
INTELLIGENCE SUMMARY
(Erase heading not required.)

250th (Northumbrian) Bde RFA (T)

Vol XIX

Imp. Hav., 26/7 — 10.000

Place	Date	Hour	Summary of Events and Information	Remarks and references to Appendices
	24th		Registration of forward sections of 18pdrs carried out, in spite of the mist which was very thick in the morning and only lifted for a short time in the afternoon. Howitzers continued firing on GALLWITZ TRENCH and took part in various organized shoots on M.G. emplacements and batteries. In the evening the remainder of the 18 pdrs were moved to forward positions. These positions afford very little cover from view and at present none from the weather or the enemy. Batteries have great difficulty in getting up ammunition an R E material, owing to their baggage wagons having been returned to the A.S.C. and the difficulty in obtaining wagons from D.A.C. whose wagons seem to be entirely alloted to the Infantry.	
	25th		A very wet & cold day spent by the 18pdrs making themselves as comfortable as possible and completing registration. Very little ~~registration~~ R.E. material had been got up to the position owing to bad roads on which G.S. wagons had stuck. Howitzers continued firing on programme. Lieut BOURDAS and 2/Lt BOBBYER posted to C and B batteries respectively.	

Army Form C. 2118

WAR DIARY
or
INTELLIGENCE SUMMARY
(Erase heading not required.)

Instructions regarding War Diaries and Intelligence Summaries are contained in F. S. Regs., Part. II. and the Staff Manual respectively. Title Pages will be prepared in manuscript.

250th (Northumbrian) Bde R.F.A. (T)

Vol XIX

Imp. Hav., 26/7 — 10.000

Place	Date	Hour	Summary of Events and Information	Remarks and references to Appendices
	26th Oct.		A finer day, 18pdr Batteries able to do more work on their positions but still very short of R.E. material. The personnel in the Batteries are suffering just as great hardships from the weather as the infantry in front line. The latter however being relieved every 48 hours, the former staying in action for anything up to 10 weeks. Firing by 18 pdrs on WARLENCOURT and a creeping barrage to drive enemy out of shell holes, in addition to ordinary day firing. Howitzers also indulge in special shoots on Battery positions.	
	27th		Another wet day chiefly spent in improving positions and firing according to programme. Difficulty in getting material up to batteries owing to bad road. Orders received that the attack is postponed to 30th. Major OMMANEY went to hospital, sick, in the afternoon.	
	28th		A dry windy day which should help to dry up the ground. Work continued on new positions. This proceeds slowly owing to the difficulty of getting the D.A.C wagons up to the position, all carting of ammunition & R.E. material has to be done at night owing to openness of positions. Fire still continued on night & day targets. Batteries visited during the afternoon by C.R.A. 15th Division. 2/Lt GRAYSON returned from hospital	

Instructions regarding War Diaries and Intelligence Summaries are contained in F. S. Regs., Part II. and the Staff Manual respectively. Title Pages will be prepared in manuscript.

WAR DIARY
or
INTELLIGENCE SUMMARY
(Erase heading not required.)

Army Form C. 2118

250th (Northumbrian) Bde RFA. (T)

Vol XIX

Place	Date	Hour	Summary of Events and Information	Remarks and references to Appendices
	29 Oct 1916		Orders received that the attack is again postponed, now till the 1st November. D/251 choose new position at M27 C 5.2 and commence preparing it. This position is to be ready by the night of the 30th Oct but not to be occupied until further orders are received from 15th D A. The position is close to that occupied by C/250.	
			Orders received to search the area behind front line trenches at 7pm. by salvoes.	
	30th		A wet day on which light was too bad for observation. Liaison Officer reported a Trench Mortar at M9 C 1½ 5, this was engaged by a rapid burst of fire from all batteries at 4pm. Parties of the enemy were engaged by A/250 during the day. Work continued on new positions, ~~at~~ especially on that of D/251 who are only commencing theirs. More batteries are now going forward to positions close to A, B + C of this Brigade. This may draw shell fire to our batteries, but they at any rate have the pick of a moderate lot of positions.	
			During the night the area behind German front line was searched at intervals on report being received that relief was taking place.	

1875 Wt. W593/826 1,000,000 4/15 J.B.C. & A. A.D.S.S./Forms/C. 2118.

Instructions regarding War Diaries and Intelligence Summaries are contained in F. S. Regs., Part II. and the Staff Manual respectively. Title Pages will be prepared in manuscript.

WAR DIARY
or
INTELLIGENCE SUMMARY
(*Erase heading not required.*)

Army Form C. 2118

250th (Northumbrian) Bde RFA (T)
Vol XIX

Place	Date	Hour	Summary of Events and Information	Remarks and references to Appendices
	31st Oct 1916.		At 2 AM. report was received that S.O.S had been sent by infantry, this proved to be a false alarm.	
			The day proved much finer than has been the case recently and the light for observation was good	
			Orders received to knock out M.G. emplacement at M9C 7.7. This was fired on slowly during the morning & a ~~?~~ rapid burst by all batteries during afternoon.	
			Day & night firing as usual.	

E. A. Johnson Lt
for
Lieut Col
250 Bde R.F.A.

1875 Wt. W593/826 1,000,000 4/15 J.B.C. & A. A.D.S.S./Forms/C. 2118.

Instructions regarding War Diaries and Intelligence Summaries are contained in F. S. Regs., Part II. and the Staff Manual respectively. Title Pages will be prepared in manuscript.

WAR DIARY

or

~~INTELLIGENCE SUMMARY~~

(Erase heading not required.)

Army Form C. 2118

50 Div

250 (Northumbrian) Bde ~~RFA~~ (T)

Vol ~~XX~~ November 1916

Vol 19

Place	Date	Hour	Summary of Events and Information	Remarks and references to Appendices
	1st Nov 1916		Little of interest; orders received that 50th Division were going to attack the BUTTE DE WARLENCOURT on the ~~—~~ 2nd Nov before the general attack. This Brigade cannot get round to support 50th Div but orders are expected for firing programme to be carried out on 15 Div front during attack. Batteries in very miserable state as all the trenches and dug outs had fallen in as result of yesterday's storm.	
	2nd Nov		Another very wet day; relief of ~~—~~ 15th Div by 48th (S Midland) Div (infantry only) commenced. Artillery to be relieved later. General attack postponed till 5th November, also attack by 50th Division, date of this latter attack not given. Work continued on positions and usual firing on day and night programmes.	
	3rd		On the whole a quiet day, batteries continued firing on their night + day lines, and building the positions. Good progress made with D/251 position. During the evening A+B batteries were shelled with a new kind of shell, which ricochetted leaving a trail of sparks. No smell of gas was noticed, although there was a very feeble detonation. Attempts made to find a blind were unsuccessful.	

1875 Wt. W593/826 1,000,000 4/15 J.B.C. & A. A.D.S.S./Forms/C. 2118.

Instructions regarding War Diaries and Intelligence Summaries are contained in F. S. Regs., Part II. and the Staff Manual respectively. Title Pages will be prepared in manuscript.

WAR DIARY
on
~~INTELLIGENCE SUMMARY~~
(Erase heading not required.)

250 (Northumbrian) Bde RFA (T)

Army Form C. 2118

Vol XX

Place	Date	Hour	Summary of Events and Information	Remarks and references to Appendices
	4th Nov		Firing continued on normal targets, C/250 fired on a battery in action at G36A07 as result of message from aeroplane; they were also able to observe the flashes from their O.P. but the light was bad and they could not correct for range. Orders received that 50th Div were going to attack GIRD TRENCH + BUTTE DE WARLENCOURT on 5th Nov. and that this Brigade was to fire on 48th Div front during the attack. Little enemy shelling during the day; a British aeroplane was seen to fall in BOIS LOUPART.	
	5th Nov		At 9.10 a.m. 50th Div attacked GIRD TRENCH from M18C37 Northwards to the BUTTE + QUARRY in M17A07. The batteries of this Brigade fired at a ~~rf~~ rapid rate for 12 minutes on GALLWITZ TRENCH from M9D65 to M9C 8½.4½, after which any movement seen was to be fired on. Reports soon received that our infantry were seen on and beyond the BUTTE, but after that no news was received. Various parties of enemy fired on and troops massing at M5C50. were dispersed.	

1875 Wt. W593/826 1,000,000 4/15 J.B.C. & A. A.D.S.S./Forms/C. 2118.

Instructions regarding War Diaries and Intelligence Summaries are contained in F. S. Regs., Part II. and the Staff Manual respectively. Title Pages will be prepared in manuscript.

WAR DIARY

or

~~INTELLIGENCE SUMMARY~~

(Erase heading not required.)

Army Form C. 2118

250 (Northumbrian) Bde RFA (T)

Vol XX

Place	Date	Hour	Summary of Events and Information	Remarks and references to Appendices
	6th Nov 1916		News was received that the 50th Division had been driven out of GIAD TRENCH and BUTTE during the night and were back in their original positions. It was impossible to organise another attack at once. Firing continued on usual targets and at various parties of Germans who were seen at suspected battery position in LOUPART WOOD. The Batteries' horses are now in very poor condition owing to heavy work on ~~[illegible]~~ bad roads chiefly at night. Almost every day some horses die from exhaustion.	
	7 Nov 1916.		A very wet and cold day on which no observation was possible. Firing reduced to 400 rds per 18 pdr battery per day, owing to difficulty of getting up ammunition.	
	8th Nov.		An uneventful day, orders received that Bde would be going out of action in a day or two, but that probably we would have to take our guns out. Batteries are of opinion that this could only be done with great difficulty owing to poor condition of horses and bad state of ground. Firing continued at new rate on old targets	

1875 Wt. W593/826 1,000,000 4/15 J.B.C. & A. A.D.S.S./Forms/C. 2118.

Instructions regarding War Diaries and Intelligence Summaries are contained in F. S. Regs., Part II. and the Staff Manual respectively. Title Pages will be prepared in manuscript.

WAR DIARY

~~or INTELLIGENCE SUMMARY~~

(Erase heading not required.)

Army Form C. 2118

250 (Northumbrian) Bde RFA (T)

Vol XX

Place	Date	Hour	Summary of Events and Information	Remarks and references to Appendices
	Nov 9th 1916		Roads reconnoitred with a view to batteries taking their guns out, roads from MARTINPUICH to BAZENTIN and HIGH WOOD to BAZENTIN left impracticable for guns at night, a possible road found from MARTINPUICH to POZIERES. 3.15 pm batteries fired on a barrage on GALLWITZ LINE during Chinese attack; enemy were slow in opening their barrage. 4. to 5 pm A, B, + C Batteries all shelled with 5.9's and all suffering a few casualties A, one O.R badly wounded, B 2 O.R wounded, C 1 Killed and 3 wounded. Orders received in the evening that on relief we would not take our own guns out.	
	Nov. 10		Orders received that the batteries were to move out of action on 10th + 11th. C/250 + B/250 being relieved by batteries of 71st Bde and A/250 by A/105. D/251 pulled its own guns out. B + C pulled guns out of positions vacated by B + C/71. B + C were completely relieved by midnight and one section each of D + A. ~~[illegible]~~	
	Nov 11		D/251 completely out of action by 9 AM and remaining section of A/250 relieved by 4 pm; all batteries wait in wagon lines for orders	

1875 Wt. W593/826 1,000,000 4/15 J.B.C. & A. A.D.S.S./Forms/C. 2118.

Instructions regarding War Diaries and Intelligence Summaries are contained in F. S. Regs., Part II. and the Staff Manual respectively. Title Pages will be prepared in manuscript.

WAR DIARY

~~or~~

~~INTELLIGENCE SUMMARY~~

(Erase heading not required.)

Army Form C. 2118

250 (Northumbrian) Bde RFA (T)

Vol XX

Place	Date	Hour	Summary of Events and Information	Remarks and references to Appendices
	Nov 11 1916.		to march to rest area. 3 guns of D/250 left in action under guard were pulled out by A/250, one of them becoming stuck in very deep + invisible shell hole in road had to be left till the following morning; a caterpillar was asked for to help but was refused.	
	Nov. 12.		The gun of D/250 was got out by a large working party of 50 men in 1½ hours. Orders received at 10pm that Bde was to march to rest area at BEHENCOURT on 13th head of column to reach ALBERT at 9AM. This necessitated moving off at 7.45 AM	
	Nov 13.		March to rest area leaving wagon lines 7.45 AM reaching ALBERT at 9AM and thence by main AMIENS road to BEHENCOURT. The batteries were short of horses + march was slow leading battery reaching BEHENCOURT at 1.30 pm. Billets not so poor as had been expected, except in case of A/250 whose officers + mens billets were both poor.	
	Nov 14		Batteries commence to clean themselves up. Preparations made to reorganize into 3 six gun 18 pdr batteries + one 4 gun how battery	

1875 Wt. W593/826 1,000,000 4/15 J.B.C. & A. A.D.S.S./Forms/C. 2118.

Instructions regarding War Diaries and Intelligence Summaries are contained in F. S. Regs., Part II. and the Staff Manual respectively. Title Pages will be prepared in manuscript.

WAR DIARY
or
~~INTELLIGENCE SUMMARY~~

(Erase heading not required.)

Army Form C. 2118

250 (Northumbrian) Bde RFA (T)

Vol XX

Place	Date	Hour	Summary of Events and Information	Remarks and references to Appendices
	Nov 15		Orders received as to reorganisation of Brigade. Each battery to consist of 6 guns, batteries each to receive a section from 255 Bde who are to be disbanded	
	Nov 16		Reorganization took place at 12 noon. The following officers posted to 250 Bde. Major N.L. PARMETER, Capt G. CHAPMAN Capt. E.H. CAUSTON, LT JAMES, 2Lt S. MITTON. 2Lt CLEGG 2Lt SMITH. Considerable surplus of stores + N.C.O's to be dealt with. Batteries move to new billets at TRECHENCOURT.	
	Nov 17		Improvements made to new horse lines + cleaning up continued. Billets at TRECHENCOURT very poor both for officers + men.	
	Nov 18		Owing to poor state of billets B/250 move back to BEHENCOURT.	
	Nov 19		No church parades held owing to cold weather.	
	Nov 20		Nothing of interest	
	Nov 21		D/250 went into action with 251 Bde, D/251 is attached to 250 Bde for administration etc.	

1875 Wt. W593/826 1,000,000 4/15 J.B.C. & A. A.D.S.S./Forms/C. 2118.

Instructions regarding War Diaries and Intelligence Summaries are contained in F. S. Regs., Part II. and the Staff Manual respectively. Title Pages will be prepared in manuscript.

WAR DIARY

~~or~~

~~INTELLIGENCE SUMMARY~~

(Erase heading not required.)

Army Form C. 2118

250 (Northumbrian) Bde R.F.A. (T)

Vol ~~XX~~

Place	Date	Hour	Summary of Events and Information	Remarks and references to Appendices
	Nov. 22		Col BELL proceeded to England on 14 days leave. Major PARMETER assumed command of Brigade. Lieut U.W. DICKINSON appointed Adjutant vice Capt. H. PYBUS struck off the strength 13/10/16.	
	No 23. Nov 24		Cleaning up + improving billets	
	Nov 25		Horse lines + Billets inspected by Brig-Gen STOCKLEY. Some of the billets were not considered good enough, but no others are vacant at present. It is decided to move the billets as soon as a vacancy occurs in the village Sites for winter horse lines decided on	
	Nov 26		No church parade owing to bad weather	
	Nov 27		Training continued; gun drill impossible as only two guns are left in Brigade. Class commenced for all signallers in the Brigade	
	Nov 28.		A + C Batteries shift to better billets in BEHENCOURT vacated by 9th D A. arrangements made with town major to take these billets over permanently	

1875 Wt. W593/826 1,000,000 4/15 J.B.C. & A. A.D.S.S./Forms/C. 2118.

Instructions regarding War Diaries and Intelligence Summaries are contained in F. S. Regs., Part II. and the Staff Manual respectively. Title Pages will be prepared in manuscript.

WAR DIARY

~~or~~

~~INTELLIGENCE SUMMARY~~

(Erase heading not required.)

Army Form C. 2118

250 (Northumbrian) Bde R.F.A. (T)

Vol XX

Place	Date	Hour	Summary of Events and Information	Remarks and references to Appendices
	Nov 29		Training continued as much as state of ground + weather permits. Sites for winter standings finally settled + work continued. Information received that R.E. material would not be forthcoming to make overhead cover, harness rooms etc for winter rest area stables.	
	Nov 30		Training continued; but much hampered by large number of sick, and number of men required for fatigues etc.	

N. L. Parmeter
Major
for O.C. 250th Bde R.F.A.

1875 Wt. W593/826 1,000,000 4/15 J.B.C. & A. A.D.S.S./Forms/C. 2118.

Instructions regarding War Diaries and Intelligence Summaries are contained in F. S. Regs., Part II. and the Staff Manual respectively. Title Pages will be prepared in manuscript.

WAR DIARY
or
~~INTELLIGENCE SUMMARY~~
(Erase heading not required.)

250 (NORTHUMBRIAN) Bde R.F.A. (T)

Vol ~~XXI~~

DECEMBER 1916

Army Form C. 2118

Vol 20

Place	Date	Hour	Summary of Events and Information	Remarks and references to Appendices
	Dec 1 1916		Capt SOUTHEAN rejoined from England.	
	Dec 2		Nothing of interest	
	Dec 3		Church parade 10 A.M.	
	Dec 4		Nothing of interest	
	Dec 5		C.R.A inspected one subsection per battery in marching order. He considered turn out satisfactory. Capt G. CHAPMAN joined the Brigade from the Base, whither he had gone, sick, from 253 Bde.	
	Dec 6. Dec 7		Nothing of interest.	
	Dec 8		Lt Col BELL returned from leave, orders received that 250 Bde (less 1 18pdr battery) was to relieve 252 Bde, on 12th + 13th Dec. HQ 250 to relieve HQ 252 on 13th. D/251 to relieve D/252 on 8th + 9th	
	Dec 9th		Batteries inspected by Lt Col BELL during the morning.	
	Dec 10th		Battery commanders go to make arrangements about details of relief. Batteries lines + Billets visited by Major General P.S. WILKINSON G.O.C 50th (Northumbrian) Division during the morning.	

1875 Wt. W593/826 1,000,000 4/15 J.B.C. & A. A.D.S.S./Forms/C. 2118.

Instructions regarding War Diaries and Intelligence Summaries are contained in F. S. Regs., Part II. and the Staff Manual respectively. Title Pages will be prepared in manuscript.

WAR DIARY
or
~~INTELLIGENCE SUMMARY~~
(Erase heading not required.)

Army Form C. 2118

250 (NORTHUMBRIAN) Bde R.F.A. (T)

Vol ~~XXI~~

Place	Date	Hour	Summary of Events and Information	Remarks and references to Appendices
	Dec 11th 1916.		Batteries get ready to move up to wagon lines at 7.30 AM on 12th + 13th. Weather very wet + cold which makes it unpleasant weather to go into action. All Batteries very short of both men + horses.	
	Dec 12.		One section each of A + C/250 move up leaving at 7.30 in a very heavy storm of rain + snow.	
	Dec 13		Remaining sections + H.Q. moved up to relieve remainder of 252 Bde. The column was inspected by C.R.A who was dissatisfied with the turn out – particularly of A/250. H.Q. relieved HQ 252 but have no tactical command, the batteries are under the command of Col HINTON 26th Bde R.F.A.	
	Dec 14		Foggy day on which no observation was possible. The batteries have very wet + uncomfortable positions, flashes not covered. Ammunition + rations have to be brought up ~~at night~~ by pack. This can be done in daylight if the weather is not clear.	
	Dec 15		Wagon lines visited by O.C. Bde. They are very muddy + the accommodation for horses is nil + for men very poor.	
	Dec 16		Batteries visited by C.R.A. 1st Div.	

1875 Wt. W593/826 1,000,000 4/15 J.B.C. & A. A.D.S.S./Forms/C. 2118.

Instructions regarding War Diaries and Intelligence Summaries are contained in F. S. Regs., Part II. and the Staff Manual respectively. Title Pages will be prepared in manuscript.

WAR DIARY
or
~~INTELLIGENCE SUMMARY~~
(Erase heading not required.)

Army Form C. 2118

250 (NORTHUMBRIAN) Bde RFA (T)

Vol XXI

Place	Date	Hour	Summary of Events and Information	Remarks and references to Appendices
[illegible] 1916	17 Dec 1916.		Report received as result of C.R.A. 1st Div.'s inspection of Batteries. This report was not very satisfactory & was forwarded to C.R.A 50th Div. who supported the Brigade.	
	18th Dec.		Nothing of interest to report.	
	19th		New position for wagon lines reconnoitred. A suitable position found for horse lines on top of the hill in S. 20 A & for the huts on the other side of German road, between it & MAMETZ WOOD. Our present wagon lines are outside Corps Area & huts for personel will not be issued till a position in the area is found.	
	20th		For the first time since the Batteries have been in their present positions, there was a really good light. Considerable hostile artillery ~~action~~ & aerial activity. About 300 4.2s & 5.9s were fired among our batteries, only causing one very slight casualty.	
			Wagon lines visited by O.C. Bde. D/251 & H.Q. horses in good condition & well groomed. A & C/250 horses in poor condition. This is partly due to the shortage of men in these batteries.	

1875 Wt. W593/826 1,000,000 4/15 J.B.C. & A. A.D.S.S./Forms/C. 2118.

Instructions regarding War Diaries and Intelligence Summaries are contained in F. S. Regs., Part II. and the Staff Manual respectively. Title Pages will be prepared in manuscript.

WAR DIARY
or
~~INTELLIGENCE SUMMARY~~
(Erase heading not required.)

250 (NORTHUMBRIAN) Bde R.F.A. (T) Army Form C. 2118

Vol XXI

Place	Date	Hour	Summary of Events and Information	Remarks and references to Appendices
	Dec 21 1916.		Nothing of interest. B.S.M. S. Harris C/250 was awarded D.C.M for bravery in the C Battery position at MARTINPUICH when it was shelled heavily he assisted in removing wounded etc. This W.O. has on several previous occasions shown coolness + bravery under fire.	
	Dec 22.		The light was good at intervals + in the afternoon there was considerable enemy artillery activity. C/250 position was shelled from 3.30 pm onwards + they had 2 men killed + a gun put out of action. Ammunition for the batteries was brought by train to LONGUEVAL station within about 1000 yards of the guns. This is intended to be the normal method of ammunition supply + will be a great saving to horses.	
	Dec 23		A gun of C/250 destroyed by a direct hit, and two of the detachment hit. Another gun was buried but not damaged. The batteries were shelled intermittently throughout the day, but no other damage was done. The ammunition from LONGUEVAL station was taken up to batteries in the early morning when the air was misty. Shelling was drawn to the neighbourhood of H.Q. by an Australian pack train which chose the clearest time of day to go over the crest.	

Instructions regarding War Diaries and Intelligence Summaries are contained in F. S. Regs., Part II. and the Staff Manual respectively. Title Pages will be prepared in manuscript.

WAR DIARY

or

~~INTELLIGENCE SUMMARY~~

(Erase heading not required.)

Army Form C. 2118

250 (NORTHUMBRIAN) Bde R.F.A. (T)

Vol XXI

Place	Date	Hour	Summary of Events and Information	Remarks and references to Appendices
	Dec 24 1916		A quiet day. The following postings + transfers have taken place during the last day or two. Capt. ARMSTRONG Adjt 50th D.A.C. to be attached to 250 Bde. 2Lt J.O. SE posted to B/250 LT WARRENS posted to D/250.	
			Capt E.H. CAWSTON to D.A.C. 2/Lt G. SMITH to D.A.C.	
	Dec 25		Nothing unusual to mark Xmas day; if anything rather more firing than usual.	
	Dec 26.		A wet + cold day. A good deal of R.E. material has been brought to railhead at LONGUEVAL for the batteries. It is taken up to Battery positions by trench tramway, + on the whole is very satisfactory; as it saves both time + horses. A difficulty arises owing to the truck load of R.E material having to be stopped at a different place almost every day, sometimes close to the trench tramway, but very often right at the other end of the yard, when a good deal of time is wasted transferring from train to tramway. In the same way the ammunition train is sometimes stopped 300 to 400 yards from the road where the pack animals wait	
	27		A bright day with the result that there was a great deal of aerial activity. It is noticeable that neither our own aeroplanes or the enemy's show any anxiety to fight.	

1875 Wt. W593/826 1,000,000 4/15 J.B.C. & A. A.D.S.S./Forms/C. 2118.

Instructions regarding War Diaries and Intelligence Summaries are contained in F. S. Regs., Part II. and the Staff Manual respectively. Title Pages will be prepared in manuscript.

WAR DIARY
or
~~INTELLIGENCE SUMMARY~~
(Erase heading not required.)

250/NORTHUMBRIAN Bde R.F.A. (T)
Vol XXI

Army Form C. 2118

Place	Date	Hour	Summary of Events and Information	Remarks and references to Appendices
	Dec	28	Nothing of Interest	
	Dec	29	Lieut SAMPLE returned from leave.	
		30	Lieut DICKINSON ~~w~~ went on leave. Lieut J.P. HUTCHINSON of C battery appointed acting adjutant during his absence. very heavy rain during the night.	
		31	Nothing of Interest	

H.P. Bell Lieut-Col
Comdg: 250 (Nbn) Bde RFA (T).

1875 Wt. W593/826 1,000,000 4/15 J.B.C. & A. A.D.S.S./Forms/C. 2118.

VOLUME ~~22~~ 250 BRIGADE R F A (T F)

WAR DIARY
or
INTELLIGENCE SUMMARY

Vol XXII

January 1917

Vol 21

Army Form C. 2118

Instructions regarding War Diaries and Intelligence Summaries are contained in F. S. Regs., Part II. and the Staff Manual respectively. Title Pages will be prepared in manuscript.

(*Erase heading not required.*)

Place	Date	Hour	Summary of Events and Information	Remarks and references to Appendices
	Jan 1		A fairly quiet day	
	2		Lt Col Bell visited the wagon lines which were in a very bad condition owing to the mud. 2nd Lt R B CLEGG of C battery proceeded on leave.	
	3		2nd Lt SCOTT reported back from a signalling course. Weather wet & dull. German artillery rather more active than usual.	
	4		Lt Col Bell took over command of Centre Artillery Group from Major FAIRBANK 26th Bde 1st Div, the group consisting of 6 batteries A/250 B/250 C/250 D/251 117th battery & 30th battery. Group Hqrs at S 15 c 6 1	
	5th		nothing of interest. Weather rainy and unsettled	
	6		Lt Col BELL attended a meeting at Infantry Brigade Hqrs to arrange a combination of night firing between artillery & machine guns. Captain SOUTHERN appointed acting Divisional Trench Mortar officer ~~[illegible]~~ to 50th DA. Captain SHIEL reported back from leave.	
	7th		Lt Col BELL visited the front line trenches this morning at 3 am	
	8th		Capt CHAPMAN of A/250 went on leave	
	9th 10 11		Bombardment of enemy trenches carried out in cooperation with the neighbouring	

Army Form C. 2118

Instructions regarding War Diaries and Intelligence Summaries are contained in F. S. Regs., Part II. and the Staff Manual respectively. Title Pages will be prepared in manuscript.

WAR DIARY
or
INTELLIGENCE SUMMARY
(Erase heading not required.)

Place	Date	Hour	Summary of Events and Information	Remarks and references to Appendices
	12th		[illegible] Bell visited the wagon lines horses in very poor condition plenty of food, but very much exposed to cold wet weather	
	13		A fairly heavy bombardment of enemy trenches was carried out	
	14		Lt Hutchinson returned from leave	
	15		Hutchinson went back to a battery	
	16		Battery positions visited by General [illegible] [illegible] he was very pleased with the amount of work which had been done [illegible] had seen the positions [illegible] the clean state of positions & guns	
			One section of D/152 relieved by D/160 [illegible] D/152 [illegible] that section for D/160 [illegible]	
			Relief of D/152 by D/160 completed	
	17		[illegible] difficult for transport by reason of frost	
	18		[illegible] report received from the infantry that a working party of the enemy could be seen in the MAZE [illegible] D/150 was ordered to fire [illegible]	
	19		[illegible] rapid burst. The infantry [illegible] reported the [illegible] as having been [illegible] The light was too bad to see whether there were any casualties	
			Orders received that the grouping of Left [illegible] group was to be altered. 5th Batty & 3rd Batty to come under command of Left Sub Group. D/152 to take over the position of 5th Battery	
			Orders issued to batteries altering zones in accordance with above	
	20		Hard frost again [illegible] a working party dispersed.	

1875 Wt. W593/826 1,000,000 4/15 J.B.C. & A. A.D.S.S./Forms/C. 2118.

Instructions regarding War Diaries and Intelligence Summaries are contained in F. S. Regs., Part II. and the Staff Manual respectively. Title Pages will be prepared in manuscript.

WAR DIARY
or
INTELLIGENCE SUMMARY
(Erase heading not required.)

250 (Northumbrian) Bde RFA (T)

Vol XXII

Army Form C. 2118

Place	Date	Hour	Summary of Events and Information	Remarks and references to Appendices
	21/1/17		252 (Northumbrian) Bde RFA split up, their batteries going to 72nd & 142 Army Brigades RFA. Preliminary instructions for relief of 50 Div by 1st Australian Div received. Heavy stores in possession to be taken to rest area by DAC who are moving empty. Both batteries & DAC very short of horses which may necessitate sending back for stores.	
	22/1/17		Very hard frost 18 degs at 8 AM, but atmosphere thick & hazy. On the whole a quiet day. B/250 take over position of 54th Batty, their own position being taken over by 115 who pull out the guns at once. B/250 have to reconnoitre road out for guns from their new position. Centre sub group now consists of six batteries A, B, C & D/250 (the 54th Batty ~~having~~ & 30th (How) Batty having been transferred to left sub group. A & B zones are on the E side of the front of the MAZE and C & D enfilade the trench to the W. of it.	
	23/1/17		Still very hard frost. Enemy aeroplanes very active all day unmolested by ours. Everything shows up very clearly in the snow. Only usual night firing.	
	24/1/17		Another clear frosty day 20° at 8 AM. All three batteries in S. 6 were shelled between 10 AM & 10.30 AM. C/250 having some casualties and D/250 having a gun destroyed & some ammunition exploded; one man wounded & 1 killed. At 10.30 AM a bombardment of the MAZE by our H.A commenced, our 18 pdrs sweeping & searching area between front & support line. This was repeated	

Army Form C. 2118

Instructions regarding War Diaries and Intelligence Summaries are contained in F. S. Regs., Part II. and the Staff Manual respectively. Title Pages will be prepared in manuscript.

WAR DIARY
or
INTELLIGENCE SUMMARY
(Erase heading not required.)

[illegible] R.F.A. (T)

Vol XXII

Place	Date	Hour	Summary of Events and Information	Remarks and references to Appendices
	24/1/17		[illegible]	
	25/1/17		[illegible]	
	26/1/17		[illegible]	
	27/1/17		[illegible]	
	28/1/17		[illegible]	First section moved to TIERRIEFOT
	1/1/17		[illegible]	
			Lt Col G. I. STEVENSON	

Instructions regarding War Diaries and Intelligence Summaries are contained in F. S. Regs., Part II. and the Staff Manual respectively. Title Pages will be prepared in manuscript.

WAR DIARY
or
INTELLIGENCE SUMMARY
(Erase heading not required.)

Army Form C. 2118

Vol XXIII

Place	Date	Hour	Summary of Events and Information	Remarks and references to Appendices
	1917		[illegible]	

Robert Chapman
Major
OC 250 Brigade RFA TF

1875 Wt. W593/826 1,000,000 4/15 J.B.C. & A. A.D.S.S./Forms/C. 2118.

Instructions regarding War Diaries and Intelligence Summaries are contained in F. S. Regs., Part II. and the Staff Manual respectively. Title Pages will be prepared in manuscript.

WAR DIARY
or
~~INTELLIGENCE SUMMARY~~
(Erase heading not required.)

Army Form C. 2118

250 (Northumbrian) Bde
R.F.A. (T.F.)
Vol XXIII February 1917

Vol 22

Place	Date	Hour	Summary of Events and Information	Remarks and references to Appendices
	1st Feb 1917		Weather still frosty. Day spent in cleaning up & inspection. Billets & horse lines in PIERRECOT satisfactory. Owing to the hard frost all watering places are frozen up. C.R.A. visited the village in the afternoon & walked round some of the horse lines etc.	
	2nd Feb		Day again spent in cleaning up. O.C. Bde inspected personnel [illegible] in the afternoon. Still a good deal to be done in the way of cleaning up. Frosty weather continues, on the whole suitable for the [illegible].	
	3rd Feb.		Nothing of interest	
	4th Feb		Brigade marched to new area (FOUILLOY) leaving PIERRECOT at 9.15 A.M. The turn out was good (B/D being the best). The C.R.A. passed the Bde on the march & expressed his satisfaction but called attention to the fact that some men were riding [illegible]. FOUILLOY reached about 2 pm, billets on the whole were good.	
	5 Feb		O.C. Bde & Adjutant went to forward area to see the positions to be taken over from the French. These were all very good, a great deal of work having been spent on all positions, supplied with deep dug-outs. All the positions must change [illegible] was expected & very few tracks showing in the snow.	
	6th Feb		O.C. Bde inspected horse lines etc. The personnel of batteries are showing results of dry weather in cleaner appearance.	
	7th Feb		O.C. Bde & B.Cs went to forward area & saw positions & made arrangements as to details of relief. O.P. [illegible] was seen but did not appear to be satisfactory	

1875 Wt. W593/826 1,000,000 4/15 J.B.C. & A. A.D.S.S./Forms/C. 2118.

Instructions regarding War Diaries and Intelligence Summaries are contained in F. S. Regs., Part II. and the Staff Manual respectively. Title Pages will be prepared in manuscript.

Army Form C. 2118

WAR DIARY
or
~~INTELLIGENCE SUMMARY~~
(Erase heading not required.)

250 (Northumbrian) Bde R.F.A. (T.F.)

Place	Date	Hour	Summary of Events and Information Vol XXIII Feby 1917	Remarks and references to Appendices
	8th Feby		Nothing of interest. Lt Col BELL returned from leave & resumed command	
	9th Feby		C.O. Bde & B.Cs again went to forward area to complete details of relief. Wagon lines were seen but did not appear satisfactory as they are not being vacated by the French till some days after we go in. Otherwise the relief appears to be fairly simple.	
	10th Feb		Nothing of interest	
	11th "		Officers from batteries went to forward area to see wagon lines	
	12th Feb		D/250 & sections C/250 marched to wagon lines leaving FOUILLOY at 8 AM & arriving at wagon lines at 1.30 pm. They occupied empty positions in the evening & got up a fair amount of ammunition. The French guns were taken out. B/72 are being attached to the Brigade & put in 4 guns.	
	13th		Lt Col BELL & Adjt went to HQ of Col TEULIER. Remaining batteries marched up from FOUILLOY to wagon lines. Remaining sections of C/250 & B/72 occupied positions vacated by French. One section each of A/250 & B/250 occupied a complete French battery position. The command of batteries remains with Col TEULIER.	
	14th		Arrangements made with 149 I.B. as to liaison with them. Their left battalion to be covered by A & B Batts who provide a liaison officer alternately at Battalion HQ at night & in the trenches by day. The right battalion	

1875 Wt. W593/826 1,000,000 4/15 J.B.C. & A. A.D.S.S./Forms/C. 2118.

Instructions regarding War Diaries and Intelligence Summaries are contained in F. S. Regs., Part II. and the Staff Manual respectively. Title Pages will be prepared in manuscript.

WAR DIARY
or
~~INTELLIGENCE SUMMARY~~
(Erase heading not required.)

Army Form C. 2118

250 (Northumbrian) Bde
R F A (T.F.)
Vol XXIII (February 1917)

Place	Date	Hour	Summary of Events and Information	Remarks and references to Appendices
	14 Feb 1917		is similarly covered by C/250 & B/72 [illegible] is arranged by C & D in same [illegible] as for left battalion. B/72 [illegible] O.P. (PISENLITS) T 28 [illegible] (Ref 62 C) by day & night from which the best general view of the Bde zone can be had.	
			Remaining section of A & B relieved French Batteries in the evening [illegible] complete by midnight. 3 French batteries which were not being relieved remained in action till after A & B were complete to maintain the barrage	
			Commander passed [illegible] Bde at 8 pm	
	15th		Col TEULIER & his headquarters moved off at 6 AM. Registration completed. The light has been fairly good & registration completed on the morning after arrival of each section. Battery commanders began to reconnoitre for O.Ps as the O.Ps used by the French command the zone rather too much to the North.	
	16th		Registration [illegible] C/250 [illegible] their [illegible] Ammunition still being brought up [illegible] to 600 rounds per Batty. Considerable difficulty experienced in getting [illegible] of ammunition [illegible] only [illegible] late at night [illegible] following day [illegible] at 7 AM	
	17		[illegible] 2/Lt R.B. CLEGG killed by a shell in the battery position C/250.	

1875 Wt. W593/826 1,000,000 4/15 J.B.C. & A. A.D.S.S./Forms/C. 2118.

Instructions regarding War Diaries and Intelligence Summaries are contained in F. S. Regs., Part II. and the Staff Manual respectively. Title Pages will be prepared in manuscript.

WAR DIARY
or
~~INTELLIGENCE SUMMARY~~
(Erase heading not required.)

Army Form C. 2118

Place	Date	Hour	Summary of Events and Information	Remarks and references to Appendices
	18 Feb 1917		Col BELL went round trenches to inspect enemy wire which is to be cut. Trenches now [illegible] bad. Sgt [illegible] forward [illegible] brought one gun to forward position near DELL [illegible] (N 3 2 c 2.5) to cut wire at range of 1600 to 2000 yds. 2Lt PRIESTMAN & Sgt USHER did well to get this gun into a very difficult position on a very bad & dark night. It had to be taken through Park Woods & over trenches	
	19 Feb		2/Lt SCOTT [illegible] detached [illegible] for wire cutting at N35 a central. This was in the nature of a feint only but was fairly successful. A lane about 20 yds wide was cut. Forward gun of C/232 & guns from A/232 position are used.	
	20		Trenches getting rapidly worse, knee deep in places but often up to the waist in mud. Attempt made to cut wire at T4 B3 a & T4 B9 but owing to difficulties with communication, the F.O.O. could not get through to their batteries till 5pm when not more than 12 rounds could be fired.	
	21		Efforts again made to cut wire. Enough D5 wire being sent down to lay a line from Battn HQ to front line & from forward guns to Battn HQ. Communication was established at 1pm but was almost immediately broken & not re-established till 3pm. A little wire was cut at T4 B16 but on the whole it was a very disappointing day. Raid postponed till 23/24th	

1875 Wt. W593/826 1,000,000 4/15 J.B.C. & A. A.D.S.S./Forms/C. 2118.

Instructions regarding War Diaries and Intelligence Summaries are contained in F. S. Regs., Part II. and the Staff Manual respectively. Title Pages will be prepared in manuscript.

WAR DIARY
or
~~INTELLIGENCE SUMMARY~~

(Erase heading not required.)

250 (Northumbrian) Bde R.F.A. (T)

Vol XXIII Feby 1917

Army Form C. 2118

Place	Date	Hour	Summary of Events and Information	Remarks and references to Appendices
	22 Feb 1917		Wire cutting continued with success. A good gap was cut at T.4.B.1.6 [illegible] gap commenced at T.1.B.0.4. A telephone line (D5) had to be [illegible] the open from Battalion HQ to the front line. The line held very well [illegible] connected to all 3 forward guns which were fired in turn, the [illegible] in the front line observing for all 3 batteries.	
	23 "		Wire cutting continued. Gap at T.4.D.1.6 cleared & widened & new gaps made at T.4.D.0.4. The telephone line held all day. The chief difficulties are [illegible] for the party to get to the front line through the very deep & holding mud in the C.T's. No gum boots are being issued to R.A. with the result that telephonists get wet to the waist & thoroughly exhausted & on returning to the battery have no dry clothes.	
	24		Wire cutting continued at [illegible] & N.34.a [illegible] with the object of [illegible] a diversion. Owing to very bad weather & state of trenches the raid has been postponed. Also the departure of A/250 & D/12 is postponed.	
	25 "		As the infantry are now satisfied with gaps cut [illegible] for purposes [illegible] batteries took opportunity to register various points. An S.O.S. was put up c. 8.55 pm. [illegible] fire came very quickly. This proved to be a false alarm as the Germans appear to have [illegible]. [illegible] Fine day on which more registration was done.	
	26		[illegible] commencement of relief of 149 I.B. by 150 I.B.	

1875 Wt. W593/826 1,000,000 4/15 J.B.C. & A. A.D.S.S./Forms/C. 2118.

Instructions regarding War Diaries and Intelligence Summaries are contained in F. S. Regs., Part II. and the Staff Manual respectively. Title Pages. will be prepared in manuscript.

WAR DIARY
or
~~INTELLIGENCE SUMMARY~~
(Erase heading not required.)

250 (Northumbrian) Bde R.F.A. (T.F.)
Vol XXIII Feb 1917

Army Form C. 2118

Place	Date	Hour	Summary of Events and Information	Remarks and references to Appendices
	27 Feb 1917		Wire cutting continued, the forward guns shot erratically on this occasion, for no apparent reason with the result that more rounds per yard than is usual were required. Orders received that a demonstration would be made on Div front on following morning to help an attack further North.	
	28th		At 5.25 AM all batteries fired a rapid rate (5 rounds per gun per minute) on enemy front line, lifting at plus 3 to support line & at +20 coming back to front line till +45. This bombardment was ~~[illegible]~~ timed very well all batteries starting absolutely together. It drew practically no retaliation from the enemy, none of it being on front line. Owing to possibility of enemy retiring patrols are out all night & fire kept up on approaches etc. Up to now there is no sign of any such movement on our front	
			H. S. Bell Lieut Col. C. C. 250th (Northn) Bde. R.F.A.	

1875 Wt. W593/826 1,000,000 4/15 J.B.C. & A. A.D.S.S./Forms/C. 2118.

Instructions regarding War Diaries and Intelligence Summaries are contained in F. S. Regs., Part II. and the Staff Manual respectively. Title Pages will be prepared in manuscript.

WAR DIARY
or
INTELLIGENCE SUMMARY
(Erase heading not required.)

250 (Northumbrian) Bde RFA T.F.

Army Form C. 2118

Vol XXIV March 1917

Vol 23

Place	Date	Hour	Summary of Events and Information	Remarks and references to Appendices
	1 March 1917		Wire cutting continued. Orders received that A/250 & B/72 would move to 48th Div Area on 3/4 & 4/5 March. Reconnaissance of Battery positions in neighbourhood of BELLOY made & positions selected for use in case of our making an attack. Positions also selected in no mans land for use in case of an advance beyond VILLERS-CARBONNEL	
	2 March		Wire cutting continued. Ground rapidly drying up	
	3 March		Raid now to be on night 4/5 March only 2 18pdr batteries & 1 how battery to support in addition to which A/251 is being lent. The intention is to put a heavy barrage 500 yards N of point of entry at zero at which time raiding party enter enemy's trench. Batteries are to be prepared to switch over to form a box barrage ~~behind~~ round raiding party to cover their return in the event of any mishap. The signal for this is to be the III Corps SOS. Units on flanks are being warned.	
			One section each of A/250 & B/250 go out of action	
	4 March		Orders received that move of A/250 & B/72 is cancelled. Guns still in action in this area to remain & guns & wagons which have gone to new area, to return. Thus 4 guns of A & 4 of B/72 are available to assist in raid. These are to be used to stand by & [illegible] barrage only open fire if SOS is put up. Liaison officer arranged to be at Company HQ during raid.	
	5th March		2 AM. orders received that owing to snow which made concealment impossible raid was to be postponed.	

1875 Wt. W593/826 1,000,000 4/15 J.B.C. & A. A.D.S.S./Forms/C. 2118.

Instructions regarding War Diaries and Intelligence Summaries are contained in F. S. Regs., Part II. and the Staff Manual respectively. Title Pages will be prepared in manuscript.

WAR DIARY
or
INTELLIGENCE SUMMARY
(Erase heading not required.)

250 (Northumbrian) Bde R.F.A

Army Form C. 2118

Place	Date	Hour	Summary of Events and Information	Remarks and references to Appendices
	6 April 1917		Batteries fired to assist in raid by 1st Div. This raid failed to [illegible] capture any prisoners. The synchronisation did not appear to have been good as the start of the barrage was very ragged.	
			Day quiet	
	7th		Batteries again assisted 1st Div. whose raid again failed	
	8th		[illegible] Major E. K. D. JOHNSTON returned to C/250 from England	
	9th		Infantry of 50 Div relieved by infantry of 59th Div	
	10th		Large number (? 36) remounts arrived to replace casualties of horses which had gone to D.A.C. with mange.	
	11th		[illegible] daily [illegible] few [illegible]	
	12		[illegible] signs of the enemy preparing to [illegible] further to the [illegible]	
			[illegible]	
			A new O.P. established near DAMSOUP COPSE from which a good view can be obtained (front German line from ST ELOI round to HOLLNY) a very good view of [illegible] country. [illegible] the country E of the SOMME can be plainly seen.	
			[illegible] ammunition has [illegible] + [illegible] to be [illegible] in preparation for a demonstration in aid of a French attack	

1875 Wt. W593/826 1,000,000 4/15 J.B.C. & A. A.D.S.S./Forms/C. 2118.

Army Form C. 2118

Instructions regarding War Diaries and Intelligence Summaries are contained in F. S. Regs., Part. II. and the Staff Manual respectively. Title Pages will be prepared in manuscript.

WAR DIARY
or
INTELLIGENCE SUMMARY

(Erase heading not required.)

Imp. Hav., 26/7 — 10.000

Place	Date	Hour	Summary of Events and Information	Remarks and references to Appendices
	[illegible]		[illegible]	
	17th		[illegible]	

Instructions regarding War Diaries and Intelligence Summaries are contained in F. S. Regs., Part. II. and the Staff Manual respectively. Title Pages will be prepared in manuscript.

WAR DIARY
or
INTELLIGENCE SUMMARY
(Erase heading not required.)

Army Form C. 2118

RFA (T)
Vol XXIV March 1917

Imp. Hav., 26/7 — 10.000

Place	Date	Hour	Summary of Events and Information	Remarks and references to Appendices
	17 March 1917		& sent back excellent reports as to the situation, laying a telephone wire as he went.	
			At 2pm 2/Lt WALBANK proceeded due East laying a wire as he went. The wire was cut at M T 12 B but the party of [illegible] was [illegible] by a few shells.	
			The infantry advanced to the line MAZANCOURT – junction of CROCODILE trench & LILLE road, CROCODILE TRENCH, HANNIBAL TRENCH and ARGOS TRENCH which was the line held during night 17/18.	
	18th		2/Lt WALBANK extended his telephone line up to BRIE reaching the village at 9.30 AM & finding no signs of enemy. This was reported at once by wire. 2/Lt BECKINGHAM also reached the CANAL further North. The infantry still held the same line. During the afternoon reconnaissances were made of the whole area between the front line & the SOMME, & an attempt was made to cross the river at ST CHRIST. The canal was crossed but it was found impossible to improvise crossing of river.	
			1st Sections of relieving Bde arrived at our present battery position which is about 3000 yards behind front line, [illegible] position beyond the river. [illegible] no signs of enemy.	
			During the evening one section of each battery 285 Bde relieved one section of each battery of 286 Bde personnel only in positions [illegible]	

Army Form C. 2118

WAR DIARY

or

INTELLIGENCE SUMMARY

(Erase heading not required.)

Instructions regarding War Diaries and Intelligence Summaries are contained in F. S. Regs., Part. II. and the Staff Manual respectively. Title Pages will be prepared in manuscript.

Imp. Hav., 26/7 — 10.000

Place	Date	Hour	Summary of Events and Information	Remarks and references to Appendices
	18th		150 Bde moved over 5000 yds behind line held by [illegible]. No orders were received from [illegible] about moving forward. [illegible] of infantry seemed [illegible] the progress of [illegible] was eventually decided that although [illegible] should not take place till 23rd [illegible] 24th Bn would [illegible] whether [illegible] were forward or not [illegible] infantry [illegible] at all [illegible] and [illegible] they were likely to come from.	
	19th		[illegible] that night [illegible] the [illegible] then until it was light [illegible] villages [illegible] and [illegible] by St [illegible] by [illegible] at St [illegible] advanced [illegible] that all villages had been [illegible] from [illegible]	

Army Form C. 2118

Instructions regarding War Diaries and Intelligence Summaries are contained in F. S. Regs., Part. II. and the Staff Manual respectively. Title Pages will be prepared in manuscript.

WAR DIARY
or
INTELLIGENCE SUMMARY
(Erase heading not required.)

Imp. Hav., 26/7 — 10.000

Place	Date	Hour	Summary of Events and Information	Remarks and references to Appendices
	19th (cont'd)		A beginning was made carting all the ammunition dumped at battery position to A.R.P. except enough to fill echelon.	
	20		Definite orders received that relief would be complete on night 21/22 and that Bde would march to RAVIGNY [illegible] on 22nd. Remainder of ammunition returned to A.R.P. and [illegible] [illegible] withdrawn [illegible]. No [illegible] yet made at ST CHRIST [illegible] transport [illegible] during afternoon [illegible]	
	21		HQ [illegible] at noon by HQ [illegible] Bde at which [illegible] of [illegible] [illegible] [illegible] ST CHRIST [illegible] withdrawn to wagon lines. 2nd Lt. R.S. BELL [illegible] Major [illegible]	
	22		Bde [illegible] from wagon lines [illegible] FOUILLOY [illegible]	
	23		Cleaning up.	
	24		Drilling [illegible]	
	25		[illegible] unloaded and [illegible] to [illegible]	

Instructions regarding War Diaries and Intelligence Summaries are contained in F. S. Regs., Part. II. and the Staff Manual respectively. Title Pages will be prepared in manuscript.

WAR DIARY
or
INTELLIGENCE SUMMARY
(Erase heading not required.)

Army Form C. 2118

[illegible] Bde R.F.A. (T.F.) Vol. [illegible] March 1917

Imp. Hav., 26/7 — 10.000

Place	Date	Hour	Summary of Events and Information	Remarks and references to Appendices
	March 26		Brigade marched at 8 AM [illegible]	
	27		A [illegible] day spent in resting [illegible]	
	28		Brigade marched at 7 AM [illegible]	
	29th		Moved off at 7 AM [illegible]	
	30th		Bde moved from [illegible]	
	31st		Bde HQ [illegible] ammunition	

1.4.17 [illegible] OC [illegible] Bde R.F.A.

Army Form C. 2118

250 (NORTHUMBRIAN) Bde RFA (T.F.) 50 Div

Vol XXV April 1917

Vol 24

WAR DIARY
or
INTELLIGENCE SUMMARY

(Erase heading not required.)

PAGE I

Instructions regarding War Diaries and Intelligence Summaries are contained in F. S. Regs., Part. II. and the Staff Manual respectively. Title Pages will be prepared in manuscript.

Imp. Hav., 26/7 — 10.000

Place	Date	Hour	Summary of Events and Information	Remarks and references to Appendices
Sheet 51B S.W. Hqrs M.3.c.4½.½	April 1 1917		Work continued on battery position first section registered and second section brought into action during evening. Ammunition being taken up all day.	
A/250 M.9.D.9¼.¼	April 2		Next section registered + remaining two sections brought into action. Carting of ammunition + working positions continued. Positions are fair but very crowded	
B/250 M.9.D.8¾.1½			+ very little accommodation. Approximately in British Front line W of BEAURAINS.	
C/250 M.10.c.1.1½				
D/250 M.9.D.7¾.¾	April 3		Registration completed + selection of O.P.s. Orders received that bombardment would now be four days V, W, X + Y "V" day being April 4. Targets for 18pdrs trenches in enfilade, wire + approaches; for 4.5 hows trenches + wire with instantaneous fuze.	
	April 4		Bombardment commenced, at 7AM and continued all day with short intervals for photography. Only 4 guns per battery in action at the same time to give the time for cleaning, rest + overhaul. Bombardment effective.	
	April 5.		Bombardment continued also practise Barrage. Equipment standing the firing well. Observation from O.P's good but light not very good most of day. Night firing on gaps in wire + C.T's.	
	April 6		Bombardment continued Orders received that Z day would be April 9th instead of 8th, thus giving one more day for bombardment. April 7th to be called Q day. Major PARMETER returned from hospital. O.P established in front of MERCATEL from which whole Brigade barrage zone can be seen.	
	April 7.		Bombardment continued D/250 have 2 guns out of action owing to dial sights working loose.	

Instructions regarding War Diaries and Intelligence Summaries are contained in F. S. Regs., Part. II. and the Staff Manual respectively. Title Pages will be prepared in manuscript.

WAR DIARY
or
INTELLIGENCE SUMMARY
(Erase heading not required.) Page II

250 (Northumbrian) Bde RFA (T)

Vol XXV

April 1917

Army Form C. 2118

Imp. Hav., 26/7 — 10.000

Place	Date	Hour	Summary of Events and Information	Remarks and references to Appendices
	8th April		Final preparations made for attack on 9th. also bombardment continued throughout day + night. During night 8/9 bombardment with Gas shells commenced. On day of the attack in addition to battery O.Ps. One forward O.P. is to be manned by 2 officers and another officer is to have a roving commission to collect information from stragglers, prisoners, wounded etc. ACHICOURT ammunition dump heavily shelled + set on fire by the enemy	
	9th		Zero time 5.30 AM. 56th Div attack at 7.45. No difficulty experienced in ~~[illegible]~~ taking NEUVILLE VITASSE + up to the "Blue Line" which was taken according to time table. Divisions on left + right also successful.	
			Position became obscure as soon as attack on Brown line commenced. Eventually news was received that the 30th Div on the right was being held up + the right of 56 Div could not get beyond N20 D S.E of NEUVILLE VITASSE. Divisions on left advancing well. Throughout the day information was received from F.O.Os which proved accurate and arrived early. Visual signalling was used from points in NEUVILLE VITASSE after it was captured. Very valuable accurate reports received from MAJOR C.L.WILKINSON D.S.O & Lt A.F.BOURDAS. At 6pm orders were received to reconnoitre + occupy positions for batteries West of + close to NEUVILLE VITASSE. These were occupied by 1 AM and ammunition brought up. These positions were quite unprepared + had no cover for men or guns. A/250 B/250 C/250 in M.24.C A/250 M.29.C Sheet 51B. S.W.	
	10th		Orders received early in the morning that an attack was to be	

Army Form C. 2118

Instructions regarding War Diaries and Intelligence Summaries are contained in F. S. Regs., Part. II. and the Staff Manual respectively. Title Pages will be prepared in manuscript.

WAR DIARY
or
INTELLIGENCE SUMMARY
(Erase heading not required.)

250 (Northumbrian) Bde R.F.A. (T) Vol XXV Page [illegible] April 1917

Imp. Hav., 26/7 — 10.000

Place	Date	Hour	Summary of Events and Information	Remarks and references to Appendices
.	10th April Cont.		by 14th & 56th Divisions in a S.E. direction on the salient in the German line in N20D & N21C. A barrage was put up by 250 Bde on ~~[illegible]~~ left flank of 56 Div. The attack was held up to start with by M.G. fire but later a bombing attack succeeded and the line was advanced to NEPAL TRENCH. The 14th Div on left during afternoon entered WANCOURT but later had to withdraw. & during the night the enemy held Hill 90 S.W of WANCOURT. Attacks on night by 30th & 21st Divs failed. Major F.G.D. Johnston made very valuable reconnaissance from Hill 90. Wagon lines moved to AGNY.	
	11th		During the early morning attacks were made on WANCOURT, HILL 90 and the HINDENBURG line further to the right. The attacks failed at first, but later about 10.30 Hill 90 was reported taken.	
Sheet 51B S.W. A/250, B/250, C/250 } N.13.C & D	12		Orders received that Batteries would relieve 123 Bde of 37th D.A. Guns being exchanged in situ. New positions were close to & N. of ~~[illegible]~~ NEUVILLE VITASSE & were very little in advance of those we were leaving. H.Q. at RONVILLE. Orders for this relief very vague & late but it was completed by 6 p.m. Bde under command of 14th D.A. No firing by batteries.	
D/250 N.19.A	13.		A quiet day spent in registering guns & improving gun positions and wagon lines. Latter are in RONVILLE & ACHICOURT. Orders received that batteries would have to move during night to ~~[illegible]~~ positions just W of WANCOURT to support attack early on morning of 14th. Owing to road being very bad this move was postponed till early morning of 14th. 14th D.A relieved by 50 D.A. & 14th Div by 50th.	

Instructions regarding War Diaries and Intelligence Summaries are contained in F. S. Regs., Part II. and the Staff Manual respectively. Title Pages will be prepared in manuscript.

WAR DIARY
or
INTELLIGENCE SUMMARY
(Erase heading not required.) PAGE IV

Army Form C. 2118

250 (Northumbrian) Bde R.F.A. (T.F).

Vol XXV April 1917

Place	Date	Hour	Summary of Events and Information	Remarks and references to Appendices
	14 April		Batteries moved limbers + full echelons from Wagon lines at 2 AM and moved from positions between 4 + 5 AM ~~from~~ to new positions which had to be occupied by 7 AM. when batteries opened fire on barrage to cover attack by ~~a~~ 151 Bde on WANCOURT TOWER and CHERISY. The first objective including ridge on which WANCOURT TOWER stands was taken, but ~~a~~ the attack was then held up by heavy M.G fire from GUEMAPPE. No further progress was made during the day. Batteries did very well to move + get into action in short time at short notice. A/250 N.16.c.6.1 B/250 N.16.c.5.2 C/250 N.16.c.3.1 D/250 N.16.c.4.4 Bde HQ. move to position previously occupied by B/250 N of NEUVILLE VITASSE N.13.B.1.6 Sheet 51B S.W.	
	15.		Batteries looked for new O.Ps + continued work at positions which have no cover for men + very little cover from view. Some calibration done.	
	16		Considerable activity on the part of the enemy during the day a good deal of movement being reported near WANCOURT TOWER and on spur running E from it. A new O.P established in N35B05 S.E of HENINEL from which the valley running through N30D + O25 C + B down to VIS EN ARTOIS can be ~~seen~~ observed. At 8.5 pm heavy enemy barrage was opened round about WANCOURT TOWER which was attacked + taken by the enemy. Preparations at once made for counter attack.	

1875 Wt. W593/826 1,000,000 4/15 J.B.C. & A. A.D.S.S./Forms/C. 2118.

Instructions regarding War Diaries and Intelligence Summaries are contained in F. S. Regs., Part II. and the Staff Manual respectively. Title Pages will be prepared in manuscript.

WAR DIARY
or
INTELLIGENCE SUMMARY

(*Erase heading not required.*) Page V

Army Form C. 2118

250 (Northumbrian) Bde
R.F.A. (T.F.)
Vol XXV April 1917.

Place	Date	Hour	Summary of Events and Information	Remarks and references to Appendices
	17 April		Counter attack planned for dawn but it was later decided to put it off until artillery could register. The attack was eventually made at noon after 5 minutes intense bombardment with field artillery. Our casualties slight and 40/50 prisoners taken. A telegram of thanks & appreciation for Barrage received from G.O.C. 149 Inf Bde.	
	18th		Quiet day; a new O.P established at N35B05, from which a good view of country towards VIS EN ARTOIS can be had. This is manned daily by batteries in turn. It is shelled considerably. Noticeable increase in hostile artillery activity. Weather still bad, rain most of day & night.	
	19th		Another uneventful day with weather still remaining bad. D/48 attached to Bde	
	20		A fine day, light becoming good in afternoon. Enemy artillery very active, batteries shelled intermittently during day. During night batteries were constantly shelled. One man killed & one officer Major WILKINSON wounded.	
	21.		Orders received to commence slow bombardment which is to last two days previous to an attack on large scale. Neighbourhood of batteries heavily shelled Major Johnston being wounded and 1 Gun of D/250 hit at battery position and 2/Lt McALLUM being wounded at an O.P. The enemy shelled back areas heavily all day as if he expected attack on next day	
	22.		Preparations for attack & bombardment continued. Enemy shelling not so heavy as on previous day. Lt GRAHAM & 2/Lt MUSGRAVE returned.	

1875 Wt. W593/826 1,000,000 4/15 J.B.C. & A. A.D.S.S./Forms/C. 2118.

Instructions regarding War Diaries and Intelligence Summaries are contained in F. S. Regs., Part II. and the Staff Manual respectively. Title Pages will be prepared in manuscript.

WAR DIARY
or
INTELLIGENCE SUMMARY
(Erase heading not required.) PAGE VI Vol XXV

Army Form C. 2118

250 (Northumbrian) Bde RFA (T)

April 1917

Place	Date	Hour	Summary of Events and Information	Remarks and references to Appendices
	23 April		Attack started at 4.45 AM, batteries forming a creeping barrage in front of attack. The attack at first was successfull and the infantry reached their first objective. The light was bad and there was ~~a~~ difficulty in distinguishing British from Germans from the O.Ps + communications to the front did not hold well.	
			At 10 AM reports were received that Germans were massing in low ground in O21c + later they counter attacked strongly and although heavily shelled by shrapnel they regained the ground they had lost.	
			Heavy fire was kept up on their front line and dead ground behind it until 6pm when another attack was made. This attack regained the ground on the left up to the first objective but on the right owing to the division on the right not advancing there was an exposed flank + for some time the situation was obscure, eventually more battalions were brought up to fill in the gap.	
			Batteries fired a lot of ammunition during the day; ~~the~~ C/250 fired nearly 3000 from 4.45 AM to 8pm; During the barrages this battery thickened the barrage formed by the other two 18 pdr batteries of the Bde + ~~it~~ was used for engaging any fleeting targets that appeared. This proved very satisfactory as many parties of the enemy were engaged and casualties inflicted. Capt F.R.A. Shiel rendered valuable services at the O.P. Capt. CHAPMAN was wounded and 1 O.R killed an 6 wounded during the day, in addition a gun of D/250 was hit and completely destroyed.	
	24		Division on right which had ~~been~~ behind came up and line was straightened	

1875 Wt. W593/826 1,000,000 4/15 J.B.C. & A. A.D.S.S./Forms/C. 2118.

Instructions regarding War Diaries and Intelligence Summaries are contained in F. S. Regs., Part II. and the Staff Manual respectively. Title Pages will be prepared in manuscript.

WAR DIARY
or
INTELLIGENCE SUMMARY
(Erase heading not required.)

Page VII Vol XXV

250 (Northumbrian) Bde RFA (T) April 1917

Army Form C. 2118

Place	Date	Hour	Summary of Events and Information	Remarks and references to Appendices
	April 24 Cont		New O.P's were established near wood in O 19 D but these were heavily shelled all day and were given up as very little could be seen from them which could not be seen from old O.P's.	
	25th		Nothing important occurred. Creeping barrages were fired during the day as enemy were said to be in shell holes.	
	26		A quiet day on the whole. at 10.35 pm the Division on our left attacked the buildings in O.14.a. batteries of this brigade fired on selected targets for an hour before zero to assist. Enemy replied with a fairly heavy barrage, along the whole front. 14th Div relieved 50th DAV, CRA 14th taking command of artillery.	
	27th		visibility poor, nothing of interest during the day	
	28th		1st Army and VI corps attacked at 4-25 AM Brigade barrage on S.O.S lines and 300 yds behind. B/250 moved to new position at N.23.c.6.9 and D/250 to N.23 A 80.	
	29th		Very quiet day. A/250 moved to new position at N.23.A.50 and C/250 to new position at N.23.A.30 B/250 & D/250 registered from new positions.	
	30th		at 2 a.m and at intervals during the early morning enemy put a number of gas shells into new position. A/250 & C/250 registered all guns.	

Robert Chapman
Lt Col
O.C. 250 Brigade RFA T 1 May 1917

1875 Wt. W593/826 1,000,000 4/15 J.B.C. & A. A.D.S.S./Forms/C. 2118.

Instructions regarding War Diaries and Intelligence Summaries are contained in F. S. Regs., Part II. and the Staff Manual respectively. Title Pages will be prepared in manuscript.

WAR DIARY
or
INTELLIGENCE SUMMARY
(Erase heading not required.)

Army Form C. 2118

250th (NORTHUMBRIAN) BRIGADE R.F.A (T)
MAY 1917.

50th

Vol XXVI

Vol 25

Place	Date	Hour	Summary of Events and Information	Remarks and references to Appendices
	1	4 a.m.	All batteries opened barrage on S.O.S. lines, lifting 100 yds at 4-3 a.m. and returning to original line at 4-6 a.m., ceasing fire at 4-8 a.m. Enemy's barrage came down at 4-4 a.m. Very heavy but erratic.	
			During afternoon our batteries were rather heavily shelled by 4-2s. 3 men were killed and 4 wounded. One howitzer was knocked out. This reduces D/250 to 2 Hows in action.	
			Major Johnston returned to duty from hospital.	
	2		During early morning batteries were again shelled by 4-2s and gas shells. 1 man killed and 3 wounded. Forward positions were reconnoitred by B.C.s during morning, and lines were laid to forward O.Ps. Also to infantry Battalion H.Q. O.19.A. Batteries were again shelled during afternoon. Heavies turned on and shelling stopped.	
	3.	3.45 a.m.	Barrage opened and attacks by 3rd, Vth and 1st Armies commenced. ~~[illegible]~~ Rate of fire 2 Rds per gun per minute.	
		3.47	Heavy enemy barrage put down.	
		4.52	F.O.O. (N.36.D.8½) reports infantry on right went over but were came back. Very heavy M.G. fire.	
		5.30	Great difficulty in keeping up lines to infantry & very little news coming back.	
		5.45	F.O.O. (N.11.C.16) reports infantry on left held up by machine gun fire. Enemy barrage on our line increasing.	
		~~6.30~~	~~Barrage~~ lifted	
		6.40.	F.O.O. on left came forward & reports from N.18.B.88 that infantry on left hold Cavalry farm and Lanyard Trench and are advancing. Enemy barrage reported very ragged. Wounded report we hold 1st objective.	
		7.40.	Batteries shelled by 10.5 c.ms.	
		8.0	Some of our infantry reported beyond CHERISY. Triangle Wood held by us & infantry digging in. Orders received for Barrage to be continued at slow rate of fire 1 Rd per gun per 3 minutes till 9-15.	
		8.52.	F.O.O. reports enemy still hold CAVALRY FARM but our infantry beyond it on either side.	
		10.20	B/250 stopped firing. A, C, & D/250 stopped protective barrage and fired occasional bursts on same line.	
		11.25.	Counter attack on Triangle wood reported probable. Barrage opened 1 Rd per gun per 2 minutes.	
		11.35	S.O.S. received from B.M. 2 Rds per gun per minute on Zero + 24 minutes line.	
		noon.	All batteries lifted 250 yards.	
		12.40 pm	Reduced rate of fire to 1 Rd per gun per 2 minutes.	
		12.55.	Enemy reported massing Triangle Wood. D/250 fired 1 Rd per gun per minute on wood.	
		1.5 p.m.	Infantry reported back in their original front line.	

1875 Wt. W593/826 1,000,000 4/15 J.B.C. & A. A.D.S.S./Forms/C. 2118.

Instructions regarding War Diaries and Intelligence Summaries are contained in F. S. Regs., Part II. and the Staff Manual respectively. Title Pages will be prepared in manuscript.

WAR DIARY
or
INTELLIGENCE SUMMARY
(Erase heading not required.)

250th (NORTHUMBRIAN) BRIGADE. R.F.A.

Army Form C. 2118

May. 1917.

Place	Date	Hour	Summary of Events and Information	Remarks and references to Appendices
	3	1-35pm	Barrage ceased; only occasional burst of fire ordered.	
		2.50pm	Enemy seen in NARROW TRENCH; C/250 turned on them	
		3.30	F.O.O.s with infantry (Lieut GRAHAM & 2/Lt Scott) telephoned that all was quiet and infantry were back in their original line. They had gone forward with infantry as far as St ROHART FACTORY where they were sniped and lost 2 telephonists, who were wounded and had to be left behind with ... of some infantry.	
		5.30.	Enemy reported by F.O.O. on left to be advancing in open order from Triangle Wood. A, B & C Batteries opened on line O.21.A.2.1 to O.15.C.2.2 & searched eastwards 300 yards. D/250 opened on N.W. corner Triangle wood. Round per gun per minute all batteries.	
		5.37	Rate of fire reduced to 1 Rd per gun per 2 minutes	
		5.48	Rate of fire reduced to 1 Rd per gun per 4 minutes.	
		6.47	Ceased firing.	
		7.57	S.O.S. from Brigade Major; 2 Rds per gun per minute.	
		8.20	Rate of fire reduced to 1 Rd per gun per minute.	
		8.50.	Ceased firing. Guns remaining on original S.O.S. lines. During the evening 78th Division, on our Right, made fresh attack on CHERISY which was unsuccessful.	
		10.40.	S.O.S. went up. Batteries opened slow rate of fire, 1 Rd per gun per 2 minutes. No attack was made by enemy on our front, and batteries were ordered to cease firing.	
			F.O.O.s. On left 2/Lieut TROTTER & 2nd Lt HOPWOOD. In centre Lt GRAHAM & 2/Lt SCOTT. On right Lt BROWELL and 2/Lt MUSGRAVE	
	4.	7am to 11AM.	Large number of gas shells were fired into the Batteries. Otherwise situation quiet.	
	5.		Everything quiet on our front during morning and afternoon	
		10.18pm	S.O.S. went up on our Zone. Opened at 2 Rds per gun per minute shortly reducing to 1 Rd per gun per 2 minutes	
		11.15	Ceased fire. No attack was made. Started in 5th Army & spread over our Zone.	

1875 Wt. W593/826 1,000,000 4/15 J.B.C. & A. A.D.S.S./Forms/C. 2118.

Instructions regarding War Diaries and Intelligence Summaries are contained in F. S. Regs., Part II. and the Staff Manual respectively. Title pages will be prepared in manuscript.

WAR DIARY
or
INTELLIGENCE SUMMARY.
(Erase heading not required.)

Army Form C. 2118.

250th (NORTHUMBRIAN) BRIGADE R.F.A. (T)

May 1917

Place	Date	Hour	Summary of Events and Information	Remarks and references to Appendices
	6		A certain number of gas shells and 4.2s fell near the batteries during the day but on the whole the situation was quieter.	
		7.30pm	Party of enemy seen in O.22.b.24 were fired on by D/250. Other batteries [illegible] given for 24 hours on tracks, road junctions [illegible] lines. [illegible] more or less indiscriminately. Report made to C.R.A. by O.C. on operations [illegible] seen by our F.O.O.s.	
	7		Quiet morning. Batteries slightly shelled by 4.2s.	
		1.7pm	Heavies bombarded HILLSIDE WORK. B/250 fired [illegible] on enemy as they evacuated the trench. Otherwise everything normal.	
	8		Quiet morning.	
		6pm	Batteries shelled by 4.2s. Heavies assistance obtained & shelling stopped.	
		8.15pm	Batteries again shelled. Heavies again [illegible] satisfactorily. Night quiet. Lieut. [illegible] returned from tour of duty as Brigade Major & resumed duties of Adjutant which had been carried out in his absence by the Orderly Officer. Lt. Graham returned to B/250.	
	9		Quiet morning. 3 new Howitzers received but 1 taken to I.O.M. for [illegible] alterations.	
		4pm	4 Howitzers reported registered and in action.	
	10		Quiet day except for shelling of WANCOURT. B/250 [illegible] the evening [illegible]	
	11		Batteries shelled intermittently. [illegible] in left [illegible] in the evening. [illegible]	

A5834 Wt. W4973/M687 750,000 8/16 D. D. & L. Ltd. Forms/C.2118/13.

Instructions regarding War Diaries and Intelligence Summaries are contained in F. S. Regs., Part II. and the Staff Manual respectively. Title pages will be prepared in manuscript.

WAR DIARY
or
INTELLIGENCE SUMMARY.
(Erase heading not required.)

Army Form C. 2118.

250th (NORTHUMBRIAN) BRIGADE, R.F.A. (T)
MAY 1917
Vol XXVI

Place	Date	Hour	Summary of Events and Information	Remarks and references to Appendices
	May 12		A quiet day, nothing of interest to report. WANCOURT shelled during day	
	13		Another quiet day. Visibility good in afternoon	
	14		A gun of C/250 damaged by direct hit in early morning. WANCOURT and neighbourhood of batteries heavily shelled during afternoon and evening by batteries close to ST SERVINS farm which were located by the O.P.s and shelled. Very heavy rain during afternoon.	
	15		Some shelling during early morning near WANCOURT, otherwise quiet day	
	16 } 17 }		Nothing of interest, batteries shelled intermittently but no damage done	
	18		B/250 returned into action from AGNY and reoccupied their old position. D/250 less one section were relieved by D/251. ~~the~~ One section of D/250 was left in action under D/251 who thus had 8 guns.	
	19		B/250 registered guns otherwise only normal day & night firing	
	20		Batteries supported an attack of 33rd Div. on right who attacked at 5.15 am. The attack was only a partial success in the morning.	
	21		Quiet day, good progress made with deep dug outs	
	22 23		} Quiet days, WANCOURT area shelled a little.	
	24		Lt Col Chapman went on leave. Major JOHNSTON assumed command of the Brigade	
	25		A/250 went out of action to rest. D/250 relieved D/47 in action & remained under orders of 47 Bde R.F.A.	

Instructions regarding War Diaries and Intelligence Summaries are contained in F. S. Regs., Part II. and the Staff Manual respectively. Title Pages will be prepared in manuscript.

WAR DIARY
or
INTELLIGENCE SUMMARY
(Erase heading not required.)

250 (NORTHUMBRIAN) BRIGADE R.F.A (T)

Army Form C. 2118

Vol XXVI May 1917

Place	Date	Hour	Summary of Events and Information	Remarks and references to Appendices
	26 May		Batteries shelled with 8 inch during the day from 11 AM to 5pm. Most of the rounds were over and no casualties to personel occurred. One gun of B/250 was hit and badly damaged. The deep saps which had been dug by batteries proved most useful and probably accounted for there being no casualties. The slits which were first dug + strongly revetted also proved useful before saps were complete and withstood hits from 5.9s within 6 or 8 ft without being blown in. The safest slit appears to be 5'6" or 6' deep; if shallower they do no give sufficient protection and if deeper the revetting is usually not strong enough to prevent them being blown in.	
			Bde H.Q. moved from WANCOURT about 2000 yards further West into the old Hindenburg support line.	
	27		A/250 moved from wagon lines to a rest camp near HENDICOURT. This is not as convenient or comfortable as AGNY.	
	28		Wagon lines of B, C + D/250 moved from RONVILLE up to M17 c on W. side of BEAURAINS - MERCATEL road. No accommodation in new camp, but very good situation.	
	29		Batteries warned to be prepared to shoot on trenches behind + N. of CAVALRY farm, these trenches were registered, but attack was cancelled.	
	30		Quiet day.	
	31		Very quiet day.	[signature] Major Comdg. 250. RFA T.

Instructions regarding War Diaries and Intelligence Summaries are contained in F. S. Regs., Part II. and the Staff Manual respectively. Title pages will be prepared in manuscript.

WAR DIARY
or
INTELLIGENCE SUMMARY.
(Erase heading not required.)

250 (Northumbrian) Bde R.F.A. (T)

June 1917

Vol XXVII

Vol 26

Army Form C. 2118.

Place	Date	Hour	Summary of Events and Information	Remarks and references to Appendices
	1 June		Quiet day. Batteries made use of balloon for registering with satisfactory ~~eff~~ results. Work commenced on deep dug outs and concrete protection at O.P.s.	
	2 June		Quiet day	
	3.		~~Bd~~ B/250 heavily shelled by 8 inch armour piercing shells from 11 AM to 4.30 pm. 3 guns being hit and badly damaged. No casualties to personnel who took cover in the deep saps. Empty positions of A/250 also heavily shelled and damaged. Only a few shells fell in C/250 position.	
	4.		Orders received that A/250 would return to action on night 5/6 and C/250 move to rest area. D/250 return to 250 Bde's command and move to WANCOURT area owing to shelling of positions. A/250 are to occupy position of C/250 and B/250 occupy partly their own & partly A/250's position.	
	5.		A/250 relieved C/250 in action and C/250 went to rest camp.	
	6.		Orders received that zone would be altered further south to cover FONTAINE trench between CHERISY and FONTAINE LES CROISILLES and that some of the batteries would move to positions now occupied by 281 Bde. Batteries have to be prepared to cover new zone but may be called on by VI Corps to fire N. of COJEUL to assist attack by them.	
	7.		At 12 noon 251 Bde HQ. went to rest and B, C & D/251 came under command of 250 Bde HQ. to cover the same zone as held	

A5834 Wt. W4973/M687 750,000 8/16 D. D. & L. Ltd. Forms/C.2118/13.

Instructions regarding War Diaries and Intelligence Summaries are contained in F. S. Regs., Part II. and the Staff Manual respectively. Title Pages will be prepared in manuscript.

WAR DIARY
or
INTELLIGENCE SUMMARY
(Erase heading not required.)

250 (Northumbrian) Bde RFA (T)

June 1917

Vol XXVII

Army Form C. 2118

Place	Date	Hour	Summary of Events and Information	Remarks and references to Appendices
	7 June		Batteries make alterations to emplacements so that they can reach new zone and still shoot N of COJEUL. B/250 and D/251 will both move from WANCOURT the former to S of HENINEL the latter to HENINEL. C/250 on returning to action will occupy position close to B/250 new position near HENINEL.	
	8th		Gas bombardment of QUARRY trenches near TRIANGLE wood at 2pm. Orders received that we would pass from 14 DA to 18 DA on 10th but would be lent to 61st D.A until 11th. 14th Div is being relieved partly by 18th on right and 61st on left. Arrangements made to take over from 280 Bde O.Ps suitable for our new zone on 18 Div front. Registration carried out on new front.	
	9th		Reconnaissances made for O.P. to observe front line of our zone; this can only be seen from our posts where lines are being laid.	
	10th		At 6 AM come under orders of 18 D.A but remain covering our own zone as 61st DA is not yet ready to take it over. Their batteries came into unprepared positions on night 9/10. Trenches on 61st Div zone registered in case we have to assist them.	

1875 Wt. W593/826 1,000,000 4/15 J.B.C. & A. A.D.S.S./Forms/C. 2118.

Instructions regarding War Diaries and Intelligence Summaries are contained in F. S. Regs., Part II. and the Staff Manual respectively. Title Pages will be prepared in manuscript.

WAR DIARY or INTELLIGENCE SUMMARY

(Erase heading not required.)

250 Bde. R.F.A (T) June 1917 Vol XXVII

Army Form C. 2118

Place	Date	Hour	Summary of Events and Information	Remarks and references to Appendices
	11		From 10 AM 61st Div take over our S.O.S lines and we change to S.O.S lines on 18 Div but are not responsible for covering them as VI Corps have a call on us.	
			Arrangements made to lay telephone lines to posts from where we can see front line and orders issued for liaison and manning of O.P.s	
	12		C.R.A. 18 Div visited battery positions in the morning. Positions for the advance of batteries in event of German retirement were reconnoitred.	
	13		Preparations made to assist 61st division on our left with barrage for attack by 3rd Div. towards B. du VERT. Lines laid to O.P.s to observe this fire. S.O.S lines on 18 Div. front taken over. Liaison officer found with left infantry battalion.	
	14.		Assisted 7th Corps by barraging LANYARD TRENCH and STIRRUP lane + putting smoke barrage N of ST ROHARTS factory. The attack was successful. Smoke barrage was effective and rates of fire appeared right; if anything the rate of 3 rounds per gun per min was kept up too long.	
			A counter attack in the evening failed.	
			Arrangements made to take over liaison with infantry Bde.	
			3/250 moved one gun to their position in N34D to register it.	

1875 Wt. W593/826 1,000,000 4/15 J.B.C. & A. A.D.S.S./Forms/C. 2118.

Instructions regarding War Diaries and Intelligence Summaries are contained in F. S. Regs., Part II. and the Staff Manual respectively. Title pages will be prepared in manuscript.

WAR DIARY
or
INTELLIGENCE SUMMARY.
(Erase heading not required.)

250 Bde RFA (T.F.)
June 1917
Vol XXVII

Army Form C. 2118.

Place	Date	Hour	Summary of Events and Information	Remarks and references to Appendices
	15		C/250 and A/251 return to action. C/250 occupies new position in N 34 D previously occupied by 250 Bde. No dug outs except some which had been commenced by by T.M. men attached. A/251 reoccupied their old position. A Liaison officer supplied nightly in turn by the 250 Bde Batteries with the centre battalion in the line.	
	16.		B/250 + B/251 go out of action to rest. C/250 + A/251 register and take over their zones. Liaison officer with left Bde in line found, Lt HUTCHINSON C/250 detailed.	
	17		D/251 go out of action to rest. Orders received that Lt Hutchinson must go to Rt Brigade	
	18		50 D.A. relieve 18 D.A. 46th + 47th Bdes RFA are relieved and their zones taken over by 250 + 251 who still retain part of the old zone. 281 Bde attached to 50 D.A. in place of 46 + 47 Bdes. S.O.S. lines for all batteries changed. Battalion liaison officer now goes to left battalion and Bde liaison officer returns to left Bde. New O.Ps manned to observe new zone.	
	19.		A/250 fire shrapnel intermittently during the night on narrow trench to cover patrol who reconnoitred a detached trench and found it occupied by the enemy	
	20.		A/250 again fired during night to cover patrol who intended to occupy detached trench. The enemy forestalled us by raiding one of our posts opposite capturing 2 prisoners but leaving 3 or 4 dead behind.	

A5834 Wt. W4973/M687 750,000 8/16 D. D. & L. Ltd. Forms/C.2118/13.

Instructions regarding War Diaries and Intelligence Summaries are contained in F. S. Regs., Part II. and the Staff Manual respectively. Title pages will be prepared in manuscript.

WAR DIARY or INTELLIGENCE SUMMARY.

(*Erase heading not required.*)

250 (Northumbrian) Bde R.F.A. (T) Army Form C. 2118.

Vol XXVII

June 1917.

Place	Date	Hour	Summary of Events and Information	Remarks and references to Appendices
	21		New orders issued for Liaison and O.Ps to simplify lines and duties. Orders received that 82, 83 and 281 Bdes are going out and 162 Bde coming in. Artillery covering division to consist of two groups covering right and left infantry Bde in the line respectively.	
	22		C/162 come into action and are attached to 250 Bde group. B/250 return to action. S.O.S lines readjusted so that batteries remaining under 250 Bde when alteration is complete, take over their eventual S.O.S. lines. Other Batteries superimposed on them.	
	23		D/162 attached to 250 Bde. C/251 return to 251 Bde. Trenches quiet except for some fishtails during the night for which D/250 retaliate. A/251 shelled heavily with aeroplane observation from 9 am to 1 pm. Battery call taken by our wireless and battery engaged by heavies.	
	24.		One section of C/250 moved to a forward position within 1500 yards of the trenches in order to engage fleeting targets, which are numerous, more effectively. Orders received that 2 18pdr batteries + 1 how battery would be attached to 251 Bde group to assist them in operation on night 25/26. A + C/250 + D/162 detailed	

Instructions regarding War Diaries and Intelligence Summaries are contained in F. S. Regs., Part II. and the Staff Manual respectively. Title pages will be prepared in manuscript.

WAR DIARY
or
~~INTELLIGENCE SUMMARY.~~
(Erase heading not required.)

250 (Northumbrian) Bde R.F.A. (T) Army Form C. 2118.

Vol XXVII
JUNE 1917

Place	Date	Hour	Summary of Events and Information	Remarks and references to Appendices
	25.		C.R.A 50 Div. visited H.Q and some of the batteries during the morning. B/250 were heavily shelled with 5.9 + 8 in during the morning no guns were hit + no damage done to personnel who took refuge in deep sap which had just been completed. At 5.30 pm FONTAINE Trench between CHERISY and FONTAINE was bombarded with 4.5 + 6" hows about 900 rounds of 4.5 and 400 6" being fired. The enemy did not retaliate at all + no movement was seen. At 11.30 pm gas was projected into CHERISY aaa	
	26		At 12.30 AM Right Inf Bde attacked some posts N.W of FONTAINE assisted by 251 Bde group R.F.A to which A + C/250 + D/162 were attached the objectives and 28 prisoners were taken and two ~~att~~ counter attacks driven off by 9 AM.	
	27		Batteries which had been attached to 251 Bde group for operation on right were returned at 10 AM and again covered their normal S.O.S lines. Trenches heavily shelled all day in the area of the attack. Sniping at small parties continued. The enemy now carries out any movements within range at the double.	
	28.		Enemy counter attacked our position we had taken from him and drove us out of the front line after shelling it very heavily + obliterating the trench.	

A5834 Wt. W4973/M687 750,000 8/16 D. D. & L. Ltd. Forms/C.2118/13.

Instructions regarding War Diaries and Intelligence Summaries are contained in F. S. Regs., Part II. and the Staff Manual respectively. Title pages will be prepared in manuscript.

WAR DIARY
or
INTELLIGENCE SUMMARY.
(Erase heading not required.)

250 (Northumbrian) Bde R.F.A. (T)
June 1917
Vol XXVII

Army Form C. 2118.

Place	Date	Hour	Summary of Events and Information	Remarks and references to Appendices
	28 (cont)		during the evening enemy's headquarters in a quarry were bombarded with chemical shell. Wagon lines visited by O.C. Brigade.	
	29.		A quiet day. Trenches shelled a little and one of the O.P.s blown in. This O.P. is well concealed & is in a shaft driven straight into a bank and then upwards with a loophole at the top; the whole being timbered out. A 5.9 hit one entrance & blew it in. The O.P. itself and the second entrance are all right.	
	30		A quiet day: the weather which has been fine for some time has suddenly changed to cold & wet	

Robert Chapman
Lieut Col
O.C. 250 Brigade RFA T

1 July 1917

A5834 Wt. W4973/M687 750,000 8/16 D. D. & L. Ltd Forms/C.2118/13.

Instructions regarding War Diaries and Intelligence Summaries are contained in F. S. Regs., Part II. and the Staff Manual respectively. Title pages will be prepared in manuscript.

WAR DIARY
or
INTELLIGENCE SUMMARY.
(Erase heading not required.)

Army Form C. 2118.

250 (NORTHUMBRIAN) BRIGADE. R.F.A. (T)

July 1917. Vol XXVIII

Page I

Place	Date	Hour	Summary of Events and Information	Remarks and references to Appendices
	July 1st		A cold windy day. Orders received that Right Infantry Brigade of 50th Div were to be relieved on night 1/2nd July by 21st Div and in consequence artillery zones would be readjusted. 250 Bde group zone is slightly extended N.wards and 251 Bde ~~dragged~~ closing up ~~from the~~ S of our zone ~~[illegible]~~. Only slight readjustment of battery zones required. Enemy field guns active on SACKDAW Trench which he can enfilade whilst is well clear of his own lines. Forward section of C/250 retaliated by enfilading NARROW TRENCH. Hows bombarded trench junctions. Some sniping on small parties during the day.	
	July 2nd		Hostile artillery more active on trench system. Some organised shoots on enemy's trenches were arranged & carried out.	
	3.		2.10 AM enemy opened heavy barrage on our front line & to the left slow rate of fire opened on S.O.S lines. No attack or raid was made on our front but battalion on left drove off raiding party and captured 2 prisoners. Trenches and back areas fairly quiet during day. Sniping of small parties carried out during afternoon with ~~success~~.	
	4.		Some persistent shelling of front system during the day. Some small bombardments organised in retaliation but these did not have the effect of stopping the hostile shelling.	

A5834 Wt. W4973/M687 750,000 8/16 D. D. & L. Ltd. Forms/C.2118/13.

Instructions regarding War Diaries and Intelligence Summaries are contained in F. S. Regs., Part II. and the Staff Manual respectively. Title pages will be prepared in manuscript.

WAR DIARY
or
INTELLIGENCE SUMMARY.
(Erase heading not required.)

250 (Northumbrian) Bde R.F.A. (T)

July 1917 Vol XXVIII

Army Form C. 2118.

PAGE II

Place	Date	Hour	Summary of Events and Information	Remarks and references to Appendices
	July 4 (contd)		Position for forward section of B/250 reconnoitred to the South from which Fontaine trench could be enfiladed at short range.	
	July 5.		Grouping of batteries altered. 250 Bde group loses D/162 - has A+B/162 attached in addition to C/162. Brigade zone is extended to the South as far as FONTAINE wood. The front covered by 6 18pdr + 1 4.5how battery being about 2000 yards. Almost every battery is short of one or two guns which are only being replaced very slowly.	
	July 6.		C.R.A visits Bde HQ + discusses question of separating batteries when the front is eventually covered by only a small amount of artillery.	
	July 7.		Information received that the enemy is digging saps out in front of his line on our front. A+B/162 ordered to fire intermittently on no mans land and the front line day + night in order to hinder the work. Hostile artillery fairly quiet.	
	July 8.		Fire on enemy front line + saps kept up during day and night. Registration carried out on NARROW trench in preparation for a bombardment to take place on 9th July in which heavy artillery and T.M.s are to take part.	
	July 9.		Quiet day, some hostile shelling near battery positions but no damage done	

A5834 Wt. W4973/M687 750,000 8/16 D. D. & L. Forms/C.2118/13.

Instructions regarding War Diaries and Intelligence Summaries are contained in F. S. Regs., Part II. and the Staff Manual respectively. Title pages will be prepared in manuscript.

WAR DIARY
or
INTELLIGENCE SUMMARY.
(Erase heading not required.)

250 (Northumbrian) Bde R.F.A (T)

July 1917. Vol XXVIII Page III

Army Form C. 2118.

Place	Date	Hour	Summary of Events and Information	Remarks and references to Appendices
	July 10		A quiet day; much sniping of small parties carried out by batteries with good effect.	
			Orders received that A, B & C/162 would be withdrawn on night 11/12th to wagon lines and that A/50 would be attached.	
	July 11.		Position of A/162 heavily shelled with 5.9 during morning, no casualties to personnel or guns. At 9 pm. A/162 B/162 & C/162 move out and A/50 is attached. The group now consists of 4 18/pdr + 1 4.5 how batteries to cover a front of approximately 2000 yards. S.O.S lines of batteries are so laid out that only dangerous portions of the front are covered by artillery. Position of A/162 heavily shelled as they withdrew.	
	July 12.		Enemy is digging saps out from FONTAINE trench; in order to hinder this work harassing fire is kept up day & night on the sap heads judging by aeroplane photographs showing one nights work previous to harassing fire and each nights work afterwards, the fire was most effective.	
			One section of A/50 moved to position vacated by C/162 in HENINEL. The intention is that each battery shall have a gun or section detached. This gun will be used for most of the ordinary day & night firing, in order to keep the main position quiet. If shelled the gun or section can easily be moved.	

A5834 Wt. W4973/M6-7 750,000 8/16 D. D. & L. Forms/C.2118/13.

Instructions regarding War Diaries and Intelligence Summaries are contained in F. S. Regs., Part II. and the Staff Manual respectively. Title pages will be prepared in manuscript.

WAR DIARY
or
INTELLIGENCE SUMMARY.
(*Erase heading not required.*)

250 (Northumbrian) Bde R.F.A. (T.F.)

Vol XXVIII July 1917.

Army Form C. 2118.

Page IV

Place	Date	Hour	Summary of Events and Information	Remarks and references to Appendices
	July 13.		A quiet day; little hostile shelling; very little movement seen behind the German lines.	
			A German aeroplane brought down just behind our front line. The two airmen being captured. The plane was heavily shelled by the enemy for the rest of the day.	
	July 14.		D/250 fired at 6. AM with aeroplane observation; This shoot was not a success; the battery did not fire owing to hostile aircraft being about. The plane went up again at 10. AM + again had difficulty in observing. At 6pm it was carried out successfully.	
	July 15.		A quiet day; very little shelling. At night D/250 bombarded points close behind the enemy's line with gas shell.	
	16.		Bombardment of new hostile work in front of FONTAINE trench carried out by D/250 in conjunction with 6" hows + heavy + medium trench mortars. Effects of this bombardment could not be seen as all the targets were invisible from our lines. Many stretcher cases seen being carried away as result of gas bombardment during the night.	
	"		The gas bombardment was repeated.	
	17.		Intermittent shelling of front line + supports throughout the day. At 10pm S.O.S lights were put up + fire opened. Rounds fell short but it was impossible to trace from which battery.	

A5834 Wt. W4973/ 750,000 8/16 D. D. & L. Ltd. Forms/C.2118/13.

Instructions regarding War Diaries and Intelligence Summaries are contained in F. S. Regs., Part II. and the Staff Manual respectively. Title pages will be prepared in manuscript.

WAR DIARY
or
INTELLIGENCE SUMMARY.
(Erase heading not required.)

250 (Northumbrian) Bde RFA. (T.F.)

Army Form C. 2118.

Vol XXVIII July 1917. Page V

Place	Date	Hour	Summary of Events and Information	Remarks and references to Appendices
	July 18		Nothing out of the usual in the morning. During the afternoon hostile artillery was active on our front line + supports during the afternoon. Considerable movement of small parties observed behind the German lines.	
	July 19		4.10 AM heavy hostile shelling of our line. 4.20 AM 1 S.O.S light noticed + slow rate opened. S.O.S rate started at 4.25. Later infantry reported enemy had attempted an attack but had failed leaving one dead Sgt Major in our hands. He belonged to a "STOSS TRUPP" and had a map showing the objective. Difficulty experienced in distinguishing the S.O.S signal.	
	July 20		Quiet day, normal shelling of trench area.	
	July 21		Quiet day; a lot of movement seen behind enemy lines. A new S.O.S signal tested at 10 pm, a rifle grenade bursting into 2 white + 2 green stars. This did not appear satisfactory, the green stars were outshone by the white and ~~the~~ it did not burst into stars until it had fallen too low, making it difficult to distinguish from the ordinary VERY light. On the whole the Red light which was unmistakeable when put up although fire was liable to be opened for German lights appears preferable.	
	July 22		Orders received that wire cutting must commence at 6 or 7 different points to assist a raid to be carried out about 25th. Preparations made by all batteries for observation and a few rounds fired by some batteries but without much success. Wire is difficult to observe and hidden in long grass + weeds	

Army Form C. 2118.

Instructions regarding War Diaries and Intelligence Summaries are contained in F. S. Regs., Part II. and the Staff Manual respectively. Title pages will be prepared in manuscript.

WAR DIARY
or
INTELLIGENCE SUMMARY.
(*Erase heading not required.*)

250 (Northumbrian) Bde RFA (T)

July 1917 Vol XXVIII Page VI

Place	Date	Hour	Summary of Events and Information	Remarks and references to Appendices
	July 23		Wire cutting continued during the day.	
			C.R.A visits the wagon lines during the afternoon.	
	July 24		Wire cutting continued during the day. Owing to grass and lie of the land wire is difficult to see; fair progress made at some points.	
	July 25		11AM point to be raided at night is bombarded by field & heavy artillery and heavy & medium T.M's, the latter using instantaneous fuzes to assist in cutting the wire. Wire cutting continued during the afternoon and gaps made in wire where it could be seen.	
			Arrangements made for an artillery officer to be in the parapet during the raid to assist in sending back signals etc to batteries.	
	July 26		12.30AM raiding party left our trenches without artillery assistance. If in difficulties O.C. raiding party would call for fire by putting up red lights, the signal would be passed on from parapet by succession of red & white lights. Unfortunately enemy put up one red light which was taken to be the signal from the raiding party and was repeated at the parapet. Batteries opened fire on the box barrage but were stopped after 10 mins on word being received that all was clear.	
			Raiding party entered trench but found it unoccupied and returned at 3.30.	
			Wire cutting continued during the day as another raid is to be carried out to attempt to get prisoners.	

A5834 Wt. W4973. 750,000 8/16 D. D. & L. Ltd. Forms/C.2118/13.

Instructions regarding War Diaries and Intelligence Summaries are contained in F. S. Regs., Part II. and the Staff Manual respectively. Title pages will be prepared in manuscript.

WAR DIARY
or
INTELLIGENCE SUMMARY.
(*Erase heading not required.*)

Army Form C. 2118.

250 (Northumbrian) Bde R.F.A. (T)

July 1917 Vol XXVIII Pest VII

Place	Date	Hour	Summary of Events and Information	Remarks and references to Appendices
	July 27		1 AM raiding party went out and batteries stood by; no call for fire was sent up and batteries stood down at 2.30. AM. Raiding party was driven off by bombs.	
			From 10 AM to 4 pm A/250 was heavily shelled by 8 inch + 5.9. enfilade extreme 2 casualties in A + 2 in D were caused but no guns hit. S.P. of A/250 was knocked in at one side.	
	July 28		Quiet day, considerable amount of sniping done in back areas and usual firing during the night.	
	July 29.		Dull misty day on which there was little activity on either side. Back areas quiet.	
	July 30.		C/251 return to action and receive the gun back which they had lent to A/250 the latter in addition lends another gun to them and one to B/251 preparatory to withdrawing from action on the night 31st/1st.	
	July 31.		Quiet day, visibility improving; A/250 hand over 2 guns to B/250 and withdraws to wagon line. O.P arrangements altered by withdrawal of A/250. Their O.P duties taken over by C/250.	
			Wagon lines visited by D.D.V.S.	
			Orders received at A/50 will be relieved on 2nd August by a battery of 290 Bde.	
			A/250 withdraw to wagon lines, their guns being taken over by B/250	

Robert Chapman, Lieut Col
OC 250 Bde R.F.A.T.

A5834 Wt. W4973 750,000 8/16 D. D. & L. Ltd. Forms/C.2118/13.

Instructions regarding War Diaries and Intelligence Summaries are contained in F. S. Regs., Part II. and the Staff Manual respectively. Title pages will be prepared in manuscript.

WAR DIARY
or
INTELLIGENCE SUMMARY.
(*Erase heading not required.*)

250 (NORTHUMBRIAN) BRIGADE R.F.A. (T) Army Form C. 2118.

~~July~~ August 1917

Vol ~~XXXIX~~ Vol 28

Place	Date	Hour	Summary of Events and Information	Remarks and references to Appendices
	Aug 1.		A quiet day.	
	Aug 2.		Half personnel of A/50 move off in the morning, the whole six guns being kept in action by the remaining half until the afternoon when half personnel of A/290 arrived. Very wet & cold day.	
	Aug 3.		Very wet & cold. The enemy's shelling has been noticeably less the last week or so, presumably the result of the attack in the North.	
	Aug 4		Another quiet but wet day. Orders received that an O.P. must be established in PLUM LANE and that forward section of c/250 will be withdrawn to main position.	
	Aug 5.		A/50 relieved by A/290, the latter taking over the S.O.S lines and tasks of the former.	
	Aug 6		A quiet day, orders received that A/290 forward section would relieve c/250 forward section, the latter being withdrawn to main position. Little shooting during the day owing to poor light.	
	Aug 7.		Forward section of c/250 relieved by forward section of A/290; tunnellers from 181 tunnelling coy who is working on deep dug outs remains at the position to continue the work.	
	Aug 8.		A quiet day, weather which has been bad is improving.	
	9 10		} quiet, poor visibility	

A5834 Wt. W4973/M6 750,000 8/16 D. D. & L. Ltd. Forms/C.2118/13.

Instructions regarding War Diaries and Intelligence Summaries are contained in F. S. Regs., Part II. and the Staff Manual respectively. Title pages will be prepared in manuscript.

WAR DIARY
or
INTELLIGENCE SUMMARY.
(Erase heading not required.)

Army Form C. 2118.

Place	Date	Hour	Summary of Events and Information	Remarks and references to Appendices
	Aug 11		Lt Dickinson proceeded on leave. Lt Hutchinson C/250 acting adjutant during his absence.	
	Aug 12		D/250 took part in bombardment of enemy trenches at U.1.b.5.5 to U.1.b.7.8 B/250 also fired on C.T.s in this vicinity	
	13		4 days slow bombardment of enemy trenches in O.26.c & a commenced at 8/am. howitzers to fire by day 2 18 pr batteries of this brigade to fire during the night. Weather unsettled & wet	
	14		G.O.C. VI Corps & G.O.C. R.A visited battery positions	
	15		A/250 came into action, returning from rest camp this afternoon	
	16		batteries ordered to wire themselves in.	
	17		weather greatly improved	
	18		HENINEL battery positions received considerable attention during the day from hun 5.9 Hows	
	19		C.R.A visited WANCOURT positions. weather much finer. Howitzers bombarded enemy TM emplacements during the day. TMs are proving troublesome at present.	
	20		A/290 withdrawn from line, & replaced by 108th A.F.A battery of 23rd A.F.A brigade.	
	~~21~~		a four days slow bombardment commenced today in which our 4.5 hows participated. two 18 pdr batteries are to fire on bombarded area by night.	
	21		bombardment continues.	

A5834 Wt. W4973/M687 750,000 8/16 D. D. & L. Ltd. Forms/C.2118/13.

Instructions regarding War Diaries and Intelligence Summaries are contained in F. S. Regs., Part II. and the Staff Manual respectively. Title pages will be prepared in manuscript.

WAR DIARY
or
INTELLIGENCE SUMMARY.
(Erase heading not required.)

Army Form C. 2118.

Place	Date	Hour	Summary of Events and Information	Remarks and references to Appendices
	Aug 22		a quiet day	
	23	3.15 pm	M.G.R.A Army visited battery wagon lines.	
	24			
	25		a quiet day	
	26	5 am	our 18 pdrs cooperated with trench mortar shoot on enemy front line enemy balloons which were up at the time evidently spotted the firing. between 7 and 11 am A & D batteries were heavily shelled with 5.9" & 4.2". D. battery suffered three casualties and had one howitzer put out of action. A battery had two guns completely destroyed and another slightly damaged & put temporarily out of action. C/250 also received attention but no damage resulted.	
	27, 28		stormy weather very strong wind, no artillery activity on either side	
	29		B/250 withdrew (personnel) to wagon lines for a rest, their position being taken over by A/250.	
	30		our howitzers co-operated with the heavies in a slow bombardment of enemy front line, which is to last for four days	
	31		a quiet day	

Robert Chapman Lieut Col
Sept 1. 1917 [illegible] Brigade R F A

A5834 Wt. W4973/M687 750,000 8/16 D. D. & L. Ltd. Forms/C.2118/13.

Instructions regarding War Diaries and Intelligence Summaries are contained in F. S. Regs., Part II. and the Staff Manual respectively. Title pages will be prepared in manuscript.

WAR DIARY
or
INTELLIGENCE SUMMARY.
(Erase heading not required.)

250 (Northumbrian) Bde RFA (T)

Army Form C. 2118.

Vol ~~XXX~~

~~August 1917~~ September 1917.

Vol 29

Place	Date	Hour	Summary of Events and Information	Remarks and references to Appendices
	Sept 1 } 2 }		a quiet day	
	3		"	
	4		Bombardment of enemy trenches commenced this is to last for 4 days. hours to fire by day 18 pdr battery to fire harassing fire by night. Gas was projected at 10 30 pm from our front lines.	
	5th		gas bombardment at 11am successfully carried out the target being TRIANGLE WOOD.	
	6th		enemy artillery extremely active in carrying out counter battery work B/250 was heavily shelled with 5.9s & 4.2s during the morning. One gun rather badly damaged, and another buried. no casualties!	
	7		Quiet day	
	8		Visibility poor; ammunition expenditure reduced to 400 rounds 18pdr by day and 75 rounds 4.5 how for the Bde	
	9		Quiet day with fog in morning. Hostile artillery has been extremely quiet for the last day or two. a little T.M fire in trenches.	
	10		O.C. A/177 Batty came to see position to be occupied by him when attached to 250 Bde for a small operation.	
	11.		a quiet day orders received for a support to be given by artillery to a daylight raid to be made by D.L.I. on 15th. One extra battery (C/177) is to be ~~attached~~ attached to 250 Bde	

A5834 Wt. W4973/M687 750,000 8/16 D. D. & L. Ltd. Forms/C.2118/13.

Instructions regarding War Diaries and Intelligence Summaries are contained in F. S. Regs., Part II. and the Staff Manual respectively. Title pages will be prepared in manuscript.

Army Form C. 2118.

WAR DIARY
or
INTELLIGENCE SUMMARY.
(Erase heading not required.)

250 (Northumbrian) Bde R.F.A. (T.)

Vol XXX September 1917.

Place	Date	Hour	Summary of Events and Information	Remarks and references to Appendices
	Sept 11		Quiet day; position for C/177 prepared by A/250 + ammunition brought up.	
	Sept 12		Wire cutting in front of support trench commenced by 108 Battery; this wire does not appear to be very thick in most places	
			For the barrage on the day of the raid, all forward sections are to be withdrawn to main positions so that barrage will be straight over the infantry.	
			C/177 occupy their position about 10 p.m.	
	Sept 13.		Wire cutting continued. Forward sections are brought back to main positions and 1 gun of A/Battery is loaned to B/250. Making number of guns available 24.	
	Sept 14		Wire in front of NARROW trench cut by T.M. bombardment in early morning supported by shrapnel.	
			Registration carried out as unobtrusively as possible on front to be raided, only flank guns of batteries tested to ensure there being no gaps in barrage.	
			Remainder of guns calibrated on datum points well clear of objective.	
	Sept 15		During morning position of B/250 was heavily shelled by 5.9s; fortunately no guns were hit + one man only was slightly wounded.	
			4.0 pm barrage opened in support of first phase of raid. Barrage reported excellent. ~~Enem~~ Very little resistance by enemy, who put down a fairly heavy barrage after about 4 mins. On flanks of raid there were dummies + smoke + Thermit barrages. Raid carried out by 9th D.L.I. who captured 26 prisoners. Killed 70	
			7.40 pm. ~~the~~ same barrage put down for second raid carried out by 8th D.L.I. which ~~one~~ found very few Germans in front line + took 1 prisoner	
	Sept 16		4 A.M. gas projected into ~~the~~ area previously raided and area swept by 18 pdrs.	
			11 AM to 3 pm B + C/250 heavily shelled by 5.9s latter having two guns hit.	
			During the evening guns were replaced in forward positions	

A5834 Wt. W4973/M687 750,000 8/16 D. D. & L. Ltd. Forms/C.2118/13.

Instructions regarding War Diaries and Intelligence Summaries are contained in F. S. Regs., Part II. and the Staff Manual respectively. Title pages will be prepared in manuscript.

WAR DIARY
or
INTELLIGENCE SUMMARY.
(Erase heading not required.)

250 (Northumbrian) Bde R.F.A. (T.)

Vol XXX Sept 1917.

Army Form C. 2118.

Place	Date	Hour	Summary of Events and Information	Remarks and references to Appendices
	Sept 17		B/250 + C/250 shelled during the day. Hostile Artillery slightly more active when raid had taken place.	
	Sept 18.		Hostile shelling of B + C/250 still continues; hostile battery cannot be located. Enemy appears to be making use of dummy flashes, as many flashes reported by R.F.C. are engaged by heavies without effect. No casualties to personnel owing to deep saps.	
	Sept 19.		Quiet day no hostile counter battery work.	
	Sept 20		Quiet day.	
	Sept 21.		B/251 return to action + in preparation for B/250 going out A/250 collect 1 gun from them + 1 from C/250.	
	Sept 22.		A/250 collect two more guns from main position of B/250 (which is then left empty) + move them to ~~the [illegible] position in WANCOURT~~ a position between WANCOURT + HENINEL where they already have 1 gun. C/250 take over forward position of B/250 B/250 withdraw to wagon lines. Batteries are now all split up in two or three positions to try to avoid so much counter battery work.	
	Sept 23.		Position of A/250 in which they have 3 guns is heavily shelled during morning fortunately there are no casualties to men or guns.	

Instructions regarding War Diaries and Intelligence Summaries are contained in F. S. Regs., Part II. and the Staff Manual respectively. Title pages will be prepared in manuscript.

WAR DIARY
or
INTELLIGENCE SUMMARY. Vol XXX

(*Erase heading not required.*)

250 (Northumbrian) Bde R.F.A. (T.F)

September 1917.

Army Form C. 2118.

Place	Date	Hour	Summary of Events and Information	Remarks and references to Appendices
	Sept 24.		Considerable hostile shelling during the day	
	Sept 25.		Quiet day; Bombardment of trenches opposite FONTAINE ~~&~~ bombarded with Hows.	
	Sept 26		Poor light nothing of importance to report.	
	Sept 27		Quiet day	
	Sept 28.		9th D.L.I made a small raid on enemy trench opposite FONTAINE wood; these were supported by C/250 who fired on trenches in vicinity of raid. One prisoner captured. Forward gun of A/250 hit & put out of action.	
	Sept 29.		Quiet day with poor light. Labour delegates from Birmingham were shown battery positions & O.Ps & entertained to lunch at Brigade H.Q.	
	Sept 30		A quiet day; a little hostile shelling of back areas. Battery positions visited by. M/CRA (Lt Col Moss Blundell D.S.O.) during the morning. Hostile artillery rather active on front line during afternoon.	

Sept 30 1917

Robert Chapman Lieut Col
250 Brigade R.F.A. T.F.

Instructions regarding War Diaries and Intelligence Summaries are contained in F. S. Regs., Part II. and the Staff Manual respectively. Title pages will be prepared in manuscript.

WAR DIARY or INTELLIGENCE SUMMARY.

(*Erase heading not required.*)

250 (NORTHUMBRIAN) BRIGADE R.F.A. T.F.

Army Form C. 2118.

October 1917

Vol XXXI

Vol 30

Place	Date	Hour	Summary of Events and Information	Remarks and references to Appendices
	Oct 1 Oct 2		} Quiet days.	
	3		B/250 take over position + duties of A/250. The latter move to wagon line but continue work on the new position.	
	4		Right infantry Bde (149) relieved by 153 Inf Bde.	
	5.		Quiet day. C.R.A. 51st Div. goes round positions.	
	6.		51 D.A. HQ take over from 50 D.A. H.Q. Batteries + Bde HQ remain in action. S.O.S lines are altered being evenly spread over the whole front + concentration arranged for on 4 sectors. Very wet + stormy day.	
	7.		Suggestions required by C.R.A. for regrouping of battery positions when relieving Bdes take over.	
	8.		Quiet day.	
	9.		Some men + 1 officer of 51st D.A arrive + are attached to batteries to learn about position which their batteries will occupy.	
	10		Work continued on light railway to C/250 + B/250 position so that it will be ready for incoming Bde. Work also continued on rebuilding B/250 position + on making sap at A/250 new position	
	11.		Considerable sniping on small parties of Bosch in back area.	

A5834 Wt. W4973/M687 750,000 8/16 D. D. & L. Ltd. Forms/C.2118/13.

Instructions regarding War Diaries and Intelligence Summaries are contained in F. S. Regs., Part II. and the Staff Manual respectively. Title pages will be prepared in manuscript.

WAR DIARY
or
INTELLIGENCE SUMMARY.
(Erase heading not required.)

250 (Northumbrian) Bde RFA (T)

Army Form C. 2118.

October 1917 Vol XXXI

Place	Date	Hour	Summary of Events and Information	Remarks and references to Appendices
	12 Oct		Quiet day. Orders received that 293 Army Bde RFA will take over from whole of 250 + 251 Bdes.	
	13 Oct		Quiet. Very wet + cold day.	
	14		Relief commenced C/250 is being relieved by A/293 remaining batteries are withdrawing. B/180 of 16 D.A. is attached to ~~Right~~ 250 Bde from 6pm. H.Q. 293 Bde are taking over H.Q. of 251 Bde. 4 guns C/250, 3 hows D/250 withdrawn.	
	15.		Remainder of D/250 withdraw, C/250 relief completed, B/250 withdraw. S.O.S lines covered by A/293 + B/180.	
	16		H.Q 250 Bde withdraw to wagon lines.	
	17 18 19 20		Spent in wagon lines waiting for new pieces to complete deficiencies + ~~for~~ in having ~~a~~ all stores + vehicles overhauled. Entraining orders received ~~last~~ on 19th for entraining on night 21/22	
	21.		Church Parade. First since BEHENCOURT in December 1917. Orders received at noon that Brigade + Battery commanders must travel by first train so that they may reconnoitre positions etc. 53 D.A to relieve 29 D.A. by 8 AM 24th. A/250 commenced entraining 7pm. at BEAUMETZ.	
	22.		Remainder of Bde entrained + travelled to PROVEN whence marched 18 Kilometres to wagon lines near ELVERDINGHE. Bde + Battery commanders ordered to proceed to positions at 3 AM 23rd.	

A5834 Wt. W4973/M687 750,000 8/16 D. D. & L. Ltd. Forms/C.2118/13.

Instructions regarding War Diaries and Intelligence Summaries are contained in F. S. Regs., Part II. and the Staff Manual respectively. Title pages will be prepared in manuscript.

WAR DIARY
or
INTELLIGENCE SUMMARY.
(Erase heading not required.)

250 (Northumbrian) Bde R.F.A. (T.F.)

Army Form C. 2118.

October 1917 Vol XXXI

Place	Date	Hour	Summary of Events and Information	Remarks and references to Appendices
	23.		Bde + Battery commanders reach positions by 5 AM and are followed by detachments, telephonists etc during the day; the last battery (D/250) relieving by 6 pm. They had only arrived at PROVEN 7 AM that day. Bde H.Q. took over 6 pm. + came under command of LEFT GROUP (34 D.A. H.Q.) of CENTRE ARTILLERY (H.Q. 50 D.A.) of XIV Corps covering 50th Div infantry. Battery positions practically in the open, only cover being 1 mebu per battery for officers + telephonists. Bde H.Q. close to batteries also in MEBUS. Batteries close to LANGEMARK in U22	Ref Map 28 + 20 1/40000
	24th		Orders received that 48 hours bombardment is commencing 6.30 AM for big attack to be made on 26th. About 5000 rounds per battery have to be brought up by pack, before the attack. A start made at once but there is a shortage of ammunition carriers. 2/Lt ASKWITH killed 4 O.R wounded.	
	25th		Further orders for bombardment + barrage received. Ammunition being brought up all day. Guns taken over were in very bad condition, also ammunition.	
	26th		Infantry attack 5.40 AM supported by barrage. No news was received from F.O.O until 11 AM when news was received that infantry had advanced part of way to objective but were held up by MEBUS + snipers. 149 Inf Bde made the attack + had heavy losses. Batteries were heavily shelled during barrage + had about 12 casualties. Later news was received that infantry had only isolated parties forward which were to withdraw to original line at night fall.	

A5834 Wt. W4973/M687 750,000 8/16 D. D. & L. Ltd. Forms/C.2118/13.

Instructions regarding War Diaries and Intelligence Summaries are contained in F. S. Regs., Part II. and the Staff Manual respectively. Title pages will be prepared in manuscript.

WAR DIARY
or
INTELLIGENCE SUMMARY. October 1917

250 (Northumbrian) Bde RFA (T) Army Form C. 2118.

Vol XXXI

(*Erase heading not required.*)

Place	Date	Hour	Summary of Events and Information	Remarks and references to Appendices
	27		A quiet day; spent in overhauling guns etc. Several out of action owing to the bad condition in which they were handed over. Reconnaissances made for O.Ps further S. than those used on 26th which were not very successful as line did not hold, owing to heavy shelling. Some firing carried out in bursts during the day & night.	
	28.		Orders received ~~that~~ to commence bombarding, chiefly by means of area shoots. Some gas shelling in neighbourhood of batteries during night.	
	29		Bombardment continued during day. Hostile shelling heavier during the day over back areas. Reconnaissances made for O.Ps but difficult to find any to which line could be kept up. Ammunition being packed up throughout day to increase dumps to 6000 per battery by midnight 30/31st Oct.	
	30.		Heavy barrage put down from 5.45 AM to 7.45 AM to assist operation by Division on right. No infantry action on our front. Heavy shelling of back areas during the day. Battery positions left alone. Bad weather during afternoon	

A5834 Wt. W4973/M687 750,000 8/16 D. D. & L. Ltd. Forms/C.2118/13.

Instructions regarding War Diaries and Intelligence Summaries are contained in F. S. Regs., Part II. and the Staff Manual respectively. Title pages will be prepared in manuscript.

WAR DIARY
or
INTELLIGENCE SUMMARY.
(Erase heading not required.)

250 (Northumbrian) Bde RFA (T.F.)

October 1917. Vol XXXI

Army Form C. 2118.

Place	Date	Hour	Summary of Events and Information	Remarks and references to Appendices
	31		4th E. Yorks make small advance at 2 A.M. without artillery support, batteries stand by in case of difficulties. Line advanced on front of 500 yds to depth of about 200. Very little firing during the day. Hostile artillery fairly quiet. Casualties have occurred daily in batteries in action + particularly to ammunition convoys. On still nights enemy bombards battery positions with gas + has caused casualties with it. Robert Chapman Lieut/Col 250 Bde RFA TF	

A5834 Wt. W4973/M687 750,000 8/16 D. D. & L. Ltd. Forms/C.2118/13.

Instructions regarding War Diaries and Intelligence Summaries are contained in F. S. Regs., Part II. and the Staff Manual respectively. Title pages will be prepared in manuscript.

WAR DIARY
or
INTELLIGENCE SUMMARY.
(Erase heading not required.)

250 (Northumbrian) Bde R.F.A. (T.F.)

Nov. 1917 Vol XXXII

Vol 31

Army Form C. 2118.

Place	Date	Hour	Summary of Events and Information	Remarks and references to Appendices
	Nov 1 Nov 2 Nov 3.		Orders received that little firing will be done & only 8 guns & 8 hows kept in action by the Bde. Remainder of personnel being withdrawn to wagon line. Amount of ammunition to be kept at positions is also reduced. Work to be done by batteries is thus very much reduced, the firing being gradually reduced to almost nothing. Visibility very poor & practically nothing has been done in the way of registration or calibration. Owing to heavy shelling it has been almost impossible to maintain a telephone line to an O.P. & register. Enemy artillery concentrates on area of batteries with gas shell each night usually firing about 1000 shells in 4/5 hours. Casualties from this have been heavy; apparently most cases occur through men getting gas while filling sandbags in ground that has been gas shelled, from their clothes, in one case from eating food that had been affected by it. Gas of mustard type was almost exclusively used. Practically no casualties have occurred while shelling was in progress. Casualties from shell fire have not been very heavy; but an unfortunately large proportion have been killed. Men who came to France with the Brigade have been particularly unfortunate.	

A5834 Wt. W4973/M687 750,000 8/16 D.D. & L. Ltd. Forms/C.2118/13.

Army Form C. 2118.

Instructions regarding War Diaries and Intelligence Summaries are contained in F. S. Regs., Part II. and the Staff Manual respectively. Title pages will be prepared in manuscript.

WAR DIARY
or
INTELLIGENCE SUMMARY.
(Erase heading not required.)

250 (Northumbrian) Bde
R.F.A. (T.F.)
Nov. 1917 Vol XXXII

Place	Date	Hour	Summary of Events and Information	Remarks and references to Appendices
	Nov 4.		Very heavy shelling of area including battery positions + Bde H.Q. chiefly in the form of area shoots. Practically no movement was possible throughout the day. Gas shelling at night was particularly intense.	
	Nov 5.		A quiet day; Orders received that grouping of Artillery was to be altered + that 250 Bde would be withdrawn to wagon line. Preparatory to this 4 guns + 1 how are withdrawn from 250 Bde position + handed to 251 Bde whose positions are further back. No gas near positions during night.	
	Nov 6.		Batteries assist an attack on right by putting down a barrage for 45 mins commencing at 6 AM on S.O.S lines. No shelling near positions to speak of. Further guns handed over to 251. + preparations made to leave only 4 guns with guard in our positions. During 14 days Bde has been in action in these positions it has suffered over 200 casualties.	

A5834 Wt. W4973/M687 750,000 8/16 D. D. & L. Ltd. Forms/C.2118/13.

Instructions regarding War Diaries and Intelligence Summaries are contained in F. S. Regs., Part II. and the Staff Manual respectively. Title pages will be prepared in manuscript.

WAR DIARY
or
INTELLIGENCE SUMMARY.
(*Erase heading not required.*)

Army Form C. 2118.

250 (Northumbrian) Bde
R.F.A. (T.F.)
Nov 1917 Vol XXXII

Place	Date	Hour	Summary of Events and Information	Remarks and references to Appendices
	Nov 7		Remaining personnel of Batteries & Bde HQ withdraw to W.L. a guard being left on 5 18 pdrs & How left in position. Orders received that Bde would return to action on 8th & 9th to replace. 60 reinforcements received in place of 20 casualties.	
	Nov 8.		One section per battery relieves sections of 83, 84, 85 & D/11 Batteries of 11th Army Bde positions in Langemarck. A lot of work had been done on these positions which are considerably better than those vacated.	
	Nov 9		Relief of Batteries & Bde HQ completed.	
	Nov 10		Barrage fired commencing 6.5 AM to assist attack on our right. Very wet day.	
	Nov 11		CRA visits Bde HQ. One gun per battery to be detached & do most of the firing if possible. As much ammunition as possible to be salved. Cover for men & guns to be made. 250 & 293 Bde HQ to command 8 batteries of the 2 Bdes alternately so that Bde HQ may be rested. Positions heavily shelled with gas during night. Harassing fire kept up during night.	
	Nov 12.		Fairly quiet morning, but heavy shelling round battery positions in afternoon. Brig-Gen Sandys C.R.A XIX Corps visited Bde HQ — considers O.P should be further forward. At present it is about 2000 yds from line.	

A5834 Wt. W4973/M687 750,000 8/16 D. D. & L. Ltd. Forms/C.2118/13.

Instructions regarding War Diaries and Intelligence Summaries are contained in F. S. Regs., Part II. and the Staff Manual respectively. Title pages will be prepared in manuscript.

WAR DIARY
or
INTELLIGENCE SUMMARY.
(Erase heading not required.)

Army Form C. 2118.

250 (Northumbrian) Bde RFA (T.F)

Nov 1917 Vol XXXII

Place	Date	Hour	Summary of Events and Information	Remarks and references to Appendices
	Nov 13		Heavy shelling of battery positions area	
	Nov 14		Take over command of 293 Bde Batteries in addition to 250 Bde Batteries. Bde zones remain the same the only difference being that the two Bdes are run by one Bde HQ. The intention is that Bde HQs will relieve each other weekly.	
	15, 16, 17		Normal days. Hostile shelling appears to be decreasing gradually, though still heavy at times & a good deal at nights. Harassing fire by night is carried out by us still at organized shell holes & tracks in rear of enemy lines. Ammunition about 300 18/pdrs & 100 How per Brigade per day.	
	18		Barrage put down on right at 7 AM. Otherwise quiet morning.	
	19, 20		Fairly quiet days, some shelling of tracks etc, but on the whole situation is becoming quieter.	
	21		HQ 293 Bde relieve HQ 250 Bde at 9 am & take over command of the 8 batteries of the 2 Bdes. HQ 250 Bde withdraw to a camp near wagon lines.	
	22 to 27		HQ at wagon lines batteries still in action where situation is getting quieter. Energies chiefly devoted to obtaining R.E material for wagon lines which is coming up well by light railway. Skilled R.E labour & unskilled black labour also lent to Bde wagon lines.	

A5834 Wt. W4973/M687 750,000 8/16 D. D. & L. Ltd. Forms/C.2118/13.

Instructions regarding War Diaries and Intelligence Summaries are contained in F. S. Regs., Part II. and the Staff Manual respectively. Title pages will be prepared in manuscript.

WAR DIARY
or
INTELLIGENCE SUMMARY.
(Erase heading not required.)

Army Form C. 2118.

250 (Northumbrian) Bde R.F.A. (T.F.)
Nov 1917 Vol XXXII

Place	Date	Hour	Summary of Events and Information	Remarks and references to Appendices
	28		HQ. 250 Bde relieve HQ. 293 & takes over command of 4 Batts of 250 Bde + 4 Batts of 293 Bde. Batteries are in same positions in which 293 Bde HQ took over & covering same S.O.S lines. While HQ 250 Bde have been out of the line the situation has become quieter & more work can now be done at Battery positions. Light on ~~[illegible]~~ this day good from 12 noon to 2 pm and some progress was made with calibration which owing to poor visibility and heavy shelling has not previously been satisfactorily done	
	29th		A fairly quiet day with ~~fairly~~ good visibility, especially between 2pm & 3pm. Calibration continued by batteries during the day. Harassing fire kept up in burst throughout night 29/30 including lethal shell from 4.5 hows	
	30th		Quiet day.	

Robert Chapman
Lieut Col

1 Nov 1917 250 Brigade RFA TF

A5834 Wt. W4973/M687 750,000 8/16 D. D. & L. Ltd. Forms/C.2118/13.

Instructions regarding War Diaries and Intelligence Summaries are contained in F. S. Regs., Part II. and the Staff Manual respectively. Title pages will be prepared in manuscript.

WAR DIARY
or
INTELLIGENCE SUMMARY.
(Erase heading not required.)

250 (Northumbrian) Bde R.F.A. (T.F.)

Vol XXXII Dec 1917

Army Form C. 2118.

Place	Date	Hour	Summary of Events and Information	Remarks and references to Appendices
	1 Dec.		Quiet day on the whole. Light Poor & little calibration possible. Remaining 2 hows of D/293 withdrawn to Wagon Line	
	2 Dec		2 AM. Barrage put down to assist attack by Division on Right. Orders received that Remaining batteries of 293 Bde are to withdraw on night 2/3 Dec. Orders sent to them to this effect. C & D/250 shelled during the day. S.O.S lines changed during day. Front of 17th Div now covered by 250 & 251 Bdes only.	
	3 Dec.		Quiet day with good light. Progress made with calibration of guns.	
	4 Dec.		Quiet day; poor visibility.	
	5 Dec		Quiet day with moderate visibility & hard frost. Hostile shelling has gradually quietened down recently & is now not noticeably heavy.	
	6th Dec.		Quiet day with better light; good progress made with calibration.	
	7 Dec		Poor light 50 D.A. H.Q. relieved by 58 D.A. H.Q.	
	8 Dec		Orders received that 291 Bde will relieve 250 Bde on nights 9/10 & 10/11 Dec.	
	9 Dec.		First sections of Batteries of 291 Bde come up to take over from 250 Bde also Bde Commander. A, C, & D 291 relieve A, C & D/250. B/250 occupies empty position near B/250.	
	10 Dec		Relief completed by 3pm. 291 Bde cover rather wider front than that covered by 250. 250 Bde withdraw to Wagon lines.	

A5834 Wt. W4973/M687 750,000 8/16 D. D. & L. Ltd. Forms/C.2118/13.

Instructions regarding War Diaries and Intelligence Summaries are contained in F. S. Regs., Part II. and the Staff Manual respectively. Title pages will be prepared in manuscript.

WAR DIARY
or
INTELLIGENCE SUMMARY.
(Erase heading not required.)

Army Form C. 2118.

250 (Northumbrian) Bde R.F.A. (T.F)

Vol XXXII Dec 1917

Place	Date	Hour	Summary of Events and Information	Remarks and references to Appendices
	11 Dec to 14 Dec		Spent in Wagon lines which had been made very comfortable by batteries, both for men + horses. Time spent in drilling the large proportion of reinforcements, many of whom are very poorly trained. Orders received on 13 to visit new camp to be occupied on 15th. There is absolutely no accommodation; but tents, without floor boards are being put up before our arrival remainder is to be done afterwards. This camp is to be kept for the Artillery in close support.	
	15 Dec		Wagon lines move to near POPERINGHE (VIII Corps). Turn out of all batteries quite good. Only one of the wagon lines is handed over to another battery, the remainder are left unoccupied in charge of area commandant. In Poperinghe area tents have been put up for personnel by Chinese labour + huts etc by advanced parties from batteries. As the weather has been very fine the camps and horse standings are in quite good condition.	
	Dec 16, 17		Work on camps continued; plans drawn up for camps for each battery. Gun drill gas drill + physical exercises carried out daily by batteries. Reinforcement gunners on the whole badly trained	

A5834 Wt. W4973/M687 750,000 8/16 D. D. & L. Ltd. Forms/C.2118/13.

Army Form C. 2118.

WAR DIARY
or
INTELLIGENCE SUMMARY.
(*Erase heading not required.*)

Instructions regarding War Diaries and Intelligence Summaries are contained in F. S. Regs., Part II. and the Staff Manual respectively. Title pages will be prepared in manuscript.

250 (Northumbrian) Bde R.F.A. T.F.
Vol XXXII Dec 1917.

Place	Date	Hour	Summary of Events and Information	Remarks and references to Appendices
	Dec 18.		Bde + battery commanders visit positions of 174 Bde in action near Zonnebeke which are to be taken over on 20 + 21st. Positions on the whole are poor, with very little accomodation. There appear to be far fewer MEBUS on this bit of line than near LANGEMARK. Batteries are firing at over 4000 yards but are within 1500 to 2000 yards of the line on a flank.	
	19		Wagon lines visited; these are poor + no work appears to have been done on them.	
	20		One section per battery relieves 1 section per battery of 174 Bde. Weather while at rest near Poperinghe has been frosty. The Horse lines have remained dry + men have had a good deal of leave to Poperinghe.	
	21		Remainder of batteries + H.Q. complete relief. Positions are not very much shelled + little firing is being done.	
	22.		Fine morning with good light. ~~which~~ Good progress made with calibration of guns which had not been very satisfactorily done with batteries which were relieved. A/250 heavily shelled in afternoon + 2 guns damaged No casualties to personnel.	

Instructions regarding War Diaries and Intelligence Summaries are contained in F. S. Regs., Part II. and the Staff Manual respectively. Title pages will be prepared in manuscript.

WAR DIARY
or
INTELLIGENCE SUMMARY.
(*Erase heading not required.*)

250 (Northumbrian) Bde R.F.A. (T.F.)
Vol XXXII Dec 1917.

Army Form C. 2118.

Place	Date	Hour	Summary of Events and Information	Remarks and references to Appendices
	Dec 23.		C.R.A. 50th Div accompanies Col Chapman on reconnaissance of reserve positions which could cover the corps reserve line along the ABRAHAM heights. Roughly from KEERSELARHOEK to GRAFENSTAFEL. Some permanent positions are chosen. Later orders are received that positions must be occupied on night 23/24 Dec. As selected positions cannot be occupied without considerable work being done, temporary positions on road running north from Fraezenburg are selected; + have to be occupied by 8 AM 24th. Arrangements are made for shifting guns and ammunition in the morning + work commenced on temporary positions. B/250 is to remain in present position attached to another group.	
	Dec 24		A, + D are in position by 8 AM. C/250 have difficulty in moving their guns out of their position owing to the plank road being very slippery ~~and~~ but are in action in temporary positions by 9.30 AM. Work is commenced on reserve positions which will be occupied as soon as possible.	
	Dec 25		Work continued on reserve positions.	

A5834 Wt. W4973/M687 750,000 8/16 D. D. & L. Ltd. Forms/C.2118/13.

Army Form C. 2118.

Instructions regarding War Diaries and Intelligence Summaries are contained in F. S. Regs., Part II. and the Staff Manual respectively. Title pages will be prepared in manuscript.

WAR DIARY
or
INTELLIGENCE SUMMARY.
(Erase heading not required.)

250 (Northumbrian) Bde
RFA (TF)
Vol XXXII Dec 1917

Place	Date	Hour	Summary of Events and Information	Remarks and references to Appendices
	26 Dec		Work continued on positions. It is hindered by very frosty state of the ground. The Mebus which are being cleaned out are full of dead British & Germans, otherwise they are in fairly good condition but very wet.	
	27 Dec		Work continued. Difficulty is found in making arrangements for R E material to come up by light Railway, as the trains are very irregular.	
	28 Dec		Work still continued. Ground still very hard. Visibility good & many hostile aeroplanes over.	
	29 Dec + 30 Dec		Work on positions continued. A partial thaw enabled drainage to be proceeded with under better conditions.	
	31 Dec		S.O.S. was sent up at 6.15 am on Right + Left Divisional fronts. Work on positions continued + ammunition transferred further forward to establish dumps of 300 rds per 18 Pr + 200 per 4.5 How to be ready when guns go in.	

Robert Chapman Lieut Col
250 Bde RFA TF

A5834 Wt. W4973/M687 750,000 8/16 D. D. & L. Ltd. Forms/C.2118/13.

APPENDIX NO 1

[illegible] D. A.

DETAILS OF ARTILLERY SUPPORT.

1. ORGANISATION.
Divisional Artillery supporting the [illegible] Division consists of 3 Brigades, [illegible] and [illegible] Bdes of [illegible] D.A. and the [illegible] Army Bde R.F.A. These are allotted Group numbers as follows:-

No. 1 Group. Lt.-Col. J.A.BUTCHART, [illegible] Army Bde RFA.
No. 2 Group. Lt.-Col. F.B.MOSS BLUNDELL. [illegible] R.F.A.Bde.
No. 3 Group. Lt.-Col. R.CHAPMAN, [illegible] R.F.A.Bde.

No.3 Group is at long range.

There are also reinforcing positions selected and prepared for two more Brigades R.F.A.

2. LIAISON ARRANGEMENTS.
See [illegible] D.A.G.Instructions No.[illegible] (already issued)

3. CONTROL.
(a) The whole of the Divisional Artillery is under the command of the B.G.R.A. [illegible] Division, who receives his orders from the G.O.C. of the Division.

(b) Subject to orders that may be issued from Div. H.Q. the Brigadier in the line arranges direct through his Liaison Officer for any special support that may be required and requires immediate action.

4. S.O.S.ARRANGEMENTS.
S.O.S. lines are shown on Map 'A' (already issued).
The point of junction of A/[illegible] and B/[illegible] barrages is [illegible].

Concentrations Right and Left are arranged as shown on Map 'B' (already issued)
The point of junction of A/[illegible] and B/[illegible] barrages in CONCENTRATION RIGHT is [illegible].

Rates of fire for S.O.S. as in [illegible] D.A.G.Instructions No.[illegible] :-

	18-pdrs.	4.5" Hows.
From time Signal is seen to plus 5 minutes.	3	[illegible]
From plus 5 minutes to plus 10 minutes.	2	1
From plus 10 minutes to plus 15 minutes.	1	[illegible]

5. MUTUAL SUPPORT D.A's RIGHT and LEFT.

Given to	Given by	Action.
[illegible] Div.	D.A. on right.	Their left Group opens on S.O.S.lines.
Div. on right.	[illegible] D.A.	Our Right Group opens on S.O.S. lines.
Div. on left.	[illegible] D.A.	Our left Group opens on S.O.S. lines.
[illegible] Div.	D.A. on left.	Their Right Group opens on S.O.S lines

6. COUNTER PREPARATION.

(a) This is put in force if a hostile bombardment of such a nature as would preface an attack commences.

(b) On the order "COUNTER PREPARATION" all 4.5" Hows. and 1/3 of 18-pdrs. will search dead ground and communications for 1000 yards grid EAST beyond their S.O.S. lines: remainder of 18-pdrs remain on their S.O.S. lines ready to fire. C/331 will normally be the 18-pdr battery to carry out searching fire as above.

(c) The order for counter Preparation on a Divisional Front is given by Div. H.Q. who report action taken to Corps H.Q.

(d) Corps H.A. have their own scheme for counter Preparation.

(e) Rates of fire for Div. Artillery :-

18-pdrs.	...	1 R.P.G.P. 3 minutes in bursts.
4.5" Hows.	...	1 R.P.H.P. 6 minutes in bursts.

507
31/12/17

Instructions regarding War Diaries and Intelligence Summaries are contained in F. S. Regs., Part II. and the Staff Manual respectively. Title pages will be prepared in manuscript.

WAR DIARY
or
~~INTELLIGENCE SUMMARY.~~
(Erase heading not required.)

Army Form C. 2118.

250 (Northumbrian) Bde
R.F.A. (T)
Vol XXXIII
Jany 1918
Vol 33

Place	Date	Hour	Summary of Events and Information	Remarks and references to Appendices
	1918 1 Jan		Work continued on positions	
	2 Jan		As it is probable that D Battery must move their Wagon Lines from the Asylum at Ypres work on new standings has been begun.	
			Lt Col Chapman D.S.O. has been ~~[illegible]~~ awarded the C.M.G.	
	3 Jan		Work continued on positions & new standings. Orders were received for No 3 Group (250 Bde less "B" battery) to exchange with No 1 Group (48 Bde A.F.A. with "B" 250).	
	4 Jan		One section each of A C & D Batteries relieved sections of A C & D 48 Bde in action. Section of B/250 changed with section of B/48	
	5 Jan		Two sections each of A, C & D Batteries relieved sections of A C & D 48 Bde in action. Headquarters 250 Bde exchanged with Headquarters 48 Bde who became No 3 Group. Relief complete at 10.30 a.m.	
	6 Jan		48 Brigade having been relieved by 119 Army Brigade B/48 has gone out of action - been replaced by B/119	
	7 Jan		One section of each battery of 250 Bde has been relieved by one section of ~~[illegible]~~ each battery of 156 Bde 33rd Div.	

A5834 Wt. W4973/M687 750,000 8/16 D. D. & L. Ltd. Forms/C.2118/13.

Instructions regarding War Diaries and Intelligence Summaries are contained in F. S. Regs., Part II. and the Staff Manual respectively. Title pages will be prepared in manuscript.

WAR DIARY
or
INTELLIGENCE SUMMARY.
(Erase heading not required.)

250 (Northumbrian) Bde R.F.A. (T)

Vol XXXIII Jany 1918

Army Form C. 2118.

Place	Date	Hour	Summary of Events and Information	Remarks and references to Appendices
	1918 Jan. 8		Relief by 156 Bde 33rd Div. was completed by 10 a.m. Brigade Headquarters removed to Poperinghe. The guns having been left in action the 18 Pr Batteries drew 6 guns each from the Corps Pool. The batteries remained at Wagon Lines.	
	9 Jan		Wagon lines were handed over to 33rd Divn. this Brigade moving to lines recently occupied in G.15 (Sheet 27 N.W.) near Poperinghe.	
	10 Jan		Working parties of 20 men per battery were sent up to build positions in Army Defence Line in [illegible].	
	11 Jan		Work on reserve positions continued.	
	12 Jan		Advance party of 29th Div. Art. arrived to take over camp occupied near Poperinghe.	
	13 Jan		Brigade moved from Wagon Lines at 8 a.m. travelling through Abeele and Steenvoorde to Oudezeele arriving at midday.	
	14 Jan		Brigade left Oudezeele at 9 a.m. travelling via Wemaers Cappel and Zuytpeene to Le Nieppe. Hard frost made travelling very difficult as the roads had been wet.	
	15 Jan		Left Le Nieppe at 8 a.m. travelling through Arques, Wizernes Clety to Thiembronne.	

A5834 Wt. W4973/M687 750,000 8/16 D. D. & L. Ltd. Forms/C.2118/13.

Instructions regarding War Diaries and Intelligence Summaries are contained in F. S. Regs., Part II. and the Staff Manual respectively. Title pages will be prepared in manuscript.

WAR DIARY
or
INTELLIGENCE SUMMARY.
(Erase heading not required.)

250 (Northumbrian) Bde R.F.A. (T) — Army Form C. 2118.

Vol XXXIII Jany 1918

Place	Date	Hour	Summary of Events and Information	Remarks and references to Appendices
	1918 16 Jan to 25th		Cleaning up commenced in training area and some alterations made in allotment of billets. A + C batteries get most of their horses under cover, ~~but~~ D/250 have their lines on a good sunken road, B/250 first use a road from which they are turned out, then a field which proved too muddy + then on another road. Weather for first 4 or 5 days was bad; but it then improved and training was proceeded with. Classes were held under Bde arrangements for N.C.Os and signallers.	
	26		Preparations made to move off on 27th. Billetting party sent forward. 10 G S wagons lent to Brigade from D.A.C to move surplus stores.	
	27		March from THIEMBRONNE to RENESCURE, about 21 miles. Very fine day for marching; no incidents. Arrived RENESCURE about 4.30pm where billets had been arranged. Horses stood on roads + in yards.	
	28		March continued to OUDEZEELE (12 miles) which was reached about 1pm. Road by which we were ordered to march was very bad in parts + ~~[illegible]~~ two detours had to be made. Batteries went to same billets ~~[illegible]~~ as on march down to THIEMBRONNE	

A5834 Wt. W4973/M687 750,000 8/16 D. D. & L. Ltd. Forms/C.2118/13.

Instructions regarding War Diaries and Intelligence Summaries are contained in F. S. Regs., Part II. and the Staff Manual respectively. Title pages will be prepared in manuscript.

WAR DIARY
or
INTELLIGENCE SUMMARY.
(Erase heading not required.)

250 (Northumbrian) Bde R.F.A. (T)
Vol XXXIII
January 1918

Army Form C. 2118.

Place	Date	Hour	Summary of Events and Information	Remarks and references to Appendices
	29th		March continued from OUDEZEELE to reserve ~~[illegible]~~ wagon lines near POPERINGHE.	
			One section per battery went forward in motor buses from OUDEZEELE to relieve one section per battery of the 156 Bde. Positions to be occupied are the same as those last occupied by the Brigade.	
			Motor buses were, as usual late, but relief of sections was complete soon after noon and Brigade + battery commanders visited positions.	
	30th		Relief of Batteries + Bde. H.Q. completed by noon. Wagon lines which were to have moved to near VLAMERTINGHE remained at POPERINGHE while stables of 33rd D.A. were disinfected against mange.	
	31st		Very little firing is to be done from present positions, only registration + observed shoots. Work is to be continued on present positions and reinforcing positions are also to be worked on.	
			Roughly, each battery is responsible for its own position and one reinforcing position.	
			One battalion liaison officer at Batt H.Q. + one F.O.O. is found.	

[illegible] Major
O.C. 250th Brigade R.F.A.

A5834 Wt. W4973/M687 750,000 8/16 D. D. & L. Ltd. Forms/C.2118/13.

Instructions regarding War Diaries and Intelligence Summaries are contained in F. S. Regs., Part II. and the Staff Manual respectively. Title pages will be prepared in manuscript.

WAR DIARY
or
INTELLIGENCE SUMMARY.
(Erase heading not required.)

250 (NORTHUMBRIAN) BRIGADE RFA (T.F)

Army Form C. 2118.

Vol XXXIV Feby 1918

Place	Date	Hour	Summary of Events and Information	Remarks and references to Appendices
	1st Feb.		Work on occupied and reinforcing positions proceeded with; material for them indented for on R.E. who are assisting. Difficulty experienced in getting the material to the positions. Too much is required ~~to be~~ for the amounts of G.S. wagons available to carry it and the light railways do not give ~~an~~ any assistance and will only deliver at certain points.	
	2nd Feb.		Visibility better than on previous days & some registration carried out. Work continued on positions. Some hostile shelling of B/250 position.	
	3rd Feb		Fine day with considerable aerial activity. Liaison & O.P. duties found by the Bde are as follows, Battalion Liaison Officer (F.O.O. during day) tour of duty 48 hours. F.O.O. Tunnel O.P. just S. of Passchendaele, tour of duty 24 hours. Bde L.O. alternately with 251 Bde, tour of duty 96 hours.	
	4th Feb		Quiet day; Heavy artillery bombarded hostile Division recently arrived from Russian front, little retaliation	
	5th Feb		Quiet day; fairly good visibility in the afternoon when registration was carried out by batteries.	
	6 Feb. 7 " 8 " 9 "		Quiet days with fairly good visibility. Calibration was difficult owing to high winds. The enemy shows himself extraordinarily little during the day. Work continued on positions and on approach to the O.P.	

A5834 Wt. W4973/M687 750,000 8/16 D. D. & L. Ltd. Forms/C.2118/13.

Instructions regarding War Diaries and Intelligence Summaries are contained in F. S. Regs., Part II. and the Staff Manual respectively. Title pages will be prepared in manuscript.

WAR DIARY
or
INTELLIGENCE SUMMARY.
(*Erase heading not required.*)

250 (Northumbrian) Bde R.F.A. (T.F) Vol XXXV Feby 1918

Army Form C. 2118.

Place	Date	Hour	Summary of Events and Information	Remarks and references to Appendices
	10 Feby		Infantry of 50 Div hand over 500 yards of the N. of the line to 27th Div and take over 1000 yards from 66th Div on the South. As a result S.O.S lines are altered; Brigade now covers about 1200 yards. On the Southern end the right group has a battery superimposed on 250 Bde Front.	
			The same O.P is used and O.P & battery arrangements remain the same.	
	11 Feb.		Quiet ~~day~~ morning. 600 106' Fuzes on 18pdr shells allotted to the Bde for trial; These were tested on various points, they did not appear to give particularly good bursts. The shelling roused the enemy after the quiet of some weeks and led to some retaliation. In reply we fired some concentrations during the evening	
	12.		Quiet day, poor visibility	
	13th / 14th		Quiet days, fair visibility.	
	15 / 16		Quiet days; tests with 106 Fuzes for 18pdrs were continued they were found to range about 50/75 yards short of H.E. with 101 fuze at ranges varying from 4000/4500. Hostile artillery slightly more active	

Instructions regarding War Diaries and Intelligence Summaries are contained in F. S. Regs., Part II. and the Staff Manual respectively. Title pages will be prepared in manuscript.

WAR DIARY
or
INTELLIGENCE SUMMARY.
(*Erase heading not required.*)

250 (Northumbrian) Bde R.F.A. (T.F.)

Vol XXXV Feby 1918.

Army Form C. 2118.

Place	Date	Hour	Summary of Events and Information	Remarks and references to Appendices
	17th		Hostile artillery fairly active during the day. Visibility good but no movement observed. During the evening our battery positions were shelled with gas. A concentration with Gas shell by our batteries had the desired effect	
	18th		Heavy bombardment ~~on the~~ near POLYGON woulds from 5.30 AM to 6 AM It did not spread to our front.	
	19		Quiet day	
	20		Bde HQ. and batteries visited by VIII Corps Commander Lt-Gen HUNTER WESTON.	
	21		Quiet ~~day~~ morning C/250 shelled in after noon with 4.2s + 5.9. Preparations made for relief by 162 Bde.	
	22		First sections of relieving Bde arrive. 162 Bde H.Q arrive.	
	23		Relief by 162 Bde completed; remainder of personnel from gun positions ~~to~~ catch up wagon lines at OUDEZEELE, where wagon lines had moved on previous day.	
	24.		March continued to RENESCURE. ~~Very~~ Fine day + good turn out by batteries.	
	25		March continued to ELNES. Wet + stormy morning, but cleared up later. Billets at ELNES rather poor.	

Army Form C. 2118.

Instructions regarding War Diaries and Intelligence Summaries are contained in F. S. Regs., Part II. and the Staff Manual respectively. Title pages will be prepared in manuscript.

WAR DIARY
or
INTELLIGENCE SUMMARY.
(*Erase heading not required.*)

250 (Northumbrian) Bde R.F.A. (T.F)

Vol XXXV Feby 1918.

Place	Date	Hour	Summary of Events and Information	Remarks and references to Appendices
	Feb 26.		March continued to THIEMBRONNE; beautiful day; turn out still good in spite of long marches + bad weather on 25th. THIEMBRONNE was reached at 11 A.M.	
	Feb 27.		Cleaning up; Section training commenced. G.O.C. Division visited Batteries during afternoon.	
	Feb 28		Training continued.	

[illegible] Major.
250 Bde R.F.A.

(A7092). Wt. W12839/M1293. 750,000. 1/17. D. D. & L., Ltd. Forms/C.2118 14

50th Divisional Artillery.

250th (Northumbrian) BRIGADE R. F. A.

M A R C H   1 9 1 8

Instructions regarding War Diaries and Intelligence Summaries are contained in F. S. Regs., Part II. and the Staff Manual respectively. Title pages will be prepared in manuscript.

WAR DIARY
or
INTELLIGENCE SUMMARY.
(*Erase heading not required.*)

250 (NORTHUMBRIAN) BRIGADE Army Form C. 2118.
R.F.A. (T.F)
Vol XXXVI March 1918.
Vol 35

Place	Date	Hour	Summary of Events and Information	Remarks and references to Appendices
	March 1st to 7th		Training carried out in neighbourhood of Thiembronne. Ground very suitable for the purpose. Several fairly large stretches of stubble have not yet been ploughed out and are suitable for driving drill + manoeuvres.	
	8th		Orders received in the early morning that D.A would entrain near ST. OMER on the 9th first train leaving at 2·30pm. Destination near AMIENS. Necessary preparations for the move made.	
	9th		H.Q. + Batteries entrain at 3 hours interval at ARQUES about 20 miles from THIEMBRONNE. Train journey of about 9 hours ends at LONGEAU a French military station outside AMIENS where the detraining facilities are very good. A march of 9 miles follows to HANGARD which is reached by H.Q. at 6 AM on the morning of the 10th	
	10th		Batteries arrive at 3 hour intervals during the day.	
	11th		Spent in resting + cleaning up at HANGARD.	
	12th		March from HANGARD to BRAY where billets are very dirty and rather inadequate. Accommodation for horses good. Orders are to be in readiness to move at short notice.	

(A7092). Wt. W12839/M1293. 750,000. 1/17. D. D. & L., Ltd. Forms/C.2118 14.

Instructions regarding War Diaries and Intelligence Summaries are contained in F. S. Regs., Part II. and the Staff Manual respectively. Title pages will be prepared in manuscript.

WAR DIARY
or
INTELLIGENCE SUMMARY.
(*Erase heading not required.*)

250 (Northumbrian) Bde R.F.A. (T.F)

Vol XXXVI March 1918.

Army Form C. 2118.

Place	Date	Hour	Summary of Events and Information	Remarks and references to Appendices
	13th } 14th }		Spent at BRAY, mostly in cleaning up billets. Some training done with battery staffs.	
	15th		Orders received at 6 AM that Bde is to move to BRUSLE area near PERONNE on the 15th. March begun at 11.30 and BUIRE reached 7 pm.	
	16th		Batteries are billetted in NISSEN huts and horses in good covered standings. Training is to continue.	
	17th		Sunday; No work of importance done.	
	18th } 19th }		Training continued. Ground is very suitable. Large expanse of open rolling ground.	
	20th		3 officers per HQ and Batteries are taken forward to reconnoitre positions for counter attack by the Division in case of Army battle zone being in danger.	
	21st		Heavy German bombardment heard to commence at 4.30 AM. Stood by during day and at 5pm received orders that batteries would move into action under 66th D.A when the line had been pushed back from HARGICOURT to near ~~MONTIGNY~~ HESBECOURT. Batteries occupied positions in the dark	
	22nd		Enemy attacked about 6 AM in dense fog and advanced steadily. Fire opened on S.O.S lines but no observation was possible.	

(A7092). Wt. W12839/M1293. 750,000. 1/17. D. D. & L., Ltd. Forms/C.2118/14.

Instructions regarding War Diaries and Intelligence Summaries are contained in F. S. Regs., Part II. and the Staff Manual respectively. Title pages will be prepared in manuscript.

WAR DIARY
or
INTELLIGENCE SUMMARY.
(Erase heading not required.)

250 (Northumbrian) Bde R.FA (T.F)

Vol XXXVI March 1918.

Army Form C. 2118.

Place	Date	Hour	Summary of Events and Information	Remarks and references to Appendices
	22nd		About 10 AM enemy were reported close in front of positions and batteries were moved to positions about 1000 yds W. of NOISBECOURT FARM. When this position had only been occupied about 2 hours orders were received that batteries were to take up positions near CARTIGNY although enemy were not yet near NOISBECOURT. ~~The~~ Positions taken up & communications established with 50th Div infantry who had come into the line with H.Q near BEAUMETZ. Enemy captured NOISBECOURT FARM about 7pm after several attempts.	
			9pm batteries moved back to positions near LE CATELET.	
	23rd		5 AM Orders received that 2 Batts of 250 Bde was to cross river SOMME at BRIE to cover Bridgehead while remaining batteries fought rearguard action. Very heavy traffic on road to BRIE where river was crossed about noon by leading batteries & about 2pm by remainder. Infantry crossed & bridges satisfactorily demolished by 4pm. Positions were taken by batteries near BARLEUX. On the whole the impression was given that retirement of ~~both~~ artillery was carried out earlier than necessary. Some good targets engaged during afternoon when enemy came down towards banks of the SOMME. Almost exactly a year ago the Brigade had followed enemy across same bridges in his retreat.	

Instructions regarding War Diaries and Intelligence Summaries are contained in F. S. Regs., Part II. and the Staff Manual respectively. Title pages will be prepared in manuscript.

WAR DIARY
or
INTELLIGENCE SUMMARY.
(Erase heading not required.)

250 (Northumbrian) Bde R.F.A. (T.F.)

Vol XXXVI March 1918

Army Form C. 2118.

Place	Date	Hour	Summary of Events and Information	Remarks and references to Appendices
	24th		Enemy made several attempts to cross the river but did not succeed. Battery positions moved back towards BELLOY to get more cover. Some heavy area shelling by the enemy. Continuous fighting near bridge heads. Late at night batteries moved across to S. side of BELLOY to relieve congestion on roads	
	25th		Enemy succeeded in crossing river at ETERPIGNY and forming bridgehead. During morning he succeeded in getting fairly large numbers across and attacked towards BARLEUX + VILLERS CARBONNEL. Heavy fighting continued throughout day. Observation difficult during morning owing to fog but improved later. Great deal of useful information received from F.O.Os during day. About 6pm enemy took ridge about VILLERS CARBONNEL. Batteries were withdrawn to near FOUCAUCOURT and infantry took up line ~~near~~ from ESTREES to ASSEVILLERS. Major ANGUS + 2/Lt Ferguson wounded. About 12 casualties O.R.	
	26th		Early in the morning batteries were ordered to occupy positions ~~near~~ in RAINECOURT to cover withdrawal of infantry to line N+S through FOUCAUCOURT. Later batteries moved to positions S. of HARBONNIERES to cover line to be taken up + fought for running through FRAMERVILLE, VAUVILLERS to ROSIERES. Line occupied during afternoon.	

(A7092). Wt. W12839/M1293. 750,000. 1/17. D. D. & L., Ltd. Forms/C.2118/14.

Instructions regarding War Diaries and Intelligence Summaries are contained in F. S. Regs., Part II. and the Staff Manual respectively. Title pages will be prepared in manuscript.

WAR DIARY
or
INTELLIGENCE SUMMARY.
(*Erase heading not required.*)

Army Form C. 2118.

[illegible] R.F.A. (T.F.) Vol XXXVI March 1918

Place	Date	Hour	Summary of Events and Information	Remarks and references to Appendices
	27		Enemy attacked during morning & was several times repulsed. He succeeded in pushing through near VAUVILLERS about 4pm and seemed to be going on. A counter attack succeeded in driving him back through VAUVILLERS. He attacked again in the evening and succeeded in pushing forward some distance in spite of counter attacks. Batteries had to be withdrawn to GUILLAUCOURT. It was expected that the line would be fought for again next day.	
	28		Orders received early in the morning that batteries were to move southwards & take up positions to cover withdrawal to CAIX – HARBONNIERES line. These positions were taken up but withdrawal was continued later in the day through BEAUCOURT down to MOREUIL where river was crossed. Situation was critical for part of the time; Batteries had to occupy several positions. Sections were usually left behind and had some good shooting over the open sights. Line held by 50th Div taken over by French in the evening.	
	29		Positions occupied between MOREUIL and HOURGES to cover infantry who were holding line in front of MEZIERES. During afternoon enemy advanced & positions were taken up near DOMART.	

(A7092). Wt. W12839/M1293. 750,000. 1/17. D. D. & L., Ltd. Forms/C.2118/14

WAR DIARY
or
INTELLIGENCE SUMMARY.
(Erase heading not required.)

Army Form C. 2118.

Instructions regarding War Diaries and Intelligence Summaries are contained in F. S. Regs., Part II. and the Staff Manual respectively. Title pages will be prepared in manuscript.

250 (North[illegible]) Bde
R.F.A. (T.F.)
Vol XXXVI March 1918.

Place	Date	Hour	Summary of Events and Information	Remarks and references to Appendices
	30.		Enemy attacked again and pushed forward. Batteries had been moved N. of R. LUCE before attack began but had to withdraw further during the day. The position improved later and they advanced again to positions near HANGARD. During day 50 Div infantry were withdrawn & we covered infantry of 18th Div.	
	31st		During morning batteries were pushed forward slightly and position remained unchanged. During afternoon enemy remained quiet on our front but attacked to the South and advanced up to the valley of the LUCE thus obtaining observation of our positions. Positions reconnoitred for move in morning as present positions are too far off to cover left but are in view from the right.	

[signature] Major
Comdg. 250 Bde RFA (T)

50th Divisional Artillery.

250th (Northumbrian) BRIGADE R.F.A.

APRIL 1918.

50/

Army Form C. 2118.

Instructions regarding War Diaries and Intelligence Summaries are contained in F. S. Regs., Part II. and the Staff Manual respectively. Title pages will be prepared in manuscript.

WAR DIARY
or
INTELLIGENCE SUMMARY.
(Erase heading not required.)

250 (NORTHUMBRIAN) BDE R.F.A. (T.F)

Vol XXXVII April 1918

Vol 36

PAGE I

Place	Date	Hour	Summary of Events and Information	Remarks and references to Appendices
	1		Batteries were moved nearer to GENTELLES, one battery N.W of the village remainder S.E. B/47 attached to the Bde and moves into action close to other batteries. Day fairly quiet on our front, but the enemy advanced S. of the R. LUCE and took ground from which the battery positions are almost in view.	
	2.		Quiet on our front which runs from HANGARD northwards towards MARCELCAVE. Some activity on the Right S. of R. LUCE where British Cavalry attacked in early morning and retook RIFLE wood on the AMIENS – ROYE road S. of HOURGES. 54th Inf Bde whom we cover attempted to advance their line N.E of HANGARD under cover of barrage, but were held up by M.G. fire. During the night the French take over the line immediately S of our front.	
	3.		Quiet day. Hostile Artillery active during the afternoon	
	4.		Enemy attacked on right and left in the early morning, but no attack took place on our front. Battery positions were heavily shelled ~~and~~ from 5AM to noon with shells of all sizes	

Instructions regarding War Diaries and Intelligence Summaries are contained in F. S. Regs., Part II. and the Staff Manual respectively. Title pages will be prepared in manuscript.

WAR DIARY
or
INTELLIGENCE SUMMARY.
(Erase heading not required.)

250 (NORTHUMBRIAN) BDE, R.F.A. (T.F.)

Vol XXXVII April 1918.

Army Form C. 2118.

PAGE II

Place	Date	Hour	Summary of Events and Information	Remarks and references to Appendices
	4		Communication was maintained with the O.P. and many good targets were engaged with observation; a gun brought up close to the enemy front line was engaged and an advanced trench occupied by the enemy was cleared.	
			During the afternoon a heavy barrage was put down on our front line and the enemy attacked towards HANGARD + BOIS DE HANGARD. He advanced a short distance and occupied eastern part of BOIS DE HANGARD.	
			Fire was maintained by batteries throughout the day, between 800 + 1000 rounds per battery being expended.	
			D/250 was in an advanced position within about 2000 yards of the enemy throughout the day and fired a gas concentration in addition to much observed and harassing fire with H.E.	
			During the day Lt Col CHAPMAN CMG. D.S.O was wounded, also 16 O.R and about 20 horses were killed and wounded.	
			3 guns were put out of action with direct hits. Communication was maintained throughout the day and valuable information received from them and targets of opportunity engaged with direct observation.	
	5.		Quiet morning; weather still wet and ground now very soft–	

Army Form C. 2118.

Instructions regarding War Diaries and Intelligence Summaries are contained in F. S. Regs., Part II. and the Staff Manual respectively. Title pages will be prepared in manuscript.

WAR DIARY
or
INTELLIGENCE SUMMARY.
(*Erase heading not required.*)

250 (NORTHUMBRIAN) BDE R.F.A. (T.F)

Vol XXXVII April 1918

PAGE III

Place	Date	Hour	Summary of Events and Information	Remarks and references to Appendices
	5		and cut up by the heavy traffic, making supply of ammunition difficult. Fire was kept up on roads and places of assembly throughout the day. Communication with the O.P. was only moderately maintained through the day and little observed fire was carried out.	
			Ammunition expenditure amounted to over 1000 rounds per battery. An enemy attack in the direction of HANGARD at about 6 pm made little progress.	
			2/Lt STOCKDALE D/250 wounded.	
	6.		Very wet & fairly quiet day. Many good targets of opportunity engaged during the day by Lt HUTCHINSON who maintained communication from forward O.P to batteries during nearly the whole day. Major Wilkinson was wounded badly in the evening and died later.	
	7.		Australians whom we cover made a local attack to regain BOIS DE HANGARD; the attack succeeded & 63 prisoners were taken but later the Germans counterattacked and retook the ground. Remainder of the day was fairly quiet with poor observation.	
	8.		Heavy enemy shelling during the early morning followed by quiet day. Bde relieved at 7 pm by 169 A.F.A. Bde & moves to BOVES for the night.	

Instructions regarding War Diaries and Intelligence Summaries are contained in F. S. Regs., Part II. and the Staff Manual respectively. Title pages will be prepared in manuscript.

WAR DIARY
or
INTELLIGENCE SUMMARY.
(Erase heading not required.)

250 (NORTHUMBRIAN) BDE. R.F.A (T.F)

Vol XXXVII April 1918

Army Form C. 2118.

PAGE IV

Place	Date	Hour	Summary of Events and Information	Remarks and references to Appendices
	9.		Bde moves from BOVES to PONT DE METZ via AMIENS. Easy march on foggy day. Horses thin + everybody + everything very dirty.	
	10		Bde moves from PONT DE METZ at 4.15 AM via AMIENS, VIGNACOURT, DOMART EN PONTHIEU to FRANSU, a distance of 27 miles; FRANSU reached at 3.30 pm. A good day for marching. Horses stood the long march well, considering the hard work they have had recently. A halt of 2 hours was made at DOMART when horses were watered + fed + men had their dinners. All men very tired + sleepy after the hard work and little sleep of past 3 weeks.	
	11th		Marched from FRANSU (8 AM) to BOUBERS (abt 17 miles) ~~which~~ was reached about 3 pm; roads crowded with transport. Beautiful day for marching; billets fairly good	
	12		Marched from ~~FRAN~~ BOUBERS to VALHUON via ST POL. On arrival at VALHUON at 1 pm were ordered to march on to SACHIN near PERNES. Halted for 2 hours at VALHUON to water + feed + give men a meal; then proceeded to SACHIN, a distance of about 5 miles + arrived 5.30 pm. Billets, horse lines + watering facilities good.	
	13.		Marched at 8.45 AM to ST HILAIRE about 10 miles. On arrival at 12 noon found our destination had been altered to RELY which was reached about 1.30 pm. Very little accommodation + poor watering.	

(A7092). Wt. W12839/M1293. 750,000. 1/17. D. D. & L., Ltd. Forms/C.2118/14.

Instructions regarding War Diaries and Intelligence Summaries are contained in F. S. Regs., Part II. and the Staff Manual respectively. Title pages will be prepared in manuscript.

WAR DIARY
or
INTELLIGENCE SUMMARY.
(Erase heading not required.)

250 (NORTHUMBRIAN) BDE R.F.A. (T.F.) Vol XXXVII April 1918.

Army Form C. 2118.

PAGE V

Place	Date	Hour	Summary of Events and Information	Remarks and references to Appendices
	14		Ordered to reconnoitre positions near GONNEHEM occupied by 158 Bde which Bde was ordered to relieve on night 14/15. After ~~order~~ reconnaissance was finished ~~we~~ were informed that orders were cancelled and that batteries were to be attached to Bdes covering 3rd Div. A+B are attached to 42nd Bde, C+D to 40th Bde and move into action late on 14th near BETHUNE. Bde H.Q. are not in the line and billet for night at BURBURE. (D. Batt'y wagon reached there [illegible] at 8 a.m.)	
	15.		Batteries remain in action; positions comfortable + quiet. Bde HQ move to MARLES LEZ MINES.	
	16		Reinforcements to bring Batteries up to strength arrive, 117 in all, and men overdue from ~~leave~~ leave also rejoin (55) Some stores arrive and indents for remainder submitted to Ordnance 1st Corps Troops.	
	17 18 19 20 21		Brigade H.Q. remains at MARLES LEZ MINES + batteries remain in action attached to 3rd D.A. On the whole the batteries have fairly quiet time, + do a good deal of firing. Lt SMITTON badly wounded on the 18th.	[signature] Lt. Col. 250 Bde R.F.A.
	22 to 27		Batteries remain in action attached to 40th + 42nd Bdes; the positions are fairly comfortable. Bde H.Q. remain at MARLES + are used for reconnoitring battery positions for rear lines of defence to cover BETHUNE.	

(A7092). Wt. W12839/M1293. 750,000. 1/17. D. D. & L., Ltd. Forms/C.2118/14.

Army Form C. 2118.

Instructions regarding War Diaries and Intelligence Summaries are contained in F. S. Regs., Part II. and the Staff Manual respectively. Title Pages will be prepared in manuscript.

WAR DIARY
or
INTELLIGENCE SUMMARY

(Erase heading not required.)

250 (NORTHUMBRIAN) BDE R.F.A. (T.F)
Vol XXXVII April 1918

PAGE II

Place	Date	Hour	Summary of Events and Information	Remarks and references to Appendices
	28		One section per battery is relieved by sections of 14th D.A. on night 28/29. Sections when relieved march to AMETTES.	
	29.		Remainder of batteries relieved & move to AMETTES. Bde HQ move from MARLES to AMETTES	
	30.		Batteries & Bde H.Q. entrain from PERNES at 3 hours intervals for journey of about 30 hours duration. Two days train rations are taken.	

[signature] Lt. Col
250 Bde R.F.A. (T)

2449 Wt. W14957/M90 750,000 1/16 J.B.C. & A. Forms/C.2118/12.

50th Division

W A R   D I A R Y

250th BRIGADE R. F. A.

M A Y 1918

WAR DIARY 250 (Northumbrian) Bde RFA (T.)

May 1918. Vol XXXVIII Vol 37

Date		
May	1	HQ + Batteries detrained at FISMES + marched to UNCHAIR where billets + horse lines were good.
	2, 3 + 4	Remained at UNCHAIR; some training done and good grazing found for horses.
	5.	Marched via FISMES + MERVAL to SERVAL where billets were again good.
	6.	Bde + Battery commanders went forward to reconnoitre battery positions N of PONTAVERT on the AISNE which were to be taken over from the French.
	7.	Reconnaissance continued; Wagon lines are at Glennes where standings + camps are good
	8.	Relief commenced. Each of the 3 French batteries of the 1st Group 215th French Regt of Artillery pull out one section; A/250 put in one section, B/250 one section in main position + one section detached; C/250 + D/250 each put 4 guns in unoccupied positions. HQ, A, B + D are all in the BOIS de BEAUMARAIS + C/250 are in the open to the S.E of it
	9.	Registration of guns in action carried out. Relief completed by 9 p.m. A/250 put 2 more guns in main position + 2 detached in same position as B/250 detached section, B/250 put 2 more in their main position, + C + D each put 2 more guns in their positions. Command passes on completion of relief. A Liaison officer is found with 151 Inf Bde whose front is covered by 250 Bde. It extends from ~~CRA~~ CHEVREUX to SE of CORBENY about 3000 yds. Bde O.P on Butte d'Edmond is manned throughout 24 hours by batteries in turn. In addition each battery mans an O.P during daylight. Observation is good.
	10 to 25.	Quiet. Very little shelling by either side; a few small raids made. Practically no ~~shelling~~ movement by the enemy observed.

WAR DIARY

250 (Northumbrian) Bde R.F.A. (T)
May 1918. Vol XXXVIII

May 26. News received that enemy would probably make an attack on the 27th. Harassing fire was carried out from 9pm onwards.

May 27. At 1 AM ~~today~~ enemy bombardment commenced. All lines went down ~~and~~ within 15 mins. Bombardment was very heavy on all forward area & on battery positions & H.Q. S.O.S went up about 4 AM.

No information was received as to the position of infantry ~~&~~ or state of batteries, orderlies sent out ~~did not get~~ were almost invariably missing. News received about 6.30 AM from C/250 through an infantry officer attached to them. At 3 AM when he left only one gun was in action, remainder having been hit. About 6.30 AM Major Shiel & Lt Richardson arrive at H.Q. and say that ~~the~~ A/250 have removed sights & Breech mechanism as the creeping barrage has passed them, and the enemy are about 500 yds in front of them. Message received from Lt Leathart who had gone over to Inf Bde HQ that Yellow line was being attacked.

Major Shiel and Capt Meek (attd from Infantry) went out about 7.30 AM towards Inf Bde H.Q. and MEEK brought back report that enemy were close to Inf Bde H.Q. about 600 yds from Bde H.Q.

Lt Hopewood had reported from B/250 that they were still firing with 3 of the 4 guns at their main position.

A message had also been received that D/250 were continuing to fire. No ~~further~~ news received from C/250.

From information received later, personnel from B/250 main position nearly all got away when the enemy arrived on the position; Very few got away

WAR DIARY

250 (Northumbrian) Bde R.F.A. (T)
May 1918 Vol XXXVIII

May 27 from detached section of B, but fair number from detached section of A/250. Very few got away from D/250; ~~lost~~ Capt Darling was last seen going towards the enemy with his revolver & Lt Earle and remaining gunners were firing the last gun left in action. No one got away from main position of C/250 but most of the detachments got away from detached section where 2/Lt Coton was last seen going towards the enemy with his revolver.

Personnel that got away from batteries when the enemy reached the position went via BEAURIEUX to wagon lines at GLENNES. 11 Wagons of D/250 which went up from wagon line to take ammunition to reserve positions were fired on at close range by Machine guns; those who were not killed or wounded were captured.

On arrival at GLENNES orders were received to march to ST. GILLES which was reached about midday.

Batteries unhooked & remained until 6pm when orders were received to march to DAVREGNY which was reached at 9.30pm. The night was spent there.

May 28. 9.30 AM Brigade marched via COHAN, ~~F~~ COULONGES & GOUSSANCOURT to CHAMPVOISIN which was reached about 2pm. and where the night was spent.

May 29. Orders received to march at 6AM via GRIGNY, VANDIERES & CHATILLON to CUISLES, which was reached at 10 AM. Orders then received to halt ~~by~~ off the road and later orders were received to march via CHATILLON. and PORT A BINSON to IGNY. Great deal of traffic on roads & many blocks; ~~to~~ First battery reached IGNY 2pm, last batteries not till 2 AM 30.th.

WAR DIARY May 1918 250 (Northumbrian) Bde RFA (T) Vol XXXVIII

May 30	Orders received at 1pm. to march via BREUIL to VERDON where night was spent.
May 31	Marched from VERDON via MARGNY, JANVILLIERS, FROMENTIERES, CHAMPAUBERT, CONGY, COURJEONNET to a camp near JOCHES beside the MARAIS de ST GOND.

Reference maps SOISSONS (1/100000.) + CHALONS (1/80000).

[illegible signature]
Lt. Col
250 Bde R.F.A (T)

Statements regarding circumstances which led to the capture of Lieut.(A/Capt) Edwin Darling, "D" Battery, 250th Bde, R.F.A., 50th Division. Captured on 27/5/18 at Bois de Beaumarais.

On night 26/27 May 1918 I was temporarily in command at gun position. I had four howitzers in action at main position and one at an advanced position. Front covered was very quiet. First warning of impending attack received at 7.15 p.m. 26th. Received impression raid on large scale was expected. Took all possible precautions for protection against gas attack. Inspected all anti-gas appliances personally. Deflected ammunition to forward gun and sent an officer giving instructions to sergeant in charge to fire steady rate of fire on Corbeny - Berrieux road (enfilade) until further orders. Brigade informed me they did not consider it necessary to send an officer to remain. At 8 p.m. Brigade informed me they were notifying wagon line of impending attack. Fired harassing programme on roads and approaches from 7.30 p.m. till 10.10 p.m. when "counter preparation" programme was ordered and put into operation. I issued instructions to all concerned in reserve positions in case it became necessary to withdraw.

At 1 a.m. 27th enemy barrage opened with tremendous intensity on forward areas, battery position and rear areas. It appeared to consist of 75 per cent H.E. and 25 p.c. gas. Latter had all appearances and produced all symptoms of lethal gas. All telephonic communication broken immediately, ceaseless attempts to repair lines proved ineffectual. Three howitzers destroyed during first hour of bombardment and casualties sustained. Withdrew remaining personnel to such shelter as position afforded with exception of sufficient men to retain remaining howitzer in action. Sent out several runners to Brigade Headquarters giving information of state of affairs and asking for situation reports. About 4 a.m. received orders from Brigade to "carry on". At 4.30 a.m. gas proof dug-out where men were sheltering sustained direct hit from gas shell which penetrated and burst inside causing several casualties. From appearance of casualties and from my own experience (my respirator having been pierced by piece of shell early in barrage) I concluded gas used was lethal gas. Taking into consideration the nature of the country (heavy undergrowth for several acres) I concluded for this reason that enemy objective probably did not include Bois de Beaumarais. No infantry, either wounded or stragglers, retired through or within sight of position during whole operation. Two infantry officers, attached for instruction, (2/Lt.Bryce,N.F. and 2/Lt. Bellerby, N.F.) volunteered with 2/Lt.Willis, R.F.A. to serve remaining gun to rest detachment. At 6 a.m. Lieut.Hornsby, R.F.A returned from O.P. badly gassed and reported no visibility from O.P. nor had he seen any sign of retirement or of enemy. Owing to morning mist and gas cloud it was impossible to see more than 60 yards from position. I posted a reliable man in tree O.P. near position and personally carried out a reconnaissance of right flank (exposed flank) of position at 6.30 a.m. I despatched 2/Lt.Willis to attempt to reach Headquarters, 150th Inf. Bde in search of information. I resumed my reconnaissance of right flank at 6.45 a.m. and instructed Lieut.Earle, R.F.A. to carry out a similar operation on left flank. Remaining howitzer was maintained in action all this time by the two infantry officers mentioned above, assisted by a layer, firing on S.O.S. points. I had instructed 2/Lt.Willis to report to me at command post about 60 yards in rear of position if he got through and returned there to meet him after complete reconnaissance of right flank, which showed no sign of enemy personnel or of retiring infantry. A few minutes after returning there I was informed that enemy were coming on to position through trees on left rear. I immediately ordered all casualties near me to leave position and get away if possible. I advanced to gun pits and found enemy in large numbers advancing from both flanks and already on position. I engaged three of the enemy with my revolver and then tried to get Lewis gun into action but found dug-out where it was kept for safety had been blown in. As all seemed over on position I decided the best thing to do was to get back to command post if possible and destroy range tables and more important confidential documents. This I was successful in doing, being fortunate enough to dispose of two of the enemy who attempted to prevent me doing so. I roused Lieut. Hornsby, ordering him to ~~follow me~~ get his revolver and follow me. On emerging I found some 50 or 60 of the enemy standing outside covering us with rifles and my revolver being empty I had no alternative but to surrender.

Officers killed on position:- Lt.Earle, R.F.A., 2/Lt.Bryce,N.F.
Captured on position 2/Lt.Bellerby, N.F., at command post Lieut.Hornsby, R.F.A.

APPENDIX "A".

NARRATIVE OFEVENTS ON POSITION
OCCUPIED BY 250th. Bde. R.F.A.
ON 27th. MAY, 1918.

-*-*-*-*-*-*-*-*-*-*-*-

1.0 a.m. Heavy bombardment of H.E. and Gas commenced and, as far as H.Q. area was concerned, continued till about 6.0 a.m. at which hour the enemy barrage of H.E. appeared to reach the area. The shells were principally 77 mm. and 105 mm. with a few of heavier calibre. Respirators had to be worn at once.

Lines went almost at once and Lt. GRAHAM went to telephone dugout and got through to D.A. and 2 batteries. I reported to D.A. and ordered batteries on to S.OS. Lines at ~~xxxx~~ maximum rates.

1.15 a.m. All lines dished and in spite of repeated endeavours no communication could be established.

1.45 a.m. Owing to darkness and density of gas cloud Capt. DICKINSON, though he had a torch, failed to find his way to the telephone dugout under ten minutes searching.

Consequently I considered it useless to attempt sending orderlies till the light improved.

Gas (Lachrymatory & Sneezing) found its way into the dugout every time anyone entered or left to an appreciable extent, but no evil results have occurred to anyone who was in ~~x~~ it. The dugout was fitted with double doors - the outer one a solid one and the windows had a solid shutter; the inner windows of transparent material were broken by the vibration of the explosions, and would have been quite useless.

The C.O's dugout had both doors blown in by a shell near by and was full of gas. No other dugout was damaged by shell-fire - the dugouts were scattered over a large area, which undoubtedly minimised casualties but the objection to having to send such a long distance for orderlies etc., proved considerable under the conditions prevailing.

About 3.30 a.m. At this time there was sufficient light to justify me in sending out for information and 2 orderlies (volunteers) went off round the Batteries; these failed to get through. Lieut. LEATHART and Sapper ROBERTS who volunteered to go with him went off to EVREUX to see Infantry Brigade and with great difficulty arrived. Gas Masks had still to be worn at this time, and the wood was littered with debris which obliterated the paths.

Arrived at EVREUX they found the whole aspect of the Hill altered beyond recognition. After a time they found a dug-out with an Infantry Captain and some men. One of these men came with them to guide them but he failed to do so and it was only by luck that they found the right dug-out. (Gas masks could be removed on the top of the hill).

Lieut. LEATHART saw General MARTIN and sent Sapper ROBERTS and a Gunner back to say the enemy were in the Reserve Line of the Battle Zone on the Right Brigade front, and added at the last minute the news that the Right of the Centre Brigade was also back in ANSPACH Trench (Reserve Line).

About 4.30 a.m. A Gunner from "D" Battery arrived in an exhausted condition, and reported the battery being heavily shelled but a steady rate of fire on S.O.S. being maintained though many men seriously affected by gas. He returned to his Battery with orders to continue firing on approaches, in particular those near CORBENY.

Lieut. HOPWOOD arrived from "B" Battery and reported that at one time they had been reduced to one gun, but that 3 were now in action - all firing on S.O.S. I sent him back with orders to try and barrage ANSPACH trench on RESERVE LINE.

Lieut. TULLEY (attached Infantry Officer) arrived from "D" Battery with news - 2 guns knocked out - 2 sergeants wounded - 2 sergeants gassed - Major CHAPMAN endeavouring to collect crew to man one gun.

No news was received of "D" forward section but I have since learned that Lieut. COSTAR maintained his fire until the enemy were upon him, and he was last seen covering the retreat of his men by advancing towards the enemy with his revolver in his hand.

About 7.0 a.m. Major. SHIEL with Lieut. RICHARDSON arrived and reported he had carried on fire continuously till left. Shelling heavy and pits knocked about. He had sent Lieut. ABEK forward and this Officer returned and reported that were we were back in the Reserve Line. He went out again, but did not return. This and the fact that the barrage was now a lifting one convinced him that the enemy must be on him and he ordered breech blocks to be removed and a retirement to MONACO.

Two guns were put out of action in this Battery almost from the start, one detachment being knocked out and a number of others wounded. All four were later got into action. An orderly had been sent to H.Q. (He failed to arrive.)

At my request Major SHIEL went forward with Capt. MEEK (attached Inf. Officer). This Officer had previously been out at my request with Lieut. TULLY, and had found theirm way to EVREUX and brought back corroboration of Lieut. LEATHART'S news.

Major SHIEL went forward but after proceeding a few hundred yards was machine-gunned from EVREUX. Capt. MEEK returned to report. He then went on and ordered his detached section (E. SATIN) to retire. He then returned to Headquarters and found we had quitted.

Lieut. WILLIS from "D" Battery, who had been sent by Capt. DARLING to EVREUX for news, arrived and reported enemy in "D" Battery.

About 8.0 a.m. the Commanding Officer of one of the French Batteries came running through the wood and told Capt. DICKSINSON the enemy had taken EVREUX.

The papers in the dugout were then burnt with parrafin from the lamp - the men collected and paraded - all present except Corpl. WATSON who was busy burning papers in his Office.

Left Headquarters with Liwut. RICHARDSON and Lieut. WILLIS, RICHARDSON very beat (he fell asleep on arrival at H.Q) Capt. DICKINSON and Lieut. GRAHAM got through the wood safely after bearing to the right considerably to avoid the thickest part of the barrage which was now preceeding us. Just outside the wood Lieut. RICHARDSON mortally wounded. Carried him as far as CHAUDARDES where he proved to have expired. Decided it was not fair to the others to carry him further.

Sent Lieut. GRAHAM and 10 of Staff to MAIZY direct and proceeded towards BEAURIEUX with Capt. DICKINSON intending to report to C.R.A.

On nearing BEAURIEUX noticed machine gun fire and became aware that it was from top of the hill. Things became more unhealthy as we approached, and on arrival at turn to MAIZY BRIDGE became satisfied the enemy could see us, so made short cut across to Bridge, which we found intact and Capt. HAND and another Officer arranging for defence. Capt. HAND stated he could get no proper force together and it appeared there was no one who knew how to fire the charges laid for demolishing the Bridge.

Proceeded. to GLENNES (very unhealthy on first part of road which is in enfilade) and found wagon lines moved to St. GILLES. Horses waiting for us.

Have since learned that all guns but one of "D" Battery were put out of action finally only one Corpl. being left on his feet. Lieut. EARLE with the Corpl. and 2 Infantry

APPENDIX "B".

NARRATIVE OF EVENTS ON POSITION
OCCUPIED BY "B" BATTERY, 251st.
BRIGADE ON NIGHT OF 26/27th MAY.

-*-*-*-*-*-*-*-*-*-*-

Enemy commenced exceedingly intense bombardment on the whole of the Divisional Front and extending well to the left of the Divisional Front.

The Battery was heavily bhmbarded by 5.9 Hows., 4.2 Hows, and 77 mm. Guns.

About 30 rounds per minute were falling on the position, Much gas was used including Lachrymatory, Sneezing and Lethal.

1.5 a.m. Number 5 gun hit and put out of action.

1.15 a.m. Number 5 Gun completely destroyed, Pit and Ammunition set on fire.

1.20 a.m. Number 4 Gun hit and destroyed and set on fire.

2.30 a.m. (approx:) Number 6 Gun out of action (trigger trouble).

Lieut. WILLIAMS attempted to get this Gun into action, but was unable to do so owing to the exceedingly heavy bombardment.

3.0 a.m. Number 1 and Number 2 Guns opened on S.O.S. Lines searching and sweeping, 4 rounds per gun per minute.

4.0 a.m. (approx:) Detachment of Number 1 Gun collapsed; reliefs were arranged, and Numbers 1 and 2 continued firing.

4.30 a.m. Number 2 hit, damaged and put out of action. Number 1 Gun continued firing gun fire in bursts.

7.0 a.m. Number 6 was reported out of action, damaged by hostile shell fire (time not known). It had been impossible to get near this Pit owing to hostile shell fire, and burning and exploding ammunition from Number 5 Pit.

Up to this time three Gun Pits were on fire, and the communication trenches between the guns were knocked in in several places, making movement about the position extremely difficult, particularly as box respirators had to be worn.

7.30 a.m. Hostile shelling became less intense.

7.40 a.m. Shelling on the position ceased (the Barrage having lifted.)

Lieut. MACNAMARA and myself * immediately proceeded to the top of the bank in order to ascertain the situation, when I saw Germans on the position and advancing on it from the left. Five of the enemy were actually entering the dugout where my look-out men were. I immediately ordered the position to be cleared at once.

Whilst leaving the position we came in for bombing and heavy sniping and machine gun fire.

* Battery Commander.

-*-*-*-*-*-*-*-*-*-*-*-*-*-*-*-*-*-*-

IX CORPS. BM/1. APPENDIX "C".

Reference your No. S/25/6. of 4/6/18.

At 9.0 p.m. on the 26th May, owing to information received that an attack was impending, harassing fire was opened by all batteries of the 50th. D.A. at a rate of 30 rounds per gun and 20 rounds per how. per hour.

At 12 m.n. counter-preparation was begun.

1 a.m. At 10 a.m. 27th the enemy opened an intense bombardment of all natures of shell on all battery positions and villages in the 50th Divisiona Area.

The majority of guns used on battery positions appeared to be of 77 mm. and 105 mm. calibre, but on villages in rear, i.e., BEAURIEUX, MAIZY and GLENNES, H.V. guns up to 11-inch were employed.

This bombardment continued until 4.0 a.m. when it became concentrated on the front system and acted as a creeping barrage in front of the enemy's infantry attacking.

During this time, 1.0 a.m. - 4.0 a.m. from evidence available, it is ascertained that 50% - 75% of the 18 pdrs. and 4.5 hows. were put hors de combat by :-

(a) Direct hits of hostile shell.
(b) Spring and buffer troubles.
(c) Gas shelling affecting detachments.

Most of the gas shells contained lachrymatory, sneezing and thermite mixtures. A few lethal were reported.

Gas helmets had to be worn at all Battery positions in BEAUMARAIS WOOD. Communication with O.P's was cut almost immediately after the beginning of the hostile bombardment.

~~X/250~~

No information is available of what happened at A, C and D/251 as there are no survivors. Similarly C/250 main position. One Officer and one telephonist returned from D/250.

A/250 main position reports having fired about 2000 rounds from 4 guns; and disabled guns before leaving them.

The Officers and detachments who succeeded in getting away did so mainly owing to their knowledge of the tracks in the wood and the way out of it.

11 wagons of D/250 were captured in the neighbourhood of CUIRY-les-CHAUDARDES going up with ammunition. The only N.C.O. or man who escaped from this party did so by swimming the river and canal. He states that he saw one of the iron bridges blown up but cannot say which.

B/250 did not have any guns actually knocked out and before retiring removed dial sights and breech blocks.

O.P's. Information from O.P's on BUTTE de L'EDMOND and HILL 120.8 agrees in that :-

(a) the enemy's guns up to 5.9's were close up to their front line and in CORBENY.
Observers state that on the opening of the bombardment it was one continuous line of flame from CORBENY to the East.
In the opinion of one F.O.O. the guns must have been practically axle to axle in some places.

(b) Soon after the beginning of the bombardment the enemy put down smoke shell in the forward area, this with the N.E. wind completely obscured all further vision from the O.P's.

(c) O.P's were heavily gassed.

T.M's. An Officer from Y/50 T.M. Battery states that the 2 T.M's in the Tr. des TARBES 300 yards N.E. of CRAONNE CHURCH were knocked out by hostile shell fire before 3.0 a.m.

C.R.E., 50th. DIVISION.

DEMOLITION OF BRIDGES OVER AISNE AND CANAL.

=*=

Bridge 14 AISNE. (Officers in charge previously wounded.)

Preparation of this Bridge was not completed when enemy appeared at Bridge. Enemy artillery obtained two direct hits on bridge while our Sappers were at work on it. This damaged the bridge but did not render it impassable.

Bridge 14 CANAL.

This Bridge was blown up after the N.C.O. in charge had seen the French on his right lighting a fuze on their bridge. The Germans were within 50 yards distance and the sappers were being fired on at this range.

Bridge 14 (CANAL).

Bridge blown up when Germans were within 50 yards. Sappers under rifle fire.

Bridge 14 AISNE.

Bridge blown up wne enemy were in close proximity and after they had crossed bridge 14 AISNE.

Bridge 14 2 CANAL.

Same as above.

Bridge 15 AISNE.
Bridge prepared. Crew waited for written orders until it was too late to fire charges.

Bridge 15 CANAL (Steel).
Same as above.

Bridge 15 (Canal) (Timber).
Small footbridge not prepared owing to lack of time and to casualties. It was hoped that explosion of charges on adjacent steel bridge would damage this bridge also.

Bridge 15 2 AISNE.
Partially charged. Whole of men (including Officers) wounded while charging. Work was continued until Germans were actually on bridge.

Bridge 15 2 Canal.
Bridge blown up when Germans were within 50 yards distance on our side of bridge. (They had come over on right).

Bridge 16 AISNE.

Bridge blown up when Germans were close to it and firing upon bridge crew. A wounded Major (Infantry) was the last to cross the bridge and he ordered its immediate demolition.

Bridge 16 Canal, 17 Canal (Upstream) & 17 Canal (Downstream).
Were destroyed on orders received from Staff Major IX Corps and on written orders received from Staff Capt. TONG, 50th Division.

Bridge 17 2 AISNE. (Upstream).
Bridge was prepared and attempts made to blow it up after crew had come under very heavy rifle fire.
The Germans were then in the Village of CUIRY-les-CHAUDARDES. Failure of the charges to explode was due to faulty fuze. Four attempts were made.

Bridge 17 2 (Downstream) AISNE.
Bridge not prepared owing to lack of time and casualties. The crew

of 17 (Upstream) intended to carry on with this bridge after completing their own.

Bridge 17 3 Canal.

Bridge blown up when Germans were close to it and firing on demolition crew.

Bridge 18 AISNE.

Pontoon Bridge meant to be destroyed by knocking holes in bottoms of pontoons with picks. This bridge was not destroyed owing to lack of time and to casualties. Crew waited here for written orders until Germans appeared on our side of bridge at only about 50 or 70 yards distance (they had crossed over by MAIZY bridge on left, and by light railway bridge on right. The N.C.O. in charge lit the fuze but the charges failed to explode (owing to defective fuze).

General.

Orders were received at MONACO at 4.15 a.m. 27/5/18, to prepare bridges for demolition.

As both MONACO and BEAUREPAIRE (where some of the bridge crews were billeted) had been under very heavy shelling (gas shells etc.) since 1 a.m. great difficulty was experienced in getting the crews out. In some cases the mens' dugouts had been blown in and many of the men themselves were suffering from the temporary effects of gas.

The bridge crews were divided up into four groups each under the charge of an Officer. Each group was responsible for the demolition of from 4 to 5 bridges.

Shortly after arrival at the bridges 3 of the 4 Officers were wounded. Some of the N.C.O's and sappers became casualties on the way down to the bridges and some others while actually at work preparing the charges.

Altogether there were 30 casualties to members of bridge crews (includes the 3 Officers).

At 7 a.m. the report centre was moved from MONACO to CONCEVREUX (by order of the C.R.E.). I waited there till 1 p.m. expecting to receive written orders from C.R.E. or Divisional Staff to blow bridges. By this time the Germans had advanced South of the Canal on both my right and left flanks. The Village of CONCEVREUX was being shelled and was partly on fire. Most of the bridges had been blown about 1½ hours previously on my own responsibility.

2nd. June, 1918.

(Sgd.) J.W.McLELLAN, Major,
O.C., 446th Field Coy. R.E.

APPENDIX 3.

(Copy of Telegram.)

To :- 74th. Inf. Bde.

G.A. 107. 28/5.

(1) You will conform with new position taken up by 8th Division, and with the French who are forming a switch in the direction of COURLANDON.

(2) Bde Headquarters should be established at MONTIGNY.

(3) 50th Div. H.Q. will move after dawn today to BRANSCOURT.

From 50th. Division.

12.45 a.m. (Sgd.) E.C. ANSTEY, Lt.-Col,
G. S.

Copy to 8th Division.

-*-*-*-*-*-*-*-*-*-***-*-*-*-*-*-

S E C R E T.

APPENDIX 4.

(Copy of Telegram.)

To :- 74th Inf. Bde.

G.A. 109.   28/5.

(1) In future all references will be to 100,000 Map SOISSONS Sheet.

(2) Boundary between 8th and 50th Divisions will be the line LE MONCET FARM - MONTIGNY - JONCHERY all to 8th Div.

(3) You will keep touch as far as possible with 8th Div. on right and French troops on left, retiring fighting if necessary to conform to their movements. If it is impossible with the troops at your disposal to keep touch with both, you will keep touch for preference with 8th Division.

From 50th Division.

7.25 a.m.

(Sgd.) E.C. ANSTEY, Lt.-Col,
G. S.

-*-*-*-*-*-*-*-

APPENDIX II.

(Copy of Telegram.)

To :- 149th Inf. Bde.
5th. N. F.

G. 224. 27/5.

5th N.F. will move as soon as possible to BEAUREPAIRE and come under orders of 149th Bde AAA C.O. to report 149th Bde Headquarters at once AAA Addsd 5th N.F. reptd 149th Bde.

From 50th. Division.

2.10 a.m. (Sgd.) E.C. ANSTEY, Lt.-Col, GS.

-*-*-*-*-*-*-

APPENDIX 1.

(Copy of Telegram.)

To :- All Units of 50th Division.

G. 214. 26/5.

Information points to possibility of hostile bombardment including gas shelling against this front beginning 1 a.m. to-night lasting 2½ hours and followed by attack AAA Our counter-preparation will take place between 12 midnight and 4 a.m. AAA Harassing fire by Machine Guns between 1 a.m. and dawn AAA Troops will be warned and all necessary precautions taken AAA Acknowledge AAA Addsd all concerned.

From 50th. Division.

8.15 p.m. (Sgd.) E.C. ANSTEY, Lt.-Col, GS.

-*-*-*-*-*-*-*-*-*-

Instructions regarding War Diaries and Intelligence Summaries are contained in F. S. Regs., Part II. and the Staff Manual respectively. Title pages will be prepared in manuscript.

WAR DIARY
or
INTELLIGENCE SUMMARY.
(Erase heading not required.)

250 (Northumbrian) Bde R.F.A. (T.F.)

Vol XXXIX June 1918

Army Form C. 2118.

38

Place	Date	Hour	Summary of Events and Information	Remarks and references to Appendices
	June 1		Bde camped at LA VERRERIE Farm in the Marais de ST GOND near JOCHES. Day spent in cleaning up etc.	
	June 2 to		A composite Bde consisting of A/250, B/250, B/251 + D/251 which were made up to strength in personnel + horses from the remaining batteries + D.A.C. was formed. Lt Col Johnston in command of it. Guns + essential stores were drawn from CONNANTRE railhead. This Brigade was held in readiness to go into action if required + continued training.	
	June 8		Brigade was inspected dismounted by Brig Gen HUMPHREYS G.O.C. RA IX Corps + by Maj Gen JACKSON G.O.C. 50th Div.	
	June 9		Bde marches at 6 AM via BROUSSY LE PETIT, MONDEMENT, MONTGIVROUX + LACHY to LES EPÉES farm where it encamped. Watering facilities rather poor.	
	June 10		Composite Bde broken up, B/251 returns to 251 Bde, C/250 to 250 Bde + D/251 to take two sections back to 251 Bde, remaining section (personnel of which had been found by D/250) remains as D/250. O.R attd from other batteries return. Officers + men attd from D.A.C. + T.Ms remain.	
	June 11 to 25th		Training continued. Bde classes for signallers + N.C.O.s. Batteries devote most attention to gun drill, patrols etc, + later to drill orders etc.	

D. D. & L., London, E.C.
(A10266) Wt W5300/P713 750,000 2/18 Sch. 52 Forms/C2118/16

Instructions regarding War Diaries and Intelligence Summaries are contained in F. S. Regs., Part II. and the Staff Manual respectively. Title pages will be prepared in manuscript.

WAR DIARY
or
INTELLIGENCE SUMMARY.
(Erase heading not required.)

250 (Northumbrian) Bde RFA (T.)

Vol XXXIX June 1918.

Army Form C. 2118.

Place	Date	Hour	Summary of Events and Information	Remarks and references to Appendices
	June 26		Orders received that Bde would march on 27th inst to forward area. Positions Between IGNY LE JARD & the MARNE reconnoitred. On return orders for move on 27th were cancelled.	
	27		Training etc continued. Considerable numbers (about 60) of cases of influenza in the Brigade. Patients have high temperature for a few days & have to be evacuated.	
	28 to 30.		Training continued. On 29th warning order received that Bde would march on 1st July & entrain later for British area. During this time, a large quantity of equipment was received.	

N. L. Parmeter Major
a/OC. 250th Bde R.F.A.

D. D. & L., London, E.C.
(A10266) Wt W5300/P713 750,000 2/18 Sch. 52 Forms/C2118/16

ACCOUNT OF THE OPERATIONS
(from June 6th. (4 p.m.) to June 7th. (6 p.m.)

(TRANSLATION.)

GERMAN ATTACK OF THE 6th JUNE, 1918, ON THE FRONT OF THE COMBINED FORCES.

On the night of the 5/6th June, patrols which were out on the front of the 28th D.I. took prisoners who confirmed the order of Battle and said a strong attack would begin at 5 a.m.

At about 4.30 a.m., after an artillery preparation lasting two hours (including gas shelling of battery positions) the enemy attacked between St. EUPHRAISE WOOD (inclusive) and CHANTEREINE FARM on a front of 4½ kilometres.

On the right, the 28th R.I. maintained their positions; in the centre, the 50th who suffered heavy casualties in the bombardment and was more heavily attacked was compelled to give up MEULEUX WOOD, [illegible] WOOD and VILLERS FARM.

On the left, the British, well supported by their artillery and by the 40th held their position on the MONTAGNE de BLIGNY and in ECLISSES WOOD.

At 8.30 a.m. a Battalion of the 22nd R.I. which was in reserve in the BOUILLY area recaptured VILLERS FARM and again got in touch with the 22nd and 50th R.I.

Between 8 and 9 a.m. supported by heavy artillery concentrated on St. EUPHRAISE area, DIX HOMMES WOOD and BLIGNY, the enemy succeeded in taking BLIGNY, but our Artillery and M.G. fire, the resistance offered by the remaining elements of 50th R.I., and a counter-attack made by the 8th Coy. of 22nd R.I. prevented him from leaving the wood or holding the [illegible] cross roads.

The English Battalion which was in front of the [illegible] withdrew their right to conform with the disposition of the 50th R.I., South of BLIGNY.

The German fire increased greatly on MONTAGNE de BLIGNY; the English Battalion which was defending it, fell back about 11.45 a.m., made a counter-attack which failed, but a Battalion of 8th Brigade in close support, well placed by General JEFFRIES, attacked at 1.30 p.m. and restored the line, which the enemy shelled heavily.

The timely attack of the English enabled the 414th Regt. to prepare a counter-attack on BLIGNY. The movement of this Regiment which was placed at the disposal of the 28th D.I., was delayed by reason of the difficult nature of the ground and the necessity of passing through woods.

At 5 p.m., the 414th deployed to the West on the edge of DIX HOMMES WOOD and a counter-attack was launched at 5.30 p.m. in a Westerly direction. Well performed, the attack succeeded and the line on the Western outskirts of the Village was soon occupied. At 6 p.m. the fighting was over and at 7 p.m. all was quiet.

REFLECTIONS ON THE OPERATIONS.

Characteristics of the Attack.

On the 6th of June, the Germans made a local attack on both sides of the river ARDRE, making use only of the best Units of the Sector; 232nd D.I., 86th D.I., and a Regiment of the 53rd D.R. From the prisoners' answers and the sketches found on them, the line they had to reach would stretch through VRIGNY WOOD, [illegible] WOOD, (South part), point 231 in DIX HOMMES WOOD, CHAMBRECY and CHANTEREINE FARM.

To obtain that aim, all troops available were pushed right forward, the Regiments being in close touch with, in each Regt. two Battalions in square formation on the front line, and a Battalion as support. A strong density all along the front line was thus realised.

Officers maintained fire to the finish, Capt. DARLING keeping off enemy with his revolver.

(Sgd.) F.G.B. JOHNSTON, Lt.-Col,
250 Bde. R.F.A. (T).

1st June, 1918.

Efficacy of our Artillery.

The counter-preparation by the 28th Div. the English D.I., and the 40th D.I. was carried out under very favourable conditions and its efficacy was largely responsible for the failure of the German attack.

Deserving of special notice was the counter-preparation in RAVELLE RAVINE and the concentration on BLIGNY the defenders of which were taken by surprise and killed by our fire. No M.G. remained in action and the movement of the 41th was greatly facilitated thereby.

Conduct of the English.

The 19th D.I.W. in the line for nine days, experienced five days of hard fighting. The Div. was twice made up to strength by composite elements which stood up well against the fire.

Strict discipline obtained in that Division and great confidence is placed in the Staff and Commanding Officers who continually go and see for themselves what is happening in their Units.

The impression made on the moral of the French troops by the fine conduct of their Allies, was very good.

Counter-attacks.

The counter-attacks which were immediately made by the English as well as by the 28th Div., resulted in limiting, close to BLIGNY, the ground gained by the Germans and, in allowing the 41th to attack on a narrow front, thus making the success assured.

The German Infantry made a weak defence: they offered no resistance in open field, and showed tenacity only in sunken roads and from behind cover which could be defended with ease.

Casualties.

The casualties owing for a great part, to the shelling on a ground without any shelter, are heavy.-

	28th. D.I.		19th. D.I.W.	
	Officers.	Men.	Officers.	Men.
killed	5	80	-	75 ?
wounded	14	566	-	580
missing	-	175	-	25 ?

The moral of the French and English Infantry is excellent. Among all those who took part in the fierce fighting of that day, a strong feeling of individual superiority prevailed.

(Sgd.) PELLE,

General Commdt. the Combined Forces.

50th. DIVISION. G.X. 80

Seen by :-

G.O.C.

G.S.O.1.

G.S.O. 2. CH

G.S.O.3.

Int. Offr.

A.A. & Q.M.G.

D.A.A.G.

D.A. Q.M.G.

Send a copy to each Bde. and 4 copies for [illegible]

"A" Form

MESSAGES AND SIGNALS.

Army Form C. 2121
(In pads of 100.)

No. of Message..............

Prefix.......... Code..............m | Words. | Charge. | This message is on a/c of: | Recd. at...........m.

Office of Origin and Service Instructions

Sent

At...................m.

To......................

By......................

.... *Service.*

(Signature of "Franking Officer.")

Date..................

From..................

By....................

TO Of i/c French Mission

Sender's Number.	Day of Month.	In reply to Number.	AAA
* G 73	11/6		

Will you please have the attached account of the operations which took place on the front of the V French Corps on the 6th inst translated and returned as early as possible to this Office

From 50th Division

Place

Time ——

The above may be forwarded as now corrected. (Z)

Censor.

Major G.S.

Signature of Addressor or person authorised to telegraph in his name.

* This line should be erased if not required.

(4715) Wt. W3253/P511 1,123,336 Shts. 2/18 C. & Co. (.634)

5e Corps d'ARMEE.   Au Q.G., le 7 Juin 1918

Etat-Major
3me Bureau

No.116/3-PC

COMPTE RENDU DES EVENEMENTS

du 6 Juin (18 h.) au 7 JUIN (18 h.)

ATTAQUE ALLEMANDE du 6 Juin 1918 sur le front du Groupement.

Dans la nuit du 5 au 6 Juin, des reconnaissances, envoyées devant le front de la 28° D.I., font des prisonniers qui confirment l'ordre de bataille et annoncent une forte attaque pour 3 heures.

Vers 4 heures 30 apres une préparation de deux heures (avec obus a gaz sur la zone des batteries,) l'ennemi prononce une attaque depuis le bois de Ste-Euphraise inclus jusqu'a la Fe de Chantereine sur un front de 6 kms 500.

A droite, le 22° R.I. maintient ses positions, au centre le 30° qui a subit des pertes élevées par le bombardement et est plus fortement pressé, est contraint d'évacuer le bois des Houleux, le bois de Beneuil et la Fe de Villers.

A gauche, les anglais très bien soutenus par leur artillerie qu'appuie celle de la 40° D.I. se maintiennent sur la Montagne de Bligny et dans le Bois des Eclisses.

A 6 h.30 le Btn. du 22° R.I. en reserve dans la région de Bouilly, reprend la Fe de Villers et retablit la liaison entre le 22° et le 30° R.I.

De 8 h.à 9 h. appuyé par le puissantes concentrations de feux sur la zone Ste-Euphraise, bois des Dix Hommes, Bligny, l'ennemi réussit à s'emparer de Bligny, mais nos feux d'artillerie et de mitrailleuses, la résistance des elements restants du 30° R.I. et une contre attaque prononcée par la 3° Cie du 22° R.I. l'empechent d'en déboucher, cesse de prendre pied au carrefour de la Croix Ferlin.

Le bataillon anglais qui est appuye a l'Ardre refuse sa droite pour se lier au 30° R.I. au Sud de Bligny.

Le tir des Allemands redouble sur la Montagne de Bligny, le bataillon anglais qui la défend se replie vers 11 h.45, tente une contre attaque qui echoue, mais un bataillon de reserve locale (58° Brigade) poussé à pied d'oeuvre par le General JEFFRIES, s'élance à l'assaut et retablit à 13 h.30 l'integralite de sa ligne, que l'ennemi se contente de bombarder energiquement.

Cette belle attitude des Anglais permet la preparation de la contre attaque du 414° R.I. sur Bligny. Le mouvement de ce regiment mis dès 9 heures a la disposition de la 28° D.I. a ete lent en raison de la difficulte du cheminement et de la necessite de le faire progresser a travers bois.

A 17 h. le 414° se deploie face a l'Ouest a la lisière du bois des Dix Hommes, et la contre attaque est declanchee a 17 h.30 en direction generale de l'Ouest. Menee à grande allure, l'opération réussil et les lisières Ouest du village bientot occupees. A 18 h. tout est terminé - A 19 h. le calme est complet.

Réflexions.....

REFLEXIONS SUR L'OPERATION

Caractère de l'attaque -

Les Allemands ont fait le 6 Juin une poussée locale, à cheval sur l'Ardre en utilisant uniquement les grandes unités en secteur, la 232° D.I., la 86° D.I. et un Rgt de la 33° D.R. D'après les déclarations des prisonniers et les croquis trouvés sur eux, la ligne à atteindre était jalonnée par: le Bois de Mrigny, le Bois de la Vallotte (Corne Sud) la Cote 231 du Bois des 10 hommes, Chaumuzy et la Ferme Chantereine.

A cet effet, toutes les troupes disponibles avaient été poussées très en avant, les Régiments accolés, et dans chaque Régiment deux bataillons carrés en première ligne et un bataillon en soutien. Une grande densité en première ligne était ainsi réalisée.

Efficacité de notre artillerie -

La contre-préparation de la 28° D.I., de la D.I. anglaise et de la 40° D.I., a été réalisée dans de très bonnes conditions. Son efficacité a été pour une grande part dans l'échec de l'attaque allemande.

A citer en particulier la préparation anglaise dans la Ravin de la Ville et la concentration sur Bligny dont les défenseurs ont presque tous été surpris et tués par nos tirs, de telle sorte qu'aucune mitrailleuse n'y est restée en action ce qui a facilité grandement le mouvement du 414°.

Attitude des Anglais -

La 19° D.I.W. en ligne depuis neuf jours, a eu cinq jour de très rudes combats; elle a été recomplétée à deux reprises par des éléments disparates (Composites), qui ont très bien tenu au feu. Dans cette grande unité règne une très sérieuse discipline. On y sent la confiance dans les Chefs qui se rendent compte continuellement de ce qui se passe dans leurs unités.

L'impression produite sur le moral des troupes françaises par la belle attitude de leurs alliés a été très bonne.

Contre-attaques -

Les contre-attaques immédiates faites, tant chez les Anglais qu'à la 28° D.I., ont eu le résultat de limiter aux abords même de Bligny le terrain gagné par les Allemands, et de permettre l'engagement du 414° sur un front étroit lui garantissant le succès.

L'Infanterie allemande s'est montrée de médiocre qualité - elle n'a pas résisté en terrain découvert, et n'a montré quelque ténacité que dans les chemins creux et derrière les talus dont l'orientation permettait une résistance facile.

Pertes.

Les pertes, dues en grande partie au bombardement sur un terrain sans abri sont sévères.

/28° D.I. ....

50th. Division.
G.X. 80.

149th. Infantry Brigade. 1 Copy
150th. Infantry Brigade. 1 "
151st. Infantry Brigade. 1 "
50th. Div. Composite Brigade. 4 Copies

Herewith cop of Translation of an Account of the Operations which took place on the front of the V French Corps, on 6th June 1918, for your information.

CRH[illegible]
Major for Lt.-Col.,
General Staff,
50th. Division.

14th June, 1918.

Translation:

Account of the operations.
(from June 6th (4.p.m) to June 7th (6 p.m.)

German attack of the 6th June 1918 on the front of the Combined forces.

On the night of the 5th/6th June, patrols which were out on the front of the 28th D.I. took prisoners who confirmed the order of battle and said a strong attack would begin at 5.a.m.

At about 4.30 a.m., after an artillery preparation lasting two hours (including gas shelling of batteries positions) the enemy attacked between Ste Euphraise wood (inclusive) and Chantereine farm, on a front of 6½ kilometres.

On the right, the 28th R.I. maintained their position; in the centre, the 50th who suffered heavy casualties in the bombardment and was more heavily attacked was compelled to give up Heuleux wood, Beneuil wood and Villers farm.

On the left, the British well supported by their artillery and by the 40th's held their position on the Montagne de Bligny and in Eclisses wood.

At 6.30. a.m. a battn of the 22d R.I. which was in reserve in the Bouilly area recaptured Villars farm and again got in touch with the 22d and 30th R.I.

Between 8 and 9 a.m., supported by heavy artillery concentration on Ste Euphraise area, Dix'hommes wood and Bligny, the enemy succeeded in taking Bligny, but our artillery and M.G. fires, the resistance offered by the remaining elements of 50th R.I., and a counterattack made by the 8th Coy of 22d R.I. prevented him from leaving the wood or holding the Croix-Perlin cross-rd.

The English battalion which was in front of the Ardre withdrew their right to conform with the disposition of the 30th R.I. south of Bligny.

The German fire increased greatly on Montagne de Bligny. The English battalion which was defending it, fell back about 11.45 a.m., made a counter.attack which failed, but a battalion of 86th Brigade in close support, well placed by general Jeffries attacked at 1.30 p.m. and restored the line, which the enemy shelled heavily.

The timely attack of the English enabled the 414 Regt to prepare a counterattack on Bligny. The movement of this regiment which was placed at the disposal of the 28th D.I., was delayed by reason of the difficult nature of the ground and the necessity of passing through woods.

At 5 p.m. the 414' deployed to the West on the edge of Dixhommes wood and a counterattack was launched at 5.30 p.m. in a westerly direction. Well performed, the attack succeeded and the line on the western outskirts of the village was soon occupied. At 6 p.m. the fighting was over and at 7 p.m. all was quiet.

Reflections on the operations.

Caracteristics of the attack.

On the 6th of June, the Germans made a local attack on both sides of the river Ardre, making use only on the best units of the sector: 232nd D.I., 86th D.I., and a regiment of the 33rd D.R. – From the prisoners' answers and the sketches found on them, the line they had to reach would stretch through Vrigny Wood, Vallotte wood, south part, point 231 in Dixhommes wood, Chaumuzy and Chantereine farm.

To obtain that aim, all troops available were pushed right forward, the Regts being in close touch, with, in each Regt, two battalions in square? formation on the front line, and a battalion as support. A strong density all along the front line was thus realised.

Efficacity of our artillery.

The counter-preparation by the 28th Div., the English D.I. and the 40th D.I., was carried out under very favourable conditions and its efficacy was largely responsible for the failure of the german attack.

Deserving of special notice was the counter preparation in Laville ravine and the concentration on Bligny, the defenders of which were taken by surprise and killed by our fire. No M.G. remained in action and the movement of the 414th was greatly facilitated thereby.

Conduct of the English.

The 19th D.I.W. in the line for nine days, experienced five days of hard fighting. The Div. was twice made up to strength by composite elements which stood up well against the fire.

Strict discipline obtains in that Division and great confidence is placed in the staff and commanding officers who continually go and see for themselves what is happening in their units.

The impression made on the moral of the French troops by the fine conduct of their allies was very good.

Counter-attacks.

The counter-attacks which were immediately made by the English as well as by the 28th Div. resulted in limiting, close to Bligny, the ground gained by the Germans and in allowing the 414th to attack on a narrow front, thus making the success assured.

The German infantery made a weak defence: they offered no resistance in open field, and showed tenacity only in sunken roads and from behind cover which could be defended with ease.

Casualties.

The casualties owing, for a great part, to the shelling on a ground without any shelter are heavy:

	28th D.I.		19th D.I.W.	
	Officers.	Men.	Officers.	Men.
Killed.	5.	80.		75 ?
Wounded.	14.	368.		520
Missing	"	175.		25 ?

The moral of the French and English infantery is excellent. Among all those who took part in the fierce fighting of that day, a strong feeling of individual superiority prevailed.

Signed: Pellé

General Commd. the Combined Forces.

RELIEF TABLE.

Unit of 50th D. A.	Location.	Relieving Unit.	No. of guns each day. Jan. 7th.	Jan. 8th.	Remarks.
No. 2 Group. (251 Bde. H.Q.)	D.25.a.94	162nd Bde. R.F.A.	-	-	
A/251	D.16.c.99	B/162	2	4	
B/251	D.16.a.27	A/162	2	4	
C/251	(D.16.a.43 (D.15.b.39(2 guns)	C/162	2	4	
D/251	D.9.c.62	D/162	2	4	
No. 1 Group. (250 Bde. H.Q.)	C.30.b.88	156th Bde. R.F.A.	-	-	
A/250	D.15.a.20	A/156	2	4	
B/250	D.14.d.33	B/156	2	4	
C/250	D.21.c.77	C/156	2	4	
D/250 (Single How. (" "	D.21.d.15 D.21.c.92 D.21.c.90	D/156	2	4	

28 men of 251 Bde. R.F.A. attached to 250 Tunnelling Coy. at WIELTJE will be relieved by 28 men from 33rd D.A. by 10 a.m. on morning of 8th Jan.

12 men of 250 Bde. R.F.A. attached to 222nd Coy. R.E. at I.3.b.53 will be relieved by 12 men of 119th A.F.A. Bde. by 10 a.m. on morning of 8th Jan.

Instructions regarding War Diaries and Intelligence Summaries are contained in F. S. Regs., Part II. and the Staff Manual respectively. Title pages will be prepared in manuscript.

WAR DIARY
or
INTELLIGENCE SUMMARY.
(*Erase heading not required.*)

250 (Northumbrian) Bde R.F.A. (T.F.) July 1918 Vol ~~[illegible]~~ XL 39

Army Form C. 2118.

Place	Date	Hour	Summary of Events and Information	Remarks and references to Appendices
	July 1		Orders received that Bde marches to a staging camp on 2nd July + entrains on 3rd + 4th July.	
	July 2		Bde marches at 8 AM via LACHY BROYES + PEAS to prisoner of war camp N. of CONNANTRE. No billets available for men and very poor watering facilities.	
	July 3		A/250 move off at 5.30 pm, commence loading at 8.30 pm and train moves at 11.30 pm. from FERE CHAMPENOISE. Loading facilities very good.	
	July 4		Remaining batteries + H.Q. entrain.	
	July 5		Batteries detrain at HANGEST (W of Amiens) and march to ALLERY about 8 miles W of detraining station. Billets good but horse lines rather crowded.	
	July 6, 7, 8		Quiet days; weather very fine. No training ground available to start with; but one is allotted.	
	9		Horses inspected by D.D.R. 4th Army. A good number cast.	
	10, 11, 12, 13		Spent in training. Only ~~[illegible]~~ one training ground available but this is quite good and big although it is some distance away.	
	14		76 remounts arrived; much above usual standard.	

D. D. & L., London, E.C.
(A10266) Wt W5300/P713 750,000 5/15 Sch. 52 Forms/C2118/16

Instructions regarding War Diaries and Intelligence Summaries are contained in F. S. Regs., Part II. and the Staff Manual respectively. Title pages will be prepared in manuscript.

WAR DIARY
or
INTELLIGENCE SUMMARY.
(Erase heading not required.)

Army Form C. 2118.

250 (Northumbrian) Bde R.F.A. (T)
July 1918 Vol XL

Place	Date	Hour	Summary of Events and Information	Remarks and references to Appendices
	July 15 16 17 18 19 20 21 22 23 24 25 26		In rest area at ALLERY. Training continued chiefly in form of drill orders ~~[illegible]~~ on training ground N of HALLENCOURT. Also signalling, gun drill, riding drill, driving drill & instruction of battery staffs. Weather on the whole good. Some thunder between 19th and 23rd. Condition of horses not as good as might be expected. Sports mounted & dismounted held on training ground during the afternoon. G.O.C. (Maj Gen JACKSON) & C.R.A. (Brig gen STIRLING) both present.	
	27		Maj Gen Budworth (G.O.C. RA 4th Army) inspected batteries during stables. Orders received to move on 28th to III Corps area.	
	28.		March via LONGPRE & FLIXECOURT to BELLOY SUR SOMME area, starting at 8 AM and arriving at 1 pm. Batteries are in camp near Foret de VIGNACOURT, good situation but poor watering facilities. Headquarters of D.A. & Both Brigades in BELLOY.	
	29. 30 }		Quiet days. Watering for batteries poor.	
	31		Orders received to go into action near HEILLY SUR SOMME, relieving 10th Australian Bde RFA.	

[signature] Lt Col

D. D. & L., London, E.C. (A10266) Wt W5300/P713 750,000 2/18 Sch. 52 Forms/C2118/16

Instructions regarding War Diaries and Intelligence Summaries are contained in F. S. Regs., Part II. and the Staff Manual respectively. Title pages will be prepared in manuscript.

WAR DIARY
or
INTELLIGENCE SUMMARY.
(Erase heading not required.)

250 (Northumbrian) Bde R.F.A. T.F.

Army Form C. 2118.

Vol XLI August 1918

Place	Date	Hour	Summary of Events and Information	Remarks and references to Appendices
	Aug 1.		Bde marches from BELLOY via St VAST EN CHAUSSEE, POULAINVILLE + ST GRATIEN to wagon lines at FRECHENCOURT. One section per battery goes into action and relieves sections of 10th Australian Bde in positions S. of HEILLY.	
	Aug 2.		Remaining sections + H.Q. relieve remainder of Aust. Bde. Positions taken over are well dug in + gas proof but very obvious.	
	Aug 3.		Forward positions reconnoitred for all batts. close to BRAY CORBIE road S.W of MORLANCOURT. A + D within 2000 yards of German line + B + C within 4000. 600 rds per 18pdr + 500 rounds per how to be in new positions by morning of 6th. Very little progress made with ammunition supply on night 3/4 owing to very congested roads. No wheeled traffic allowed East of B + C's positions consequently A + D + many other batteries had to pack. Eventually traffic became entirely blocked.	
	Aug 4.		Night firing and registration carried out from rear positions. Arrangements made for allotment of different roads to Bdes and for traffic circuits for ammunition. Some packs obtained for A/250 + D/250. B/250 + C/250 make good progress with supply by vehicles.	

D. D. & L., London, E.C. (A10266) Wt W5300/P713 750,000 2/18 Sch. 52 Forms/C2118/16

Instructions regarding War Diaries and Intelligence Summaries are contained in F. S. Regs., Part II. and the Staff Manual respectively. Title pages will be prepared in manuscript.

WAR DIARY or INTELLIGENCE SUMMARY.

(Erase heading not required.)

250 (Northumbrian) Bde RFA (T.F.)

Vol XLI Aug 1918

Army Form C. 2118.

Place	Date	Hour	Summary of Events and Information	Remarks and references to Appendices
	Aug 5		Reconnaissances made for O.P.s from which to watch our projected advance. Good view can only be obtained from ~~high~~ close to front line on high ground S. of BRAY - CORBIE road. (K19 + K25) Ammunition carrying continued. B + C complete their dumps, A makes good progress; But D owing to lack of carriers only gets small number to position although full number required are dumped not far from position as far as wagons are allowed to carry them.	
	Aug 6		S.O.S reported at 4.30 AM. Our first liaison officer at Batt. HQ reports all quiet on our front but later (6.30 AM) enemy is reported to have advanced about 1000 yds W along BRAY - CORBIE road + at one time had posts in A + D's forward positions. Counter attacks are made during the morning by 54th + 55th Inf Bdes + partly restore situation. By 2pm. line is more or less fixed, the enemy holding our front line + having outposts in our supports. Relief of 18 Div by 58 Div was in progress at time of attack which added to confusion, which lasted almost all day.	

D. D. & L., London, E.C. (A10266) Wt W5300/P713 750,000 2/15 Sch. 52 Forms/C2118/16

Instructions regarding War Diaries and Intelligence Summaries are contained in F. S. Regs., Part II. and the Staff Manual respectively. Title pages will be prepared in manuscript.

WAR DIARY
or
INTELLIGENCE SUMMARY.
(*Erase heading not required.*)

252 (Northumbrian) Bde Army Form C. 2118.
RFA T.F.
Vol XLI Aug 1918

Place	Date	Hour	Summary of Events and Information	Remarks and references to Appendices
			Line immediately N. of the SOMME covered by 250 Bde remained intact.	
			From 10 AM 250 Bde covers 174 Bde 58 Div which had relieved part of 18 Div.	
			Communications poor throughout the day, partly owing to shelling but chiefly owing to large numbers of moves and reliefs.	
			During afternoon orders received that no more ammunition was to be taken up to forward positions of A & D which are now just within our lines. Fresh positions close to B & C are chosen for them and arrangements are made by which A & D assist them in getting up ammunition during the night.	
			Arrangements made for a counter attack during night 6/7 to recover ground lost in the morning before main attack is made.	
	Aug 7		4.40 AM. 54th Inf Bde make a counter attack to retake the ground lost on 6th. Attack is successful and the line is restored.	

D. D. & L., London, E.C.
(A10266) Wt W5300/P713 750,000 2/18 Sch. 52 Forms/C2118/16

Instructions regarding War Diaries and Intelligence Summaries are contained in F. S. Regs., Part II. and the Staff Manual respectively. Title pages will be prepared in manuscript.

WAR DIARY
or
INTELLIGENCE SUMMARY.
(*Erase heading not required.*)

250 (Northumbrian) Bde R.F.A. (T.F.)
Vol XLI Aug 1918.

Army Form C. 2118.

Place	Date	Hour	Summary of Events and Information	Remarks and references to Appendices
			A, C & D Batteries assisted by firing on creeping barrage. 287 prisoners captured.	
			Large quantity of ammunition got up to A & D's new forward positions.	
	Aug 8.		At Zero hour 4.20 AM Barrage opened and infantry (174 Bde) advanced preceded by tanks. Misty at 4.20 AM, cleared a little at about 5.30 but then came down worse than ever, so bad at one time about 6.30 AM that gunners could not see aiming posts.	
			2 parties of F.O.Os out each consisting of two ~~parties~~ officers and 4 signallers. Owing to fog visual was impossible and all lines went down. ~~Vis~~ Runner was only method of communication & was very slow.	
			Batteries had occupied new positions in J 15 D, on CORBIE – BRAY road. These were not shelled at all. Wagon lines moved up to S. of BONNAY.	
			At Zero and for a short time afterwards our front system was fairly heavily gas shelled.	
			As no news was received from F.O.Os, a patrol was sent out.	

D. D. & L., London, E.C.
(A10266) Wt W5300/P713 750,000 2/15 Sch. 52 Forms/C2118/16

Instructions regarding War Diaries and Intelligence Summaries are contained in F. S. Regs., Part II. and the Staff Manual respectively. Title pages will be prepared in manuscript.

WAR DIARY
or
INTELLIGENCE SUMMARY.
(Erase heading not required.)

250 (Northumbrian) Bde R.F.A. (T.F.) Army Form C. 2118.

Vol XLI Aug 1918

Place	Date	Hour	Summary of Events and Information	Remarks and references to Appendices
	Aug 8.	8. AM & 5.30	Information difficult to obtain. Wounded returning say that things are going well. Later Report received from patrol from D/250 that line runs through K21 B & D down to quarry K27 D 9.0.	
		10 AM	Report received from D.A. H.Q. that final objectives have been reached, this later turns out to be wrong.	
			Position of division on left astride BRAY CORBIE road not good. They had got forward to K22 B but their flank from that point to K16 was exposed.	
		1 pm	Information received that 58 div infantry hold MALLARD wood but nothing East of it.	
			During the afternoon various targets are fired on in the neighbourhood of CHIPILLY	
			No change to speak of in infantry line.	
			We attack again from MALLARD wood towards SOMME at 7 pm but infantry are driven back at once by a counter attack and at night our line runs along East edge of MALLARD wood, NE along spur to K 21 central	
			Normal night firing. Batteries remain in their positions.	

D. D. & L., London, E.C.
(A10266) Wt W5300/P713 750,000 2/18 Sch. 52 Forms/C2118/16

Instructions regarding War Diaries and Intelligence Summaries are contained in F. S. Regs., Part II. and the Staff Manual respectively. Title pages will be prepared in manuscript.

WAR DIARY
or
INTELLIGENCE SUMMARY.
(Erase heading not required.)

250 (Northumbrian) Bde R.F.A. (T.F.)

Vol XLI Aug 1918

Army Form C. 2118.

Place	Date	Hour	Summary of Events and Information	Remarks and references to Appendices
	Aug 9.		During morning 58 D.A ring up to say that attack will not be continued during day, but that we may have to fire barrage early next morning. O.C Bde + batteries go out to reconnoitre for O.Ps. + forward battery positions. Later in the morning orders are received that barrage to cover an attack up to East of Gressaire wood is to be fired during the evening. As many batteries as possible are to be moved forward to positions W. of MALLARD wood in K25 + K26, but batteries must be so moved that there are always 2 18pdr batteries available to fire on barrage. A + D ordered to move up into positions in K25 D. They only just get into action in time to open fire on a barrage beginning at 5 30pm in support of an attack to gain GRESSAIRE wood S of BRAY CORBIE road. B + C fire the barrage from their positions in J16. Objectives are gained and immediately on completion of barrage B/250 + C/250 move forward to positions in K26 C and Bde HQ moves to SAILLY LAURETTE.	

D. D. & L., London, E.C.
(A10066) Wt W5300/P713 750,000 2/18 Sch. 52 Forms/C2118/16

Instructions regarding War Diaries and Intelligence Summaries are contained in F. S. Regs., Part II. and the Staff Manual respectively. Title pages will be prepared in manuscript.

WAR DIARY
or
INTELLIGENCE SUMMARY.
(*Erase heading not required.*)

250 (Northumbrian) Bde RFA (T.F.)

Army Form C. 2118.

Place	Date	Hour	Summary of Events and Information	Remarks and references to Appendices
	Aug 10		During morning Bde H.Q. move up to close to Batteries in K26c. During the day the infantry occupy the whole of GRESSAIRE wood and old AMIENS defences on East and North east of it. During the afternoon, Australians relieve 58 Div. S. of BRAY CORBIE road. 58 Div whom 250 Bde cover now hold about 2000 yds N of the road.	
			During the evening (7pm.) 12th Div on left of 58 Div. advance their line thus straightening it, + joining up with left of 58 Div.	
	Aug 11		During night 10/11 Australians advance their ~~road~~ line on the right of the road + take ETINEHEM + the high ground N of it. Batteries remain in positions in K25 + K26 until the afternoon when they move forward to positions in K23A NW of GRESSAIRE wood.	
			During day Australians push on towards BRAY but retire slightly towards evening. No change on 58 Div Front.	

D. D. & L., London, E.C.
(A10206) Wt W5300/P713 750,000 2/16 Sch. 52 Forms/C2118/16

Instructions regarding War Diaries and Intelligence Summaries are contained in F. S. Regs., Part II. and the Staff Manual respectively. Title pages will be prepared in manuscript.

WAR DIARY
or
INTELLIGENCE SUMMARY.
(Erase heading not required.)

250 (Northumbrian) Bde
R.F.A. (TF)
Vol XLI Aug 1918.

Army Form C. 2118.

Place	Date	Hour	Summary of Events and Information	Remarks and references to Appendices
	Aug 12		Quiet day. No attack made near our front. Batteries fairly comfortable in new positions, making use of old German positions. The positions are rather conspicuous & get shelled. Very little firing done during the day except at targets of opportunity. Some harassing fire done by night.	
	Aug 13		Defensive positions reconnoitred further W & N of BRAY CORBIE road. As further offensive is not intended here present positions are considered too far forward. Work is to be commenced at once on new positions & they are then to be occupied. Battery positions shelled during day & a few casualties suffered.	
	Aug 14		Work commenced on positions N. of BRAY CORBIE road. Quiet day; very little shelling by either side.	
	Aug 15		Positions selected N. of Bray Corbie road and their vicinity heavily shelled all day. Other positions slightly further West chosen and batteries move two sections each into them during the night. One section per battery remains in forward positions to do normal harassing and sniping fire	
	Aug 16		Batteries settle into new positions which are to be kept silent.	
	Aug 17		Quiet day. III Corps Commander Lt Gen Godley visits Bde HQ.	

D. D. & L., London, E.C.
(A10266) Wt W5300/P713 750,000 2/15 Sch. 52 Forms/C2118/16

Instructions regarding War Diaries and Intelligence Summaries are contained in F. S. Regs., Part II. and the Staff Manual respectively. Title pages will be prepared in manuscript.

WAR DIARY
or
INTELLIGENCE SUMMARY.
(*Erase heading not required.*)

250 (Northumbrian) Bde R.F.A. (T)

Vol XLI Aug 1918

Army Form C. 2118.

Place	Date	Hour	Summary of Events and Information	Remarks and references to Appendices
	Aug 18		During early morning the infantry advance one of their posts on to the crest on the ETINEHEM MEAULTE road. Considerable artillery activity by both sides in the early morning. Counter preparation was fired by us at 3AM & 4AM as considerable hostile movement had been observed during previous afternoon.	
	Aug 19.		Orders received to reconnoitre positions E of MORLANCOURT for use in offensive operations in a few days. Positions selected in K9 B & D and arrangements made for getting up 500 rds per gun & 400 rds per how on night 19/20 & 20/21. Harassing fire with forward sections to be continued - till last moment. More than ½ the ammunition required got up during the night.	
	Aug 20		Work with ammunition continued. O.P's selected.	
	Aug 21		Final preparations made for occupying new positions. Night firing is to be continued by forward sections as late as possible. During evening main positions are changed as soon as it is dark; there is a certain amount of gas shelling but not enough to delay movement. Forward sections continue firing until 11 p.m. and then move across to new positions. H.Q. move across close to batteries.	

D. D. & L., London, E.C.
(A10266) Wt W5300/P713 750,000 2/18 Sch. 52 Forms/C2118/16

Instructions regarding War Diaries and Intelligence Summaries are contained in F. S. Regs., Part II. and the Staff Manual respectively. Title pages will be prepared in manuscript.

WAR DIARY
or
INTELLIGENCE SUMMARY.
(*Erase heading not required.*)

250 (Northumbrian) Bde R.F.A. T.F. Vol XLI August 1918 — Army Form C. 2118.

Place	Date	Hour	Summary of Events and Information	Remarks and references to Appendices
	Aug 22.		4.45 AM barrage opens and attack by 47 Div commences. Bde has two officers forward working together. At zero they are at a good O.P about 1000 yds behind our jumping off line. They are to work forward laying a line as they go.	
			At first little news is received, what there is is good. By 6.15 our infantry are reported up to time on their first objective.	
			At 6.30 AM C.O. & B.Cs go forward to reconnoitre positions to be occupied by batteries in case of an advance. If enemy resistance is weak it is intended to push on in which case 250 Bde will be artillery with advanced guard.	
			7.10 AM report that infantry are at first objective is confirmed and also reported to be going on to second.	
			Line to F.O.O.s holding well, but their information is late & vague.	
			About 8 AM news received from returning cavalry that infantry are on second objective. Cavalry & tanks had tried to exploit it but were held up by heavy MG fire.	
			By 8.5 AM all firing on final protective barrage ceased. ~~and~~ Only one gun (A/250) was out of action & sent to I.O.M. B/250 had one G.S. hit.	

D. D. & L., London, E.C. (A10266) Wt W5300/P713 750,000 2/18 Sch. 52 Forms/C2118/16

Instructions regarding War Diaries and Intelligence Summaries are contained in F. S. Regs., Part II. and the Staff Manual respectively. Title pages will be prepared in manuscript.

WAR DIARY
or
INTELLIGENCE SUMMARY.
(*Erase heading not required.*)

250 (Northumbrian) Bde
R.F.A (T.F)
Vol XLI August 1918.

Army Form C. 2118.

Place	Date	Hour	Summary of Events and Information	Remarks and references to Appendices
	22		after protective barrage had been finished numerous targets were engaged at long range as result of wireless calls. Both guns in action + movement were engaged. Observations were received but many other batteries were firing. Little information received from F.O.Os. Their line is usually down + they are inexperienced + don't show a great deal of energy. At noon infantry commence consolidating green line + intention to advance further is given up in the mean time. Probably 250 Bde will not move. As no news received from forward, Lt Hurst C/250 is sent forward mounted to find out situation. He brings back an excellent report giving line held by each battalion and saying line is very thinly held. As result of his report ground in front of our line is searched as enemy is reported advancing in artillery formation.	
		5.15pm	2/Lt Laidlaw who had been with Battalion H.Q. comes back + reports that S.O.S. went up at 5.45. Fire opened at once. Later	

D. D. & L., London, E.C.
(A10266) Wt W5300/P713 750,000 2/18 Sch. 52 Forms/C2118/16

Instructions regarding War Diaries and Intelligence Summaries are contained in F. S. Regs., Part II. and the Staff Manual respectively. Title pages will be prepared in manuscript.

WAR DIARY
or
INTELLIGENCE SUMMARY.
(Erase heading not required.)

250 (Northumbrian) Bde R.F.A. (T.F) Vol XLI Aug 1918

Army Form C. 2118.

Place	Date	Hour	Summary of Events and Information	Remarks and references to Appendices
			our infantry are reported to have fallen back to the 1st objective and S.O.S lines for the night are laid out in front of the line. A little harassing fire done during the night.	
			A new position forward was selected for D earlier in the evening but owing to withdrawal was not used.	
			On the whole an unsatisfactory day. The enemy artillery was active throughout & his M.G.s were up to their usual standard. He fought hard & our infantry suffered heavy casualties. Enemy counter attack succeeded for no apparent reason.	
	23 Aug		During the morning our line was found to run along MEAULTE BRAY road. Bursts of fire were put into HAPPY Valley throughout the day. Orders received to get up 450 rounds per gun by 11 pm. Later orders received that attack would be made to retake old green line at 1 AM, barrage to be fired. Arrangements made for patrol to go out at dawn under Lt Fowler.	

D. D. & L., London, E.C.
(A10266) Wt W5300/P713 750,000 2/18 Sch. 52 Forms/C2118/16

Army Form C. 2118.

WAR DIARY
or
INTELLIGENCE SUMMARY.
(Erase heading not required.)

Instructions regarding War Diaries and Intelligence Summaries are contained in F. S. Regs., Part II. and the Staff Manual respectively. Title pages will be prepared in manuscript.

250 Northumbrian Bde R.F.A. T.F.

Vol XII Aug 1918

Place	Date	Hour	Summary of Events and Information	Remarks and references to Appendices
	24th	1 am	Barrage opens and our troops advance to the attack. The objective being the Green Line F20a 6.0 to F20d 2.4 to F26b 1.0.2	
			[illegible] shells falling near Battery.	
		1.15am	[illegible]	
		2.15am	Orders [illegible] out for [illegible] barrage [illegible] new S.O.S. lines [illegible] out.	
		3.30am	[illegible] on left are pushing out patrols and in consequence we have orders not to fire north of Divisional Boundary.	
		4.50am	Ordered by B.M. to fire the Hows at normal rate for 15 mins on F40b 0.3 to F[illegible]	
		4.55am	B Battery fired 60 rounds into N.E. corner F14d.	
		5.20am	[illegible] communication [illegible] at cemetery in F25d	
		5.22am	[illegible] STRAGGLY TREE reports S.O.S. [illegible] answered by all Batteries	
		5.35am	[illegible] Tanks [illegible]	
		5.40am	At this hour our front line was OK but support [illegible] S.O.S. [illegible] and [illegible]	
		5.45am	Enemy M.G. [illegible] from F20a [illegible]	
		7.55	S.O.S. reported and answered by all Batteries.	
		8.15	Enemy M.G. [illegible] F.O.O.s [illegible]	
		9 am	Situation settling down and B.C. Batteries ordered to cease firing. [illegible] ordered to place [illegible] on F20a 9.8 – F26 b 7.7.	
		10 am 12 noon	[illegible] earthworks in F20a [illegible] held by enemy	
		12.30pm	B.M. [illegible]	
		2.30pm	Batteries [illegible] forward [illegible] C.O. with Battery Staff [illegible] CRA 47th D.A. [illegible] CRA 58th D.A. [illegible] Positions selected are A. L18[illegible] B. L16[illegible] C. L23[illegible] D. L18[illegible]	
		4.20pm	D Battery [illegible]	
		4.30pm	F.O.O.s are called in	
		8.30pm	[illegible]	
		10.??	H.Q. at K15c 3.4 closed down [illegible] at K12 5.0.	
	25th	2.30am	Barrage opens and our troops advance to the attack. The objectives on our front being BILLON FARM, BRONFAY WOOD, [illegible] COPSE. At this hour [illegible] F.O.O. [illegible]	
		9.5	[illegible]	

D. D. & L., London, E.C.
(A10266) Wt W5300/P713 750,000 c/15 Sch. 52 Forms/C2118/16

Instructions regarding War Diaries and Intelligence Summaries are contained in F. S. Regs., Part II. and the Staff Manual respectively. Title pages will be prepared in manuscript.

WAR DIARY
or
INTELLIGENCE SUMMARY.
(Erase heading not required.)

250th Northumbrian Bde. R.F.A. T.F.

Army Form C. 2118.

VOL XLII Aug 1918

Place	Date	Hour	Summary of Events and Information	Remarks and references to Appendices
	25	11.30	F.O.O. states that [illegible] is established at 103 contour in F27d. [illegible] in spite of heavy shelling [illegible] 174 Inf. Brigade 47 Div. are holding on to [illegible] [illegible] machine gun [illegible]	
		3.5 pm	[illegible] Bde. 2.3 Batteries fire for half an hour on Shipka trench, Billon trench running to [illegible] WOOD.	
		3.45 pm	Attack had to be made by 173. 174 Inf. Brigades on BILLON WOOD but owing to lack of men was cancelled. Our F.O.O. states that at 6 pm our line was E of BILLON WOOD. It is decided that C.O. goes forward with General [illegible] of the 174 Inf. Bde. who is pushing forward his headquarters. Mr. [illegible] (A Battery) goes forward [illegible] The C.O. having gone forward [illegible] that [illegible] the morning headquarters will be established at F28d 2.4. Little or no shelling of Battery Positions [illegible] headquarters. Batteries throughout the day in position at K6 a & b. [illegible]	
	26	4 am	Barrage opens as per Operation Orders No 155. The scheme being to advance our line east of BILLON WOOD. Enemy shelling a bit but only on [illegible] Headquarters move to F28d 2.4 and Batteries move to positions in L5 a & b. Wagon Lines move forward to positions in the vicinity of [illegible] Throughout the morning enemy shells gas and HE [illegible] [illegible] somewhat [illegible] [illegible] [illegible] in a South Easterly direction. We are told that we will probably take over from 210 Bde R.F.A. [illegible] [illegible] is sent to find out [illegible] at 210 H.Q. [illegible] Battery have a gun out of action owing to [illegible] Road [illegible] [illegible] for several casualties. [illegible] to expect a barrage in the [illegible] we are told that [illegible] will be [illegible]	
	27	4.55 am	Barrage opens and advance continues as per Operation Orders No [illegible] [illegible] reported to have been [illegible] [illegible] MARICOURT [illegible] 210th Bde R.F.A. take over our lines etc and the 250 Bde [illegible] 3rd Aus. D.A. The Brigade is ordered to continue the advance as per O.O. No 98 ~~[illegible]~~ Craney ~~[illegible]~~ Pearson ~~[illegible] the Brigade.~~ Little or no shell fire experienced towards evening.	

D. D. & L., London, E.C.
(A10266) Wt W5300/P713 750,000 2/18 Sch. 52 Forms/C2118/16

Instructions regarding War Diaries and Intelligence Summaries are contained in F. S. Regs., Part II. and the Staff Manual respectively. Title pages will be prepared in manuscript.

WAR DIARY *or* INTELLIGENCE SUMMARY.

(*Erase heading not required.*)

250 Northumbrian Bde R.F.A. – T.F.

Vol XLI Aug 1918

Army Form C. 2118.

Place	Date	Hour	Summary of Events and Information	Remarks and references to Appendices
28	28	4.55am	Barrage opens and our troops go forward to the attack. Positions forward are reconnoitred and Brigade ordered to move forward. Throughout the day the Australian troops have their patrols forward and we are asked not to shoot on forward area. 2nd Lieuts Garry and Ransom join this Brigade. At dusk Batteries move forward to positions on West edge VAUX WOOD and Wagon Lines moved to vicinity of SUZANNE. H.Q. is opened at CORSE P.	
	29		Brigade is ordered to move in the morning to take up positions in H3 close to HEM as per Operation Order No 50	
	30		Brigade moves forward under Major Shields to the vicinity of CURLU from which place BCs go forward to reconnoitre positions. These selected are well camouflaged just West of HOWITZER WOOD. Wagon Lines are occupied in vicinity of HEM. H.Q. is established in WORMWOOD SCRUBS. Throughout the morning enemy shells our positions with heavy shell. 2 Lieut Laidlaw goes forward as Liaison Officer and establishes himself with 10th Aus. Inf. Brigade. Mr Laidlaw goes forward to find out the situation. Reported by Brigadier General McNicoll killed in action in vicinity of Clery. 2 Lieut Dundas goes forward to take Mr Laidlaw's place. Much useful shooting done throughout the day on various targets.	
	31st	6am	Barrage opens and attack continued as per TA4 Bde OO. Much progress made and our troops continue the advance beyond original objective. Batteries fire on enemy targets and greatly facilitate the advance. B Battery has 3 guns temporarily out of action. Line in the evening runs along RANCOURT — FEUILLAUCOURT road. MONT ST QUENTIN reported to have been [illegible]	
		9pm	Batteries and Brigade H.Q. relieved by 3rd Australian Army Brigade. 250 Brigade moves to vicinity of MEAULTE via MARICOURT & FRICOURT, Batteries moving [illegible]. Last Battery arrived in MEAULTE at 5am 1/9/18	

[Remarks margin:] OM B. Wallace Lt for CO 250 Bde RFA

D. D. & L., London, E.C.
(A10266) Wt W5300/P713 750,000 2/18 Sch. 52 Forms/C2118/16

Instructions regarding War Diaries and Intelligence Summaries are contained in F. S. Regs., Part II. and the Staff Manual respectively. Title pages will be prepared in manuscript.

WAR DIARY
or
INTELLIGENCE SUMMARY.
(Erase heading not required.)

250th Northumbrian Brigade RFA (T.F.)

Army Form C. 2118.

Vol XLII September 1918.

Vol 41

Place	Date	Hour	Summary of Events and Information	Remarks and references to Appendices
	1.		The Brigade moved off at 10-30 am and marched to PAS a distance of eighteen miles. The route was via ALBERT, BOUZINCOURT, FORCEVILLE, LOUVENCOURT, MARIEUX and THIEVRES. At 6 pm the Brigade arrived at PAS where men and horses had billets for the night.	
	2.		Brigade resumed the march at 4 pm and marched to ARRAS via LAHERLIERE and BEAUMETZ arriving at destination at 11 p.m. having completed a distance of eighteen miles. The Brigade is allotted billets of a nature in ARRAS.	
	3		Spent the day cleaning up, men and horses glad of the rest.	
	4		Again most of the day spent cleaning up, all ranks having had baths and clean clothing. Warned at 10 pm that Brigade will go into action on the morrow taking over positions and wagon lines from 15th D.A. A motor lorry is arranged for to take CO and BCs forward for reconnaissance in the morning.	
	5		At 9 am CO with BCs goes forward and positions with adjacent wagon lines are inspected close to VIS-EN-ARTOIS. Arrangements are made by Batteries to march in independently and by midnight all Batteries report themselves in action. Night firing is done by all forward sections. Major Shiel takes over command of Brigade.	
	6		Nothing of interest happens and general routine carried out.	

D. D. & L., London, E.C.
(A10266) Wt W5300/P713 750,000 2/18 Sch. 52 Forms/C2118/16

Instructions regarding War Diaries and Intelligence Summaries are contained in F. S. Regs., Part II. and the Staff Manual respectively. Title pages will be prepared in manuscript.

WAR DIARY
or
INTELLIGENCE SUMMARY.
(Erase heading not required.)

250th Northumbrian Bde R.F.A. (T.F.) Army Form C. 2118.

Vol XLII September 1918.

Place	Date	Hour	Summary of Events and Information	Remarks and references to Appendices
7	7.		A quiet day, the usual routine carried out. Position selected for section of 4.5 Hows which is ultimately occupied to enable us to cut wire in front of SAILY-en-OSTREVENT.	
	8.		Section Hows start wire cutting from position in P9b S. of ETAING about 500 rounds being fired in the course of the day. Otherwise the day is very quiet.	
	9.		Wire cutting continued, considerable gaps being made in vicinity COW LANE. Outside of this the usual routine carried out.	
	10.		Receive orders to hand over to 58th Bde, N D.A who are relieving the Brigade. B. Battery vacate their positions, the other Batteries are relieved about 9pm – 10pm all marching to MAROEUIL via ARRAS where 50th DA is in 1st Army Reserve at 12 hours notice.	
	11 12 13 14		Cleaning up at MAROEUIL. Billets fairly good but only standings for a few horses. Weather is bad. Some reinforcements & remounts arrive.	
	15 16 17 18 19 20 21 22		At MAROEUIL spent in training etc. Weather on the whole fair. ~~but~~ Fair amount of grazing for horses.	

D. D. & L., London, E.C.
(A10266) Wt W5300/P713 750,000 2/18 Sch. 52 Forms/C2118/16

Instructions regarding War Diaries and Intelligence Summaries are contained in F. S. Regs., Part II. and the Staff Manual respectively. Title pages will be prepared in manuscript.

WAR DIARY
or
INTELLIGENCE SUMMARY.
(Erase heading not required.)

250 (Northumbrian) Bde R.F.A. (T.F.)
Vol XLII Sept 1918

Army Form C. 2118.

Place	Date	Hour	Summary of Events and Information	Remarks and references to Appendices
	23		Bde moves at 11 AM from MAROEUIL via ARRAS to S of FEUCHY. O.C. Bde goes forward to 56 D.A. & goes on to reconnoitre positions S of [illegible]. Ammunition up to 500 rds per 18 pdr & 700 rounds per how is to be taken up commencing night of 24/25. Night of 23/24 spent near FEUCHY.	
	24		B.Cs go up to reconnoitre positions & to make arrangements for ammunition supply. 56 D.A.C is to assist as well as No 1 Section 50 D.A.C. Wagon lines move to near [illegible].	
	25		Ammunition supply during night 24/25 had been fairly satisfactory except that 56 D.A.C had dumped ammunition at wrong place. Ammunition supply continued during night 25/26 & guns put in.	
	26		Final preparations made & guns laid in spite of hostile shelling. Final orders for barrage received.	

D. D. & L., London, E.C.
(A10266) Wt W5300/P713 750,000 2/18 Sch. 52 Forms/C2118/16

Instructions regarding War Diaries and Intelligence Summaries are contained in F. S. Regs., Part II. and the Staff Manual respectively. Title pages will be prepared in manuscript.

WAR DIARY
or
INTELLIGENCE SUMMARY.
(Erase heading not required.)

250 (Northumbrian) Bde R.F.A. (T.F.)
Vol XLII 5/10/1918

Army Form C. 2118.

Place	Date	Hour	Summary of Events and Information	Remarks and references to Appendices
	27		At 5.20 AM attack commenced. No movement was made on our front (56 Div) to begin with. The Canadians crossed the Canal du Nord S of the ARRAS CAMBRAI road near SAINS LEZ MARQUION & after forming a bridge head gradually swung left handed. The 11th Division crossed the Canal behind the Canadians & moved up Northwards on the East side of the Canal du Nord.	
			9 hours after Zero they formed up on an East & West line south of SAUCHY LESTRES. They advanced Northwards under a heavy frontal enfilade barrage. The barrage was good and the infantry kept fairly well up to it.	
			Between zero and the attack of the 11th Division the ground over which they were to advance was searched & swept at a slow rate.	
			The 56 Div attacked northwards at the same time as and west of the 11th Div.	

D. D. & L., London, E.C.
(A10266) Wt W5300/P713 750,000 2/18 Sch. 52 Forms/C2118/16

Army Form C. 2118.

Instructions regarding War Diaries and Intelligence Summaries are contained in F. S. Regs., Part II. and the Staff Manual respectively. Title pages will be prepared in manuscript.

WAR DIARY
or
INTELLIGENCE SUMMARY.

(Erase heading not required.)

Place	Date	Hour	Summary of Events and Information	Remarks and references to Appendices
	28		OISY LE VERGER was captured on morning of 27th and [illegible] on 28th [illegible] continued the attack without artillery support and advanced [illegible] the canal bank N of OISY. 51 Div [illegible] the Bois de QUESNOY. [illegible] during the morning [illegible] to support an attack [illegible] towards B[illegible] [illegible] be in position [illegible] 30 Batteries were not found [illegible] got out during night.	
	29		Positions S.W. of OISY LE VERGER chosen. Orders then received that they are not to be occupied till further orders. Day spent in old positions.	
	30		Later in day orders received to move to positions selected near OISY during the night then [illegible] done. 250 Bde [illegible] now grouped under 282 Bde. No S.O.S. [illegible] during night.	[illegible]

D. D. & L., London, E.C.
(A10266) Wt W5300/P713 750,000 2/18 Sch. 52 Forms/C2118/16

Instructions regarding War Diaries and Intelligence Summaries are contained in F. S. Regs., Part II. and the Staff Manual respectively. Title pages will be prepared in manuscript.

WAR DIARY
or
INTELLIGENCE SUMMARY.
(*Erase heading not required.*)

Army Form C. 2118.

250 (Northumbrian) Bde R.F.A. (T.F.)

Vol XLIII Oct 1918

Vol 42

Place	Date	Hour	Summary of Events and Information	Remarks and references to Appendices
	1.		Quiet day. A good O.P. close to the battery position was established and considerable number of targets of opportunity engaged, including some batteries in action. During the afternoon orders received that 250 Bde was to be relieved by 280 Bde during the evening. 250 Bde was to move to wagon lines. Relief completed by 10pm	
	2.		Spent cleaning up etc in wagon lines.	
	3.		Bde moved at 6.30 AM via main CAMBRAI ARRAS road to billets previously occupied at MAROEUIL. Distance about 20 miles MAROEUIL reached at 1pm. Good day for marching. A/250 were unfortunately shelled by H.V. gun on ARRAS CAMBRAI road about 2 miles E of VIS EN ARTOIS and had 10 casualties to men + 15 to horses.	
	4th		Quiet day at MAROEUIL. Orders received that 50 D.A. to relieve 20 D.A. in front of VIMY. Reconnaissances to be made on 5th. Relief to take place of 6/7 + 7/8.	

D. D. & L., London, E.C.
(A10266) Wt W5300/P713 750,000 2/18 Sch. 52 Forms/C2118/16

Instructions regarding War Diaries and Intelligence Summaries are contained in F. S. Regs., Part II. and the Staff Manual respectively. Title pages will be prepared in manuscript.

WAR DIARY
or
INTELLIGENCE SUMMARY.
(Erase heading not required.)

250 (Northumbrian) Bde R.F.A. (T.F.)

Vol XLIII Oct 1918

Army Form C. 2118.

Place	Date	Hour	Summary of Events and Information	Remarks and references to Appendices
	5th		Bde + Battery Commanders go forward to see positions. Enemy is withdrawing slowly from the front and battery positions have advanced once. Under these conditions it is only possible to get a general idea of the situation.	
	6th		One section per battery moves up to relieve one section per battery of the 42nd Bde.	
	7		Remainder of batteries + H.Q. move into and complete relief of 42nd Bde RFA. Locations H.Q. T20 C21, A T20 D81, B T21 C87, C T20 D64, D T22 A77 (Map 44A) all due East of VIMY. Infantry covered are 36th Bde 12th Div. Situation very quiet enemy expected to withdraw at any time.	
	8th		Last day during which guns are registered and a little movement engaged. During the evening the enemy are reported to be withdrawing on the front of the Div. on our right + later begin to withdraw on our own front.	
	9th		A little progress made by the infantry during the night + MERICOURT and ACHEVILLE occupied. During the morning our infantry had	

D. D. & L., London, E.C.
(A10266) Wt W5300/P713 750,000 2/18 Sch. 52 Forms/C2118/16

Instructions regarding War Diaries and Intelligence Summaries are contained in F. S. Regs., Part II. and the Staff Manual respectively. Title pages will be prepared in manuscript.

WAR DIARY
or
INTELLIGENCE SUMMARY.
(Erase heading not required.)

250 (Northumbrian) Bde R.F.A. (T.F.)

Vol XLIII Oct 1918

Army Form C. 2118.

Place	Date	Hour	Summary of Events and Information	Remarks and references to Appendices
			towards ROUVROY but is held up just short of the village by M.G. fire.	
			In the evening batteries move forward to positions in T 16 D from which they can more easily cover the front. Infantry clear ROUVROY during the evening. Liaison with infantry + communications satisfactory and the infantry were able to get fire when + where they wanted it, ~~chiefly ... N of ROUVROY~~	
		10th	H.Q. move up to T 16 close to Batteries. Infantry continue going forward but have some difficulty from snipers + M.Gs in railway station at N. end of ROUVROY. These are engaged several times with bursts of fire + eventually the infantry get the line of the railway. Rt Battalion 9th N.F. (36th I.B) get forward quicker than left Battn. Liaison with infantry good again + produced good results. Very little hostile shelling except at night. The Enemy has only left rearguards of a few M.Gs.	
		11th	Advance continued + DROCOURT QUEANT line E of ROUVROY occupied during morning. Not much ~~hostile~~ resistance and infantry do not ask for much artillery fire. Owing to wide front held by 12th Div there are no troops available for making up roads	

Instructions regarding War Diaries and Intelligence Summaries are contained in F. S. Regs., Part II. and the Staff Manual respectively. Title pages will be prepared in manuscript.

WAR DIARY
or
INTELLIGENCE SUMMARY.
(Erase heading not required.)

Army Form C. 2118.

250 (Northumbrian) Bde. RFA (T.F.)
Vol XLIII Oct 1918

Place	Date	Hour	Summary of Events and Information	Remarks and references to Appendices
	11		and a working party from batteries is employed during the ~~next~~ whole day making a track through ACHEVILLE. This is fit for guns by dusk but as it is very narrow, A + C are only going to move at dawn on 12th. During night enemy [illegible] line of resistance is DROCOURT second support. F.O.Os had been out during day but no hostile movement was observed + better results were obtained from Battn. Liaison officer who usually got earliest information through of any points troubling infantry.	
	12		C/250 move up to ROUVROY at dawn + immediately afterwards A/250 go up to FOSSE 2 de DROCOURT. B + D remain mobile + provide working parties for the roads which are still in bad condition. A + C are both in touch with battn. H.Q and fire on request. Infantry advance quickly through HENIN LIETARD + A + C during afternoon move up to just S. of the village. 62nd + 63rd Bdes 12th D.A. come up during day to take over. They take up positions during evening near A + C and [illegible] withdrawn when they are in action. Owing to fairly rapid advance there is some difficulty in effecting satisfactory relief.	

D. D. & L., London, E.C.
(A10269) Wt W5300/P713 750,000 2/18 Sch. 52 Forms/C2118/16

Instructions regarding War Diaries and Intelligence Summaries are contained in F. S. Regs., Part II. and the Staff Manual respectively. Title pages will be prepared in manuscript.

WAR DIARY
or
INTELLIGENCE SUMMARY.

(*Erase heading not required.*)

250 (Northumbrian) Bde R.F.A. (T.F.) Vol XLIII Oct 1918

Army Form C. 2118.

Place	Date	Hour	Summary of Events and Information	Remarks and references to Appendices
	13		Batteries reach wagon lines between midnight & 9AM owing to lateness of relief, caused by congestion on roads. They then march to ACQ where ~~to~~ good billets & stabling are available.	
	14		Entraining of Bde begins at AUBIGNY at 10.30 first train leaves at 2.30 pm. and continue at 4 hrs intervals. destination PERONNE. Train journey expected to take 6 hrs.	
	15		4 AM First train reaches PERONNE after journey of 14 hrs instead of 6; remaining trains follow during day, longest time taken over train journey being 16 hrs & shortest 10½. No ~~as~~ arrangements made for watering horses or feeding men.	
	~~15~~		After detraining marched to NURLU where billets are in huts & horses under cover.	
	16.		Spent cleaning up at NURLU. Billets very dirty when taken over.	
	17		At NURLU.	
	18		At NURLU. During the evening orders were received to march the next morning.	
	19.		Moved off at 9.30 AM and marched via EPEHY, HONNECOURT and GOUY to BEAUREVOIR where there were indifferent billets for the night.	

D. D. & L., London, E.C.
(A10266) Wt W5300/P713 750,000 2/18 Sch. 52 Forms/C2118/16

Instructions regarding War Diaries and Intelligence Summaries are contained in F. S. Regs., Part II. and the Staff Manual respectively. Title pages will be prepared in manuscript.

WAR DIARY
or
INTELLIGENCE SUMMARY.
(Erase heading not required.)

250 (Northumbrian) Bde R.F.A. (T.F.)

Army Form C. 2118.

Vol XLIII Oct 1918

Place	Date	Hour	Summary of Events and Information	Remarks and references to Appendices
	20		Marched via GENEVE + MARETZ to bivouacs about a mile N.E of latter village. Positions near LE CATEAU are to be occupied on 21st by batteries and 350 Rds per gun taken up by morning of 22nd. 250 Bde is to be attached to 18 D.A.	
	21		Positions ~~North of~~ in western outskirts of LE CATEAU selected and ammunition taken up during the day. The guns are brought up at dusk. Some casualties suffered during the day as ammunition wagons came into view bringing up ammunition. Attack which was to have been on 22nd postponed. O.P. from which a general view of the advance can be had, selected and line laid to it.	
	22		Spent at LE CATEAU. Reconnaissances made of roads on which to advance. A good deal of enemy shelling of battery areas.	
	23		Barrage fired commencing 1.20 AM to cover advance of 18th Div. Batteries were able to cover advance as far as second objectives from their original positions. Little news received from O.P. owing to darkness and the fact that line was often cut. By 6.30 news came through that advance	

D. D. & L., London, E.C.
(A10266) Wt W5300/P713 750,000 2/18 Sch. 52 Forms/C2118/16

Instructions regarding War Diaries and Intelligence Summaries are contained in F. S. Regs., Part II. and the Staff Manual respectively. Title pages will be prepared in manuscript.

WAR DIARY
or
INTELLIGENCE SUMMARY.
(Erase heading not required.)

252 (Northumbrian) Bde R.F.A (T.F)

Vol XLIII Oct 1918

Army Form C. 2118.

Place	Date	Hour	Summary of Events and Information	Remarks and references to Appendices
	23		was going well. At 7.30 AM. O.C Bde + Batteries went forward to reconnoitre positions N of BOIS L'EVEQUE from which final objective can be reached. Batteries follow on and eventually take up ~~the~~ positions, with wagon lines near RICHEMONT stream.	
			Infantry advance well as far as BOUSIES where they meet with strong opposition, and only just manage to clear the village by nightfall. Liaison officer gets through good deal of information about targets to be engaged.	
	24		Infantry attack again at 4 AM under barrage, but are met with considerable resistance and during the day only advance to Eastern outskirts of ROBESART. RENUARD Farm to the North of it is also strongly held and is only taken late in the evening after being subjected to several bursts of fire. It is found after capture to have been very strongly fortified + wired. Throughout the day ~~a good deal~~ the Liaison officer with Battalion HQ sent through targets to be engaged for stated periods after which infantry attacked them. This proved successful in several instances, notably RENUART FARM.	

D. D. & L., London, E.C.
(A10266) Wt W5300/P713 750,000 2/18 Sch. 52 Forms/C2118/16

Instructions regarding War Diaries and Intelligence Summaries are contained in F. S. Regs., Part II. and the Staff Manual respectively. Title pages will be prepared in manuscript.

WAR DIARY
or
INTELLIGENCE SUMMARY.
(Erase heading not required.)

250 (Northumbrian) Bde R.F.A. (T.F.)

Vol XLIII Oct 1918

Army Form C. 2118.

Place	Date	Hour	Summary of Events and Information	Remarks and references to Appendices
	25.		Quiet day on the whole. Batteries & H.Q. move forward to positions in LANNOY during the afternoon. Positions of good in outskirts of village. A little shelling while batteries are on move causes some casualties.	
	26.		At 1 AM a barrage is fired to support an attack by the Brigade on our left. The attack makes a certain amount of progress but does not reach final objective. During the day an O.P. is manned at RENUART Farm and some targets engaged with observation. Harassing fire on roads behind front carried out at night	
	27.		Quiet day. Registration of guns checked and some observed fire in addition to day & night harassing fire carried out.	
	28 } 29 }		Quiet days. A certain amount of observed shooting done at the request of the infantry. Observation difficult owing to the enclosed nature of the country which is covered with orchards.	

D. D. & L., London, E.C.
(A10266) Wt W5300/P713 750,000 2/18 Sch. 52 Forms/C2118/16

Instructions regarding War Diaries and Intelligence Summaries are contained in F. S. Regs., Part II. and the Staff Manual respectively. Title pages will be prepared in manuscript.

WAR DIARY
or
INTELLIGENCE SUMMARY.
(*Erase heading not required.*)

250 (Northumbrian) Bde R.F.A. (T.F.)
Vol XLIII Oct 1918.

Army Form C. 2118.

Place	Date	Hour	Summary of Events and Information	Remarks and references to Appendices
	30		Quiet day. During the evening the 50th Division take over a front between the 18th Div on left and 25th Div on Right. 250 Bde covers centre of 50th Div but does not move positions.	
	31.		Quiet day.	
			[illegible] Major for O.C. 250th Brigade R.F.A.	

D. D. & L., London, E.C.
(A10266) Wt W5300/P713 750,000 2/18 Sch. 52 Forms/C2118/16

50 Div

Army Form C. 2118.

WAR DIARY
or
INTELLIGENCE SUMMARY.
(Erase heading not required.)

250 (Northum brian) Bde R.F.A. (T.F)

Vol XLIV November 1918

App 43

Instructions regarding War Diaries and Intelligence Summaries are contained in F. S. Regs., Part II. and the Staff Manual respectively. Title pages will be prepared in manuscript.

Place	Date	Hour	Summary of Events and Information	Remarks and references to Appendices
	1		Quiet day. Some observed fire and usual harassing fire. Ammunition at guns made up to 350 per gun in preparation for attack. Trench mortar men and R.E. attached to Bde for use ~~on~~ on roads + bridges.	
	2.		Quiet day. Ammunition completed to 350 rounds per gun. Preliminary orders for attack received	
	3.		Gas shelling of LANNOY during early morning. Day quiet. Final orders received.	
	4.		Zero hour 6.15 A.M. Barrage fired in support of infantry. Bde ceased firing after 88 mins + was held in readiness to advance with infantry. Position was not clear for some time as the right of attack was held up to begin with. At 8.30 A.M. a section ~~each~~ from B/250 was attached to ~~[illegible]~~ 1st K.O.Y.L.I and a section of C/250 to 4th K.R.R. These sections advanced with battalion H.Q. of the battalions to which they were attached. When the 149 + 150 Bdes had reached their objectives the above battalions went through, the K.O.Y.L.I going up ROUTE DE FONTAINE and the K.R.R by the LAIE DE MONT CARMEL.	

D. D. & L., London, E.C.
(A10266) Wt W5300/P713 750,000 2/18 Sch. 52 Forms/C2118/16

Instructions regarding War Diaries and Intelligence Summaries are contained in F. S. Regs., Part II. and the Staff Manual respectively. Title pages will be prepared in manuscript.

WAR DIARY
or
INTELLIGENCE SUMMARY.
(Erase heading not required.)

250 (Northumbrian) Bde R.F.A. (T.F)

Vol XLIV Nov. 1918.

Army Form C. 2118.

Place	Date	Hour	Summary of Events and Information	Remarks and references to Appendices
	4.		The sections of B + C fired whenever infantry were held up. It was found that whenever the sections fired, even if owing to the trees they had to fire well over the target, the enemy invariably retired almost at once.	
			At 11 AM. Remainder of Bde advanced from BOUSIES to position of assembly near ROSIMBOIS from where B + C followed their sections in support of the two battalions on left + centre while A/250 sent a section up the ROUTE de LANDRECIES with the INNISKILLING FUSILIERS and engaged some targets of opportunity on the South Bank of the SAMBRE.	
			By the evening, the infantry held a line running N. through HACHETTE Farm, A, B + C were in action in support of the infantry + D/250 were in support.	
	5.		At 6.15 AM the infantry continued the advance; Batteries fired for half an hour on points that were thought to be held and on road + railway crossings. Sections advanced with the infantry as on previous day; K.O.Y.L.I who had been on the left were withdrawn into support. During the morning 251 Bde who had been	

Instructions regarding War Diaries and Intelligence Summaries are contained in F. S. Regs., Part II. and the Staff Manual respectively. Title pages will be prepared in manuscript.

WAR DIARY
or
INTELLIGENCE SUMMARY.
(*Erase heading not required.*)

250 (Northum brian) Bde RFA. (T.F)

Vol XLIV Nov 1918.

Army Form C. 2118.

Place	Date	Hour	Summary of Events and Information	Remarks and references to Appendices
			out of action since end of the barrage on the previous day took over from 252 Bde batteries which pulled out of action and remained in readiness.	
			The weather on this day broke and rain fell steadily from 10 A.M. until dark. This made the roads through the FORET DE MORMAL very bad and ~~xxx~~ in addition to the demolitions done by the enemy delayed transport considerably.	
			A pontoon was put across the SAMBRE S of HACHETTE Farm and the infantry crossed by it, but no artillery.	
		6	Weather still very bad; and 252 Bde ordered not to move. Some artillery crosses pontoon Bridge, but approaches to it are bad.	
		7	Bde moves at 8.30 AM to SASSEGNIES where billets are available. Bridges over the river are still short and ~~–~~ great difficulty is found in keeping infantry supplied. Trestle bridge is completed at 8 pm and working parties from batteries are kept on roads during day.	
		8th	Spent at SASSEGNIES. Patrols sent out to keep in touch with situation on div front, where infantry advance in spite of strong rearguard resistance.	
		9th	Orders received early during morning to form composite battery	

D. D. & L., London, E.C.
(A10266) Wt W5300/P713 750,000 3/18 Sch. 52 Forms/C2118/16

Instructions regarding War Diaries and Intelligence Summaries are contained in F. S. Regs., Part II. and the Staff Manual respectively. Title pages will be prepared in manuscript.

WAR DIARY
or
INTELLIGENCE SUMMARY.
(Erase heading not required.)

250 (Northumbrian) Bde RFA (T.F.)

Vol XLIV Nov 1918

Army Form C. 2118.

Place	Date	Hour	Summary of Events and Information	Remarks and references to Appendices
			composed of one section each of A, B & C/250 which is to be ready to move at an hours notice to go through with mobile column formed from the division to keep in touch with the enemy who is retiring fast. Ten wagons of ammunition are taken for each gun and 4 days rations. Battery moves at 1130 hours to rendezvous at LEZ FONTAINE. Battery under command of Major MILBURN	
	10		Orders received for Bde less mobile battery to move to ST REMY CHAUSSEE, composite battery is later ordered to move there as well and sections rejoin their batteries. Good billets available.	
	11		Orders received that hostilities cease at 1100 hrs as an armistice has been signed.	
	12.		at ST. REMY.	
	13		at ST REMY. Div Arty attends thanksgiving Service & is inspected by G.O.C. Division. Maj Gen JACKSON.	
	14 15 16		at ST REMY.	

D. D. & L., London, E.C.
(A10266) Wt W5300/P713 750,000 2/18 Sch. 52 Forms/C2118/16

Instructions regarding War Diaries and Intelligence Summaries are contained in F. S. Regs., Part II. and the Staff Manual respectively. Title pages will be prepared in manuscript.

WAR DIARY
or
INTELLIGENCE SUMMARY.
(Erase heading not required.)

250 (Northumbrian) Bde RFA (T.F.)
Vol XLIV Nov 1918

Army Form C. 2118.

Place	Date	Hour	Summary of Events and Information	Remarks and references to Appendices
	Nov 17 18 19 20 21 22 23 24 25 26 27		At ST. REMY. Most of time spent in salving areas of all British & German stores. On the whole there is not a great deal. Preparations made to send back miners. Commencement made with Educational scheme. Miners interviewed by interviewing official and those found suitable sent to be despatched to England	
	28		G.O.C. 50th Div. (Maj Gen H.C. JACKSON) inspects billets, horse lines etc.	
	29		First batch of 22 miners despatched to England	
	30		50 men per Batty have been found for [illegible] by [illegible]	

[signature]
Major
O.C. 250th Brigade R.F.A.

D. D. & L., London, E.C.
(A10266) Wt W5300/P713 750,000 2/18 Sch. 52 Forms/C2118/16

Instructions regarding War Diaries and Intelligence Summaries are contained in F. S. Regs., Part II. and the Staff Manual respectively. Title pages will be prepared in manuscript.

WAR DIARY
or
INTELLIGENCE SUMMARY.
(*Erase heading not required.*)

250 (Northumbrian) Bde R.F.A (T.F.)

Army Form C. 2118.

Vol XLIV Dec 1918

Place	Date	Hour	Summary of Events and Information	Remarks and references to Appendices
	Dec 1, 2		At ST REMY	Vol 44
	3		H.M. The King visits ST REMY. 250 Bde are lined up on both sides of the road up which the King walked. No ceremonial parade or inspection	
	4, 5		At ST REMY. Billetting parties sent forward to LEVAL where Bde is moving on 6th	
	6		March to LEVAL at 1000 hrs. March only takes about 1 hour; billets in LEVAL fairly good	
	7		At LEVAL.	
	8, 9, 10, 11		At LEVAL. Education scheme continued + more classes formed. Some miners despatched to England	
	12, 13, 14, 15, 16		Brood mares inspected by A.D.V.S + best ones chosen to be repatriated.	
	17		March via BERLAIMONT + LA GRANDE CARRIERE to LE CARNOY, starting at 0930 hrs	
	18		At ~~LE~~ LE CARNOY. Billets good and all horses under cover.	
	19, 20, 21, 22, 23		At LE CARNOY.	

D. D. & L., London, E.C.
(A10266) Wt W5300/P713 750,000 2/18 Sch. 52 Forms/C2118/16

Instructions regarding War Diaries and Intelligence Summaries are contained in F. S. Regs., Part II. and the Staff Manual respectively. Title pages will be prepared in manuscript.

WAR DIARY
or
INTELLIGENCE SUMMARY.
(Erase heading not required.)

250 (Northumbrian) Bde R.F.A. (T.F)

Vol XLIV

Nov 1918

Army Form C. 2118.

Place	Date	Hour	Summary of Events and Information	Remarks and references to Appendices
	24		20 Miners despatched to Interviewing centre	
	25		Festivities rather spoilt by failure of Div Canteen to deliver goods which had been promised	
	26		Remaining miners (36) despatched, leaving the Brigade 93 men below establishment.	
	27		at LE CARNOY	
	28		Demobilization Form Z 8 showing men for dispersal by trades and dispersal areas made up, on ration strength for the day	
	29		Demobilization ordered in the following classes. (a) Coal miners (b) "Demobilizers" and "Pivotals". (c) Men claimed on AF Z 56 (2 classes) (d) "Guarantee letter" officers and men (e) Certain categories of men over 41 years of age (f) Group 43 – Students and teachers (g) men who have been longest with an Expeditionary Force.	
	30		All serving soldiers with more than 2 years unexpired colour service will be ordered home shortly to form the nucleus of the post-bellum army. There are 8 such in this Brigade.	
	31		Demobilization at a standstill because the necessary forms have not been issued.	

[signature] Major
Commanding 250 Bde. R.F.A.

D. D. & L., London, E.C.
(A10266) Wt W5300/P713 750,000 2/18 Sch. 52 Forms/C2118/16

Instructions regarding War Diaries and Intelligence Summaries are contained in F. S. Regs., Part II. and the Staff Manual respectively. Title pages will be prepared in manuscript.

WAR DIARY 250 (NORTHUMBRIAN) BRIGADE ROYAL FIELD ARTILLERY (T.F.)
or
INTELLIGENCE SUMMARY.
(Erase heading not required.)

Army Form C. 2118.

50

VOL XLVI JANUARY 1919.

WO 45

Place	Date	Hour	Summary of Events and Information	Remarks and references to Appendices
LE CARNOY.	Jan 1		Remaining miners available for demobilization despatched to CAMBRAI.	
	" 2			
	" 3			
	" 4			
	" 5		Capt. A.H. LEATHART. M.C. Despatched to CAMBRAI. Demobilized as "PIVOTAL".	
	6		2 O. Ranks sent away on demobilization.	
			Inspection of horses in Brigade with a view to classifying them prior to disposal on demobilization	
	7			
	8			
	9			
	10			
	11			
	12		Inspection of BRIGADE by M.G.R.A. Third Army.	
			Two O.Rs sent home as "WATFORD DETAILS	
	13		Three O.Rs. sent off on demobilization	
	14		Three ——— do ———	
	15			
	16		Horses classified "Y" (horses to be sent to England) "Z" (horses to be left in FRANCE) malleined.	
	17		One O.R sent off on demobilization	
	18		Ten. O.Rs. " " " "	

D. D. & L., London, E.C.
(A10266) Wt W5300/P713 750,000 2/18 Sch. 52 Forms/C2118/16

Instructions regarding War Diaries and Intelligence Summaries are contained in F. S. Regs., Part II. and the Staff Manual respectively. Title pages will be prepared in manuscript.

WAR DIARY 250 (NORTHUMBRIAN) BRIGADE ROYAL FIELD ARTILLERY (T.F.)
or
INTELLIGENCE SUMMARY.

(*Erase heading not required.*)

Army Form C. 2118.

VOL XLVI JANUARY 1919.

Place	Date	Hour	Summary of Events and Information	Remarks and references to Appendices
LE CARNOY.	Jan 19			
	20		Two O.Rs. sent off on demobilization.	
	21		Eight O.Rs " " " . 16 horses demobilized.	
	22			
	23			
	24		11 O.Rs demobilized	
	25			
	26			
	27		65 horses classified Y sent to DIEPPE by March Route for demobilization. 1 O.R demobilized	
	28		8 horses " Y " " " " " " "	
	29			
	30			
	31		Major E. G. Angus M.C. 2/LT. R.P. Mildon demobilized. 21 O.Rs. demobilized.	

During the month sufficient parades and drills have been carried out to maintain smartness. Salving has been carried out up to January 27 when state of roads + country under snow rendered it impraticable.
Sports - Football - cross country runs - officers jumping (horses) have been encouraged.
A concert party organised by Lt. R.M. Graham M.C. has proved a great success. Set on foot by contributions from Officers of the Brigade subsequent expenditure is met by funds taken from the receipts.

[illegible] Major
Comdg 250 Bde. R.F.A.

D. D. & L., London, E.C.
(A10266) Wt W5300/P713 750,000 2/18 Sch. 52 Forms/C2118/16

Instructions regarding War Diaries and Intelligence Summaries are contained in F. S. Regs., Part II. and the Staff Manual respectively. Title pages will be prepared in manuscript.

WAR DIARY
or
INTELLIGENCE SUMMARY.
(Erase heading not required.)

250 (NORTHUMBRIAN) BRIGADE ROYAL FIELD ARTILLERY

VOL XLVII

February 1919

Army Form C. 2118.

Place	Date	Hour	Summary of Events and Information	Remarks and references to Appendices
LE CARNOY	Feb 1		6 horses classified Y despatched by march route to DIEPPE for demobilization	9846
	2			
	3			
	4			
	5		10 O.Rs demobilized.	
	6			
	7			
	8			
	9		16 O.Rs. demobilized	
	10			
	11		4 L.D. horses "Z" to Paris for sale.	
	12		1 O.R: demobilized.	
	13		4 O.R. "	
	14			
	15			
	16			
	17		2/LT. C. WILLIS, D/250 demobilized.	
	18		1 R horse to 73 Bde. R.G.A.	
	19			
	20			
	21			
	22		1 O.R. demobilized 2 C.Z. Rides for sale at BERLIAMONT. 4 C.Z. L.D. " " " 10 C Z Mules " " " " LT. COL. H. HOWDEN posted from 331 Bde. 66th DIV. to command BRIGADE Major OMMANNEY re-posted to A Battery.	

D. D. & L., London, E.C.
(A10266) Wt W5300/P713 750,000 2/18 Sch. 52 Forms/C2118/16

Instructions regarding War Diaries and Intelligence Summaries are contained in F. S. Regs., Part II. and the Staff Manual respectively. Title pages will be prepared in manuscript.

WAR DIARY or INTELLIGENCE SUMMARY.

(*Erase heading not required.*)

250 (NORTHUMBRIAN) BRIGADE Army Form C. 2118.

ROYAL FIELD ARTILLERY

VOL XLVII FEBRUARY 1919.

Place	Date	Hour	Summary of Events and Information	Remarks and references to Appendices
LE CARNOY	23		BRIG. GENL STIRLING (C.R.A) inspected A Battery	
	24		" " " " B "	
	25		3 Y L.D horses to BEAUVOIS.	
	26		BRIG GENL. STIRLING (CRA) inspected C " — 3 Z L.D. horses for sale LE QUESNOY.	
	27		" " " " D " — 1 OR demobilized. 4 Z L.D. for sale at PARIS.	
	28		The General commented upon the cleanliness of the guns & parks and the harness. Each battery was good. The "Pip Squeak" Concert Party continued its performances with success throughout the month. Football matches between batteries took place throughout the month.	

[illegible] Lt Col
commanding 250 Brigade RFA

D. D. & L., London, E.C.
(A10266) Wt W5300/P713 750,000 2/18 Sch. 52 Forms/C2118/16

Vol 47

WAR DIARY

of

250th (NORTHUMBRIAN) BDE R.F.A

for

MARCH

VOLUME XLVIII

Instructions regarding War Diaries and Intelligence Summaries are contained in F. S. Regs., Part II. and the Staff Manual respectively. Title pages will be prepared in manuscript.

WAR DIARY 250 (NORTHUMBRIAN) BRIGADE
or
INTELLIGENCE SUMMARY. ROYAL FIELD ARTILLERY
(Erase heading not required.)

Army Form C. 2118.

VOL: XLVIII MARCH 1919

Place	Date	Hour	Summary of Events and Information	Remarks and references to Appendices
LE CARNOY	1st March		Demobilized 2 O.Rs.	
	2nd		" 21 "Z" animals.	
	3rd		" 25 "Z" "	
	4th			
	5th		" 8 O.Rs. 2/Lt. J.M. Harcourt & 31 O.Rs. posted 32nd Division "Rhine Army"	
	6th		Major C.H. Ommanney to U.K. for service abroad. (India) 14 ~~animals~~ O.Rs. demobilized.	
	7th		27 O.Rs. demobilized 20 Animals demobilized "Z". 51 "X" animals demobilized.	
	8th		A/Capt. V.N. Dickinson M.C. & 39 O.Rs. posted to 65th Army Bde. R.F.A. A/Capt. A.S. Fowler M.C. appointed Adjutant of Brigade as from 18.1.19 vice A/Capt. Dickinson M.C. 26 O.Rs. demobilized	
	9th		12 O.Rs. demobilized.	
	10th		66 "Z" animals demobilized.	
	11th		24 "Z" " " 3. "T" animals despatched.	
	12th		3 O.Rs. demobilized. 9 O.Rs. posted to 65th Army Bde. R.F.A.	
	13th		1 " " Capt. A.M.T. Trotter M.C. demobilized.	
	14th		53 "Z" & 6 "X" animals demobilized.	
	15th		11 horses 5 mules "Favourite" animals to be purchased in U.K.	

D. D. & L., London, E.C.
(A10266) Wt W5300/P713 750,000 2/18 Sch. 52 Forms/C2118/16

Instructions regarding War Diaries and Intelligence Summaries are contained in F. S. Regs., Part II. and the Staff Manual respectively. Title pages will be prepared in manuscript.

WAR DIARY 250 (NORTHUMBRIAN) BRIGADE or INTELLIGENCE SUMMARY. ROYAL FIELD ARTILLERY

(Erase heading not required.)

Army Form C. 2118.

VOL XLVIII MARCH 1919.

Place	Date	Hour	Summary of Events and Information	Remarks and references to Appendices
LE CARNOY	March 16th		3 ORs demobilized 36 "Y" & 1 "Z" animals demobilized	
	17th			
	18th		14 "Y" animals demobilized	
	19th		8 ORs demobilized 2 "Z" animals demobilized	
	20th			
	21st		9 "X" animals demobilized	
	22nd			
	23rd			
	24th		9 ORs demobilized	
	25th		Major B. C. St G. Warrens demobilized 3 "X" animals demobilized	
	26th		4 ORs posted to 104 A.F.A. Bde	
	27th			
	28th			
	29th		45 "X" animals demobilized 22 ORs posted to 65th A.F.A. Bde	
	30th		2 ORs demobilized	
	31st			
			Owing to lack of personnel Educational Classes and Pip Squeak Concert Party had to be discontinued. Football matches arranged.	
			A S Fowler Capt & Adjt for Lt-Col Comdg. 250 Bde RFA	

D. D. & L., London, E.C.
(A10266) Wt W5300/P713 750,000 2/18 Sch. 52 Forms/C2118/16

Instructions regarding War Diaries and Intelligence Summaries are contained in F. S. Regs., Part II. and the Staff Manual respectively. Title pages will be prepared in manuscript.

WAR DIARY 250th (NORTHUMBRIAN) BRIGADE ROYAL FIELD ARTILLERY. **Army Form C. 2118.**

or

INTELLIGENCE SUMMARY.

(Erase heading not required.)

VOL XLIX APRIL 1919.

V8 48

Place	Date	Hour	Summary of Events and Information	Remarks and references to Appendices
Le Carnoy.	3rd		The last man eligible for the Army of Occupation was posted there. This brought the Brigade down to Cadre "A" Strength.	
	7th		Capt: A.S. Fowler M.C. and Capt V.H. Jowett with 6 ORs were posted to "Z" Horse Depôt, NEUFCHATEL.	
			Capt. J. Hopwood M.C. takes Command of D/250 vice Capt V.H. Jowett.	
			Lieut H.S. Eccles MC takes over the duties of Adjutant vice Capt A.S. Fowler M.C.	
	11th		Lt. Col. H. Howden posted to 165th Bde R.F.A. (Army of Occupation)	
			Major S.W. Milburn takes Command of the Brigade vice Lt Col. H. Howden.	
	23rd		Royal Artillery Commemoration Service at Gommegnies, at which the Brigade was present. The Rev: W. Church CF took the service.	
			During the month the number of horses in the Brigade was reduced to 8, just sufficient for rations and necessary fatigues.	
			S W Milburn Major O.C. 250 Bde R.F.A.	

D. D. & L., London, E.C.
(A10266) Wt W5300/P713 750,000 2/15 Sch. 52 Forms/C2118/16

Instructions regarding War Diaries and Intelligence Summaries are contained in F. S. Regs., Part II. and the Staff Manual respectively. Title pages will be prepared in manuscript.

250 Bde R.F.A.

Army Form C. 2118.

WAR DIARY
or
INTELLIGENCE SUMMARY.
(Erase heading not required.)

VOLUME L. - MAY 1919.

49

Place	Date	Hour	Summary of Events and Information	Remarks and references to Appendices
LE CARNOY.	2/5/19.		Authorisation received for the reduction of Cadres strength 59 O.Rs.	
do do	6/5/19.		Approval granted of Capt. H.S. Eeles MC, as Adjutant, 250 Brigade, R.F.A. with Acting Rank of Captain. (acting with pay & allowances of Lieut.)	
do do	12/5/19.		25 O.Rs proceeded to Reception Camp, LE QUESNOY, for demobilisation.	
do do	13/5/19.		4 H.D. Horses received from the 50th Divisional Train, R.A.S.C.	
do do	14/5/19.		10 O.Rs proceeded to Reception Camp, LE QUESNOY, for demobilisation.	
do do	15/5/19.		6 H.D. Horses despatched to Animal Collecting Camp, BEAUVOIS.	
do do	17/5/19.		13 O.Rs proceed to Reception Camp, LE QUESNOY, for demobilisation.	
do do	23/5/19.		2 H.D & 2 L.D Horses detached with 50th Btn, M.G.C.	
do do	29/5/19.		1 O.R proceeded to Reception Camp, LE QUESNOY, for demobilisation.	
do do	30/5/19.		2 H.D & 2 L.D Horses returned from 50th Btn. M.G.C.	

[signature]
Major,
Officer Commanding 250 Brigade, R.F.A.

D. D. & L., London, E.C.
(A10266) Wt W5300/P713 750,000 2/18 Sch. 52 Forms/C2118/16

Army Form C. 2118.

Instructions regarding War Diaries and Intelligence Summaries are contained in F. S. Regs., Part II. and the Staff Manual respectively. Title pages will be prepared in manuscript.

WAR DIARY for 250 BRIGADE R.F.A.

or

~~INTELLIGENCE SUMMARY.~~

(Erase heading not required.)

VOL. XI JUNE 1919.

Place	Date	Hour	Summary of Events and Information	Remarks and references to Appendices
LE CARNOY.	2/6/19.		Authorisation received for the selection of Equipment Guards. (1 Officer & 15 O.Rs per Battery, 1 Officer & 4 O.Rs per H.Q.) remainder to proceed Home as Cadre.	
-do-	3/6/19		Stores not in use by Batteries were removed to LE QUESNOY.	
-do-	4/6/19.		Authorisation received for D/250 Brigade R.F.A to be broken up in France.	
-do-	10/6/19		D/250 Commenced handing Stores into Ordnance.	
-do-	10 - 18/6/19.		Usual Routine Work carried out.	
-do-	18/6/19		Orders received for the Cadre to proceed to the U.K. 26/6/19.	
-do-	18,-26/6/19.		Usual Routine work carried out.	
-do-	26/6/19.		Cadre, less Equipment Guard proceeded to U.K. (2 Officers and 79 O.Rs.)	
-do-	30/6/19.		Orders received for D/250 Brigade R.F.A to proceed to U.K. 1/7/19.	

****

H G Eccles
Capt,
Officer Commanding, 250 Brigade., R.F.A.

D. D. & L., London, E.C.
(A10266) Wt W5300/P713 750,000 2/18 Sch. 52 Forms/C2118/16

50

Army Form C. 2118.

Instructions regarding War Diaries and Intelligence Summaries are contained in F. S. Regs., Part II. and the Staff Manual respectively. Title pages will be prepared in manuscript.

WAR DIARY or INTELLIGENCE SUMMARY.

(Erase heading not required.)

Vol LII July 1919

250 Brigade RFA

Place	Date	Hour	Summary of Events and Information	Remarks and references to Appendices
Le Carnoy	1/7/19		D/250 Brigade proceeded to the U.K. for demobilisation.	
-do-	4/7/19		The Equipment Guard proceeded to Le Havre (4 officers & 44 ORs) prior to embarkation for the U.K.	
Le Havre	16/7/19		The Guns, vehicles & equipment loaded on to the WAR YARE.	
Le Havre	17/7/19		WARE YARE sailed for Southampton. Personnel embarked on the Lorina & sailed for Southampton	

H S Eeles Capt
for O.C. 250 Brigade R.F.A.

D. D. & L., London, E.C.
(A10266) Wt W5300/P713 750,000 2/18 Sch. 52 Forms/C2118/16

www.ingramcontent.com/pod-product-compliance
Lightning Source LLC
Chambersburg PA
CBHW080842010526
44114CB00017B/2357
9781474527699